SAP NetWeaver™ Roadmap

 PRESS

SAP PRESS and the SAP NetWeaver Essentials are issued
by Bernhard Hochlehnert, SAP AG

SAP PRESS is a joint initiative of SAP and Galileo Press. The know-how offered by SAP specialists combined with the expertise of the publishing house Galileo Press offers the reader expert books in the field. SAP PRESS features first-hand information and expert advice, and provides useful skills for decision-making.

SAP PRESS offers a variety of books on technical and business related topics for the SAP user. For further information, please also visit our Web site: *www.sap-press.com*.

Jens Stumpe, Joachim Orb
SAP Exchange Infrastructure
2005, 270 pp., ISBN 1-59229-037-X

Kessler, Tillert, Dobrikov
Java Programming on the SAP Web Application Server
2005, approx. 520 pp., DVD, ISBN 1-59229-020-5

Chris Whealy
Inside Web Dynpro for Java
A guide to the principles of programming in SAP's Web Dynpro
2005, 355 pp., ISBN 1-59229-038-8

Jo Weilbach, Mario Herger
SAP xApps and the Composite Application Framework
2005, approx. 270 pp., CD, ISBN 1-59229-048-5

Arnd Goebel, Dirk Ritthaler
SAP Enterprise Portal
Technology and programming
2005, 310 pp., CD, ISBN 1-59229-018-3

Karch, Heilig, Bernhardt, Hardt, Heidfeld, Pfennig

SAP NetWeaver™ Roadmap

SAP PRESS

© 2005 by Galileo Press
SAP PRESS is an imprint of Galileo Press,
Fort Lee (NJ), USA
Bonn, Germany

German Edition first published 2005 by
Galileo Press.

Translation Lemoine International, Inc.,
Salt Lake City, UT
Copy Editor Nancy Etscovitz, UCG, Inc.,
Boston, MA
Cover Design Silke Braun
Printed in Germany

ISBN 1-59229-041-8

Contents

5 Roadmap to SAP NetWeaver in an Automotive Supplier Company 95

6 Roadmap to SAP NetWeaver for United Gas 131

7 Roadmap to SAP NetWeaver at ABC Bank 163

8   ESA—Enterprise Services Architecture   197

9   Technology   221

1 Introduction

What is SAP NetWeaver, and how can a company benefit from it? What are the actual application fields in which SAP NetWeaver should be used? What is an Enterprise Services Architecture, and what advantages does it offer? These are just a few of the questions that will be addressed in this book.

With the increasing globalization of markets, the rules of competition are changing evermore rapidly and are forcing companies to make rapid changes as well. Given these circumstances, only those companies that can adapt their organization to make it flexible enough to meet current requirements can gain a competitive edge. However, very few companies are equipped with an information technology landscape that can cope with these ever-changing demands. The goal of the SAP NetWeaver technology platform is to act as an "Enabler of Change" by facilitating the necessary adjustments to processes.

SAP NetWeaver is an infrastructure software that supports the integration and development of heterogeneous system landscapes as they are typically found in companies today. This can take place on four different levels:

▶ At the *front end*, particularly via a portal

▶ On the *information* level, for example, with a Business Intelligence system

▶ On the *application side,* for a cross-company integration of processes

▶ At the *back end*, using the application server

This proposition is based on the concept of a company-wide integration of business data that SAP has already made so successful. Unlike SAP R/2 and SAP R/3, the focus with SAP NetWeaver lies with the *integration of all data*—even data that is saved and processed outside an SAP system. Because SAP NetWeaver is a technology software, the individual NetWeaver components have no direct relationship to processes, but function as the technical basis for enabling the processes to run across the entire system.

The SAP NetWeaver Value Proposition

With NetWeaver, SAP promises a solution that enables every company to achieve the three essential goals of *Cost Reduction* (reduction of the Total Cost of Ownership—TCO), *Innovation,* and *Flexibility.* By making Web

Overview

services and the use of these services available, SAP NetWeaver also creates the need for restructuring the IT architecture to turn it into an Enterprise Services Architecture (ESA). What sets this modern type of integration architecture apart is that processes can be adapted much more rapidly and flexibly than is possible with a client/server architecture. **Chapter 2** provides a comprehensive overview of the requirements for this architecture and how it can be technically achieved using ESA.

Evaluation

Since the end of the e-business hype, every investment decision made must now prove cost-efficient, particularly when choosing a software product. An installation must prove its usefulness by solving the problems surrounding Return on Investment (ROI) and TCO. In **Chapter 3,** the bases for an evaluation of a technology software are explained and applied to the SAP NetWeaver product in Chapters 4 to 7 using real-life examples. Here, the advantages of changing to the ESA architecture play a particularly significant role.

Real-life Scenarios

Once a company has decided to use SAP NetWeaver in its IT strategy, the necessary steps to implement this decision must be planned. In Chapters 4 to 7, four different, real-life examples based on actual customers' experiences are used to illustrate which problems can be solved with SAP NetWeaver and which kinds of approaches are appropriate. In terms of content, the scenarios and roadmaps are as follows:

▶ International automobile manufacturer (**Chapter 4**): *Automotive Inc.* wants to better serve its customers, and therefore requires detailed information from various sources, all of which must be merged into one standardized view.

▶ Module supplier (**Chapter 5**): *Car Doors Inc.* has to generate enormous growth to be able to remain independent. Successful management of the supply chain will be a key factor in deciding the future success of the company.

▶ Medium-sized gas provider (**Chapter 6**): *United Gas* must prepare its IT landscape for the requirements resulting from the liberalization of the gas market. A primary goal of United Gas is to always respond flexibly to customer requirements without this resulting in exploding costs.

▶ Large European financial institute (**Chapter 7**): The *ABC Bank* has far-reaching structural problems that can be solved only by trimming its vertical integration. Because this requires the outsourcing of parts of the process chain to partner companies, the bank must create a modern, integrated infrastructure.

Generally, it is recommended that software as comprehensive and versatile as SAP NetWeaver be implemented in a step-by-step procedure. To aid in this, planning is done using a roadmap or a development plan specifying how the IT landscape of a company should change in the next three to five years. This very planning, based on business requirements, is found in the scenario descriptions.

SAP NetWeaver forms the basis for all current SAP products and will be used even more intensively in the future. This fact alone should be reason enough for IT departments to start using NetWeaver, but there are also additional reasons. One key reason is the fundamental changes to IT architecture that are about to take place. The use of Web services for easily integrating systems has a lasting effect on systems for managing business processes. Therefore, SAP has created the concept of *Enterprise Services Architecture* (ESA), which is presented in detail in **Chapter 8**. Using NetWeaver, client/server systems are gradually converted into an ESA. On the basis of the ESA, cross-application composite applications (for example, SAP xApps) can be run.

Chapter 9 explains the individual components contained in SAP NetWeaver (corresponding to the four integration levels):

▶ *SAP Enterprise Portal* for user integration

▶ *SAP Mobile Infrastructure* as the basis for mobile business

▶ *SAP Business Intelligence* for reporting and analysis

▶ *SAP Master Data Management* for consolidating and standardizing master data

▶ *SAP Exchange Infrastructure* for cross-company integration of processes

▶ *SAP Web Application Server* for J2EE and ABAP applications

▶ *SAP Solution Manager* for process management during the entire process life cycle

▶ *Composite Application Framework* as a basis for flexibly integrated, cross-system applications

The book ends with **Chapter 10**, in which we consider the changes that lie directly ahead for companies and their IT systems. Composite applications—xApps—afford a good solution for achieving the required flexibility for remaining competitive in the future. Every company should ask itself which strategy it can use to be successful in the future, and which preparations it must undertake, particularly in terms of IT.

Acknowledgements

Writing a book is not an easy task, and the particular form of this book, as a specific reference intended to provide a clear introduction to SAP NetWeaver, has demanded a great commitment from the authors.

In addition to the authors themselves, many others were involved in producing this book. We wish to express our gratitude to them.

First, we would like to thank Andreas Mayer from IBSolution GmbH. Due to his enormous breadth and depth of experience, he has made a huge contribution to ensuring that the real-life examples used in this book are of the highest quality.

A project such as this book can succeed only if the right information is available at the right time. We therefore wish to thank the following members of the SAP staff who were always ready to help: Jeffrey Word, Mathias Haendly, Thomas Mattern, Jürgen Kreuziger, Karsten Erxleben, and Franz-Josef Fritz. Special thanks is also due to Klaus Kreplin, who made so many things possible.

Oliver Hain from the DZ BANK shared his expertise on the topic of SAP NetWeaver at the ABC Bank (Chapter 7), for which we are very thankful. We also wish to thank Thorsten Scholz from IDS Scheer for the information he provided on ARIS for SAP NetWeaver.

Our thanks are also due to Gabriela Isop for the many wonderful images. She was supported in this work by André Kirchner.

Above all, a book needs a publishing house and an editor. Huge thanks are due to the publisher and especially to Tomas Wehren and Florian Zimniak. They supported us from the very outset in our idea for an SAP NetWeaver book, and thus helped to ensure that the book could be published in a timely manner.

We are especially pleased that the book can be published by SAP PRESS, which would not have been possible without the support of Bernhard Hochlehnert, editor at SAP.

Freiberg/Neckar, March 2005
Christian Bernhardt, Andreas Hardt, Frank Heidfeld, Loren Heilig, Steffen Karch, and **Roland Pfennig**

2   SAP NetWeaver in 20 Minutes

The problems that IT strategists and consultants are confronted with change as quickly as the company itself. A modern IT landscape must therefore be prepared for the constant changes of the company and its marketing environment.

The Chief Information Officer (CIO) of a company constantly works within the magic triangle of quality versus time versus costs. Every new software solution offers the CIO the promise of optimal support for current problems within this triangle. Yesterday the Web shop promised new sales opportunities; today new OS versions promise cost reductions; and tomorrow Web service technology will promise the elimination of all interfaces. The last five years, in particular, have clearly shown how objectives can change within a very short period of time. While the years of e-business hype focused exclusively on making "things" possible, that is, via new processes using the Internet, soon afterward the focus shifted to saving money. Whereas in 1999/2000 there were investments in numerous diverse and sometimes exotic e-enabling systems, the importance of reducing costs came to the forefront in 2001/2002. In retrospect, it is apparent that very few companies in the IT landscape were prepared to tackle this rapid change of course.

Within an industry, there are often similar requirements for IT systems; however, there can be considerable differences in the detail of these requirements. For example, a growth-oriented medium-sized company in the service industry has completely different concerns than those of a multinational pharmacology corporate group with several acquired foreign subsidiaries that have specific legacy systems. Typically, every company faces highly individual challenges that make its software requirements unique. It is, however, readily apparent that a few recent trends have repeatedly proved to be significant. Typical examples of such megatrends of recent years have been:

Trends in IT

▶ **Outsourcing/Offshoring/ASP**
Outsourcing of IT and entire processes to companies that view them as within the sphere of their core competence

Megatrends of Recent Years

▶ **Cost reduction**
Discussions about Total Cost of Ownership (TCO) or Return on Investment (ROI) with a simultaneously shrinking IT budget

▶ **Best-of-Breed, automation and integration**
A growing number of systems with the simultaneous demand for integrating information from different systems and keeping heterogeneity under control

▶ **Consolidation on different levels**
Simplification of the IT landscape, beginning with the aggregation of server farms by standardizing the software landscape to the template concept in SAP implementations

▶ **Innovations**
Paradigm changes such as the transition to client/server architecture, the opening for Web business, or currently, the increasing spread of Web services

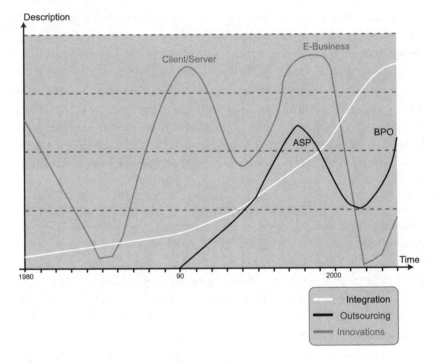

Figure 2.1 Development of Megatrends in Waves

Although some of these trends were not at the forefront for some time, they've become important again in the following years. The importance of a trend must not always be measured by how many millions of dollars of revenue was achieved (for consulting or software companies); the importance of a trend is also often reflected by how often it has been discussed in trade journals, or in the time period used to evaluate the trend.

Although the significance of individual trends for a company is determined by the CIO or a specific department, the need to be open to new trends generated by the ever-changing business environment will determine the success or survival of the company.

2.1　Requirements of an IT Landscape

Regardless of the discussions about trends and the demands on a company's IT department, every company must make a fundamental compromise in the orientation of its IT landscape. This orientation unavoidably lies at the intersection of three important objectives that ultimately are irreconcilable with one another.

1. **Flexibility**
   Flexibility is the basis for being in a position to quickly respond to trends and changing demands.

The Magic
Triangle

2. **Cost consciousness**
   Economically sensible decisions need to be made often, and not only in times of a shrinking budget.

3. **Innovation**
   The ability to optimize existing processes or to make new processes available largely determines the competitive capability of any company.

These three objectives, the reasons for pursuing them, and their respective promises of success are discussed in the following sections.

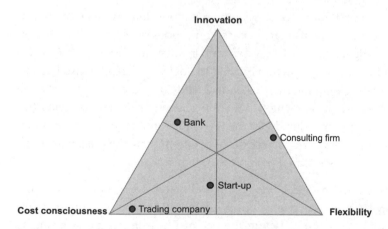

Figure 2.2 Orientation of Companies Within the Magic Triangle

2.1.1 Flexibility As a Key to Success

In the past, the main focus of interest was the depiction of processes with the help of a software solution. Enterprise Resource Planning (ERP), Customer Relationship Management (CRM), and Supply Chain Management (SCM) systems provide the best support for users in the management of their tasks in their respective areas of expertise. Since the replacement of pencil and paper by computers, whose capacity has immensely increased, great progress has been made in the management and redesigning of processes. Where it used to take weeks to draw up the annual financial statements of a company, today it can be accomplished with the touch of a button. Because processes take much less time, companies can make completely new offers. For example, real-time securities trading for end customers (so-called *intraday trading*) has become available only in recent years.

The Competitive Advantage of Process Optimization
Companies can, however, hardly achieve a competitive advantage by continuing to reduce process times. Whether a transaction is completed within a second or 0.8 seconds makes little difference for most areas of application. However, the time span a company needs to change a process and to adjust to changing market conditions is much greater. A competitor who needs a year or two to copy the processes of a company would be a clear advantage. Dell is an exemplary case of a company that succeeded in becoming the market leader by optimizing its processes. So far, no competitors have managed to catch up with Dell, let alone surpass it.

Cross-System and Cross-Company Processes
Processes aren't interested in system limitations. In most cases, a process consists of components that are based on various systems. The creation of an order originates in a CRM system and involves the ERP for BOM explosion and the CRM system for verifying the delivery date. It is also becoming increasingly important to connect and integrate systems between companies. By outsourcing production and entire functional units (for example, the purchasing department) to subcontractors, much information which, for example, is necessary for determining the availability of an article, is no longer stored within the company.

A Change of Focus
The question of the feasibility of cooperation between companies should not only be addressed from a purely technical perspective. Opening firewalls and setting configurations are not nearly as important as changing the focus of the IT landscape. For example, the capacity of smaller partner companies to afford the planning of electronic collaboration platforms is easily overestimated. Many electronic marketplaces have failed because

too much IT know-how was expected of the participants, and, in addition, this know-how differentiated heavily depending on the individual marketplaces. Small companies could not and did not want to make the necessary investments. Decisions about software products in particular should therefore be made while considering the change of focus, which now applies to relations between companies.

Strategy and Implementation

Individual business processes, also in addition to complete business models and even companies as a whole, are changing more quickly, so the pressure on a modern IT landscape to make the appropriate changes possible is continuously growing. A company merger of such magnitude as the Daimler and Chrysler merger doesn't occur daily, but it's clear that companies change in their structures to a much greater degree than they did 30 years ago. Whether it's sinking product life cycles, increasing cost pressures, or globalization, there are various changes to the structures and strategies of a company, and all of these changes have widespread effects on the IT systems of the companies. Examples include:

▶ The acquisition or sale of part of a company   Possible Changes

▶ The agreement to extensive cooperation with vendors for the development of new products

▶ Shared service center initiatives

▶ The objective of creating a simple and unified user interface for employees and partners via a portal

▶ The optimization of customer relations through Web services

▶ The need for transparent reporting on all international subsidiaries and joint ventures

▶ Business process outsourcing of purchasing

What these changes have in common is that they occur in three distinct steps:

1. Defining the strategy
2. Establishing the organization
3. Adjusting the processes

The last step, adjusting the processes, refers to the adjustment of the mapping of processes with the help of software.

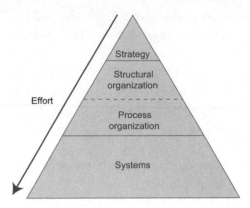

Figure 2.3 The Strategy, Organization, and Systems Pyramid

If you consider the individual areas of the pyramid in Figure 2.3 in terms of the time required for adjustments, it becomes evident that this length of time increases toward the base of the pyramid. A new strategy, for example, the taking over of a market segment, is soon necessary. The definition and adjustment of the corresponding organization (in this context, we can further differentiate between structural organization and process organization) usurps even more time. The mapping of processes in software generally requires the most time and the largest investments.

The Importance of Flexibility In the past, when structures and processes remained unchanged for years, the question as to how systems could be changed was far from the center of focus. Changing market conditions have made it necessary for information technology to concentrate much more on the adjustability of systems. Because the way that business is done is always changing, attention must be paid to all factors that could slow down the speed of adjustment. Just as flexibility is required of today's employees and those who do business with vendors in particular, systems that meet this requirement are necessary.

Such changes to the structure of a company necessitate an IT infrastructure that not only allows the appropriate adjustments to be made, but also envisions them in their conception. The actual situation, however, is completely different. Whether prompted by the best-of-breed approach of recent years or because of the use of heterogeneous IT systems in acquired subsidiaries, almost all companies are faced with the constant challenge of integrating all of their systems on a tight budget. Only rarely does this lead to a landscape which, although simple to manage and easy to maintain, can also cope with constant changes. Quite the opposite is true. Every interface that is necessary to implement processes between numerous different systems causes the IT landscape to become more rigid.

Interfaces that have already been created are changed only when it appears absolutely necessary, adhering to the principle "never touch a running system." The maintenance of an interface becomes increasingly difficult over the years. Technology changes, employees' knowledge about the technology and the details of the interface become dated, the employees responsible for managing the technology leave the company, and the documentation, if it even exists, is available only in a rudimentary form. The countless Year 2000 (Y2K) projects that required the re-engagement of retired Cobol experts clearly demonstrated that no company is immune to these problems.

The Problems of Interfaces

The question of *how* is all too often the core of discussions about pending changes. The question "How can we manage that?" must, however, not deter a company from implementing a promising strategy. Precisely because of this, the objective must be an infrastructure that makes everything possible and shifts the focus to the question of *what*. To achieve success in global competition, the question regarding which of the several possibilities available should be implemented must be answered.

"How?" Versus "What?"

The role of the IT department in the company can change along with the transformation to a diverse and flexible system landscape. Today, IT can often react only to business requirements—it determines the requirements within the scope of financial possibilities. However, if larger portions of the budget are available for innovative projects and the company has an infrastructure that allows changes to be made easily, IT can act much more proactively and work on improvements to processes. The role of IT changes—away from a pure implementer of concepts to a business consultant—so that the importance of the IT department's services increases.

2.1.2 Cost Consciousness

Even if the best-of-breed approach is no longer preferred because of its interface problems and the resulting integration expenditure, one must accept that there is always a variety of systems in individual companies. The reason for this could be previous mergers and acquisitions on which various strategies from different organizational units are based or other practical explanations, such as the size of the international subsidiaries. This diversity and heterogeneity are, however, associated with enormous costs. Every one of the systems used requires maintenance; specialized knowledge is required for support; and, as far as the hardware is concerned, usually several small- or medium-sized servers that require administrative expenditure are used.

Interfaces as Cost Drivers

The largest cost pool when using such a heterogeneous system landscape is, however, not the operation of individual systems, but rather their integration. The numerous interfaces that are often created as cost-intensive 1:1 connections consume the majority of the IT budget. Poor or missing interfaces quickly have a negative impact on the quality of the master data, since manual synchronization or multiple entries that are subject to error become necessary.

Approaches to Cost Reduction

Practically all companies take measures to reduce IT costs and make investments as economically as possible. The following approaches for reducing costs are therefore well known in most companies:

▶ Consolidation

▶ Business process outsourcing

▶ ROI analyses prior to any project decision

▶ Reduction of interface costs

▶ Automation

▶ Simplification of administration

▶ Use of widespread technologies (for example, Java instead of Cobol)

This causes money to be spent almost exclusively on the maintenance and consolidation of the status quo. This along with the trend of IT budgets shrinking rather than growing leads to a dangerous development. Innovation becomes very sluggish and rare. Companies are no longer in the position to draw competitive advantages from their IT and they are at risk of being outperformed by their competitors.

Costs Versus Value

A pure focus on consideration of costs does not take into account that constant changes are necessary to stay competitive. A typical example is the trend to *business process outsourcing* (BPO), in which subareas that don't belong to the core business are transferred to a BPO service provider. This results in the outsourcing company losing some of its influence and scope for design in this area. So, whenever deciding for or against an investment, you should consider not only costs, but the value of the investment as well, in terms of costs versus advantages and strategic opportunities.

2.1.3 Innovation

Five years ago—in the days of Internet hype—there were no discussions about the main responsibility of the CIO being the promoter of innovation. Depending on how conservative a company was at that time, the setup of a Web site meant real progress, but most important was the development and implementation of complete e-business strategies. A small revolution—certainly an innovation—was made possible by the introduction of a CRM system, which supposedly focused on customer relations, in addition to the already existing ERP system, the primary task of which had more to do with accounting. Because of discussions about costs, innovation is no longer the obvious focus, but as always it is still at least the main impetus of every IT department, if not its raison d'être. Competitive advantages can be attained only by steadily improving activities that lead to new proposals and completely new processes that are implemented in IT.

The risk that arises whenever investments are stopped and money is spent exclusively on the maintenance of the status quo must not be underestimated. Such a curtailment to investments would create an enormous backlog demand, one that would be difficult to handle financially. The overall renovation of the complete IT landscape, as was necessary in several cases, for example, at the turn of the millennium, created massive problems for some companies. The replacement of outmoded, host-based account management by modern real-time solutions, which is currently planned for European banks, is an enormous and laborious undertaking. However, sometimes there are short-term risks involved in deferring making an investment in IT. An example would be the case of a large chip manufacturer that lacked a modern reporting tool and discovered the great slump in demand in 2001 much too late; the company could not respond quickly enough, and because of that, is still in the red today.

The Risk of Investment Backlog

Of course there are innovations of all proportions. The modern integration of two systems can eliminate a daily hindrance and serve as a real improvement to the company's everyday work. The switching of IT architecture, such as the shift from SAP R/2 to SAP R/3, has completely different implications regarding time and finance. This must be considered when planning the investment capability of a company. The budget and resource plan must facilitate both long-term and medium-term objectives (for example, consolidation or IT strategy) and short-term improvements that are urgently needed. Changes such as the emergence of the Internet and its effects can hardly be predicted in the long run, and the success of the company depends primarily on the ability to react to such changes with the right innovations.

Making Solid Progress The innovative capacity of a company is expressed explicitly in its ability to implement new ideas in well-defined optimizations or new processes; an innovation is the achievement of technical or organizational progress. "Innovation" is what causes the competition to say, "Why weren't we able to invent that?" From the perspective of IT, this means making new processes possible and leveraging new technical achievements for the improvement of processes. A current example is found in RFID chips,[1] which can make automation of the supply chain possible.

The realization that IT innovations can have a value-creating and increasing effect and that they are essential for the subsistence of the company causes some companies to make investments in this area, investments that can prove themselves regardless of any specific ROI analyses. They establish a specific budget for the IT department's research and development so that IT employees can develop new ideas and improvements without the pressure of having to attain immediate results.

Trends In reality, the will to innovation means, for example, using modern tools that support trends such as the reusability of software components. In this regard, Java/J2EE is more effective than a programming language such as BASIC. Improvements that don't refer to a specific process, such as improvements to the administration of applications or the creation of a portal, should not be neglected. In view of the problems of integration, the current focus is on the use of Web services and the transformation of architecture linked with it. The client/server architecture is changed to one that is service-oriented and thus much more capable of integration and flexibility.

The famous misjudgment of Charles H. Duell, the director of the U.S. Patent Office, who in 1899 said, "Everything that can be invented, has been invented" has demonstrated one point above all: innovations will always continue to be made.

2.2 SAP NetWeaver

SAP NetWeaver provides a solution to help meet the three central requirements of an optimal IT landscape, namely, software that fulfills the

---

1 Radio Frequency Identification; a means of wireless data transfer.

demand for *flexibility* and *innovation* at manageable *costs*, not only for individual problems, but in the form of a durable infrastructure for all business processes. SAP NetWeaver is to become the basis for the changing processes of companies, and it is versatile enough to be adjusted to future changes. Therefore, SAP NetWeaver allows every company to find an individual position within the magic triangle.

NetWeaver is SAP's answer to contemporary problems in companies that led to discussions about infrastructure software, specifically IT costs, flexibility, interfaces, master data, integration, harmonization, and reusability. The central problem addressed is the integration of the diverse content and systems that are necessary to successfully managing daily work. As Figure 2.4 shows, SAP NetWeaver is positioned between that area of operating systems and databases that is close to the hardware and those applications used to map information and processes.

The Promise of SAP NetWeaver

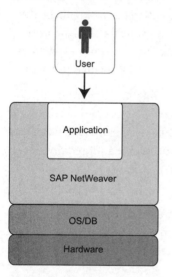

Figure 2.4 Positioning of SAP NetWeaver in Relation to OS/DB and Applications

In practically all companies, there is a status quo in which the system landscape consists of a heterogeneous combination of the most diverse software for the various applications, process areas, and organizational units. All of these systems must be integrated to make a comprehensive use of processes possible while working with high-quality master data and reporting. Wherever integration is lacking, people have to work on several systems to complete processes, which means they have to enter the same data several times, thereby forcing them to have specific knowledge of all of the applications used. The person becomes the de facto

The Challenge of Integration

point of integration, performing a task that can and should be assumed by computers.

The Wish ... People shouldn't have to waste time and energy, and they shouldn't be expected to have to familiarize themselves with a variety of applications; instead, the computer should assume such mechanical tasks. In an ideal world, with the aid of an easy-to-use user interface, the user could access any and all information necessary to implement all processes via the same user interface—one that remains flexible and can be adjusted to reflect and implement the strategies and structures of the company. It is inconsequential to the users whether they access the internal SAP system or use an outsourcing service via the Internet. But thanks to the work of the IT department, users would know that they're using the optimal processes and means to obtain the necessary information.

... and the Reality In the real world, up to 80% of the IT budget is spent on integration. Despite this high percentage, users must live with a confusing diversity of systems, unsubstantiated integration gaps, and manual data synchronization. Integration costs continuously increase and therefore prevent sensible and necessary investments in new products or innovative processes.

2.2.1 Levels of Integration

Figure 2.5 shows four different levels of an IT landscape on which integration can occur. The following paragraphs explain these integration levels in more detail:

1. **People Integration**
   The integration of all applications and information is required, especially via a portal, but also via mobile terminals. The main objective is to give the user an easy-to-use user interface for all required content.

2. **Information Integration**
   In the era of the "knowledge worker," fast and simple access to relevant information is critical. Therefore, when integrating information, one tries to combine information independently of its source and structure.

3. **Process Integration**
   Work that spans applications and companies requires that processes are connected between systems.

4. **Application Integration**
   The development and execution of applications in Java or ABAP must be ensured. Seamless cooperation, especially in heterogeneous environments (Java or .NET), is critical in this regard.

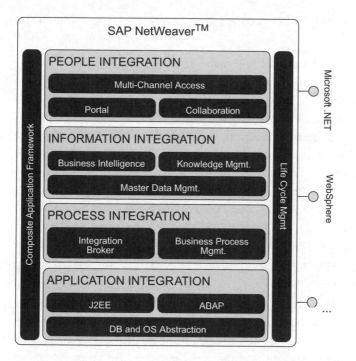

Figure 2.5 The Four Levels of Integration and Components of SAP NetWeaver

There are different explanations about the emergence of the four blocks that gave rise to SAP NetWeaver (and a service-oriented architecture in general). The existing three-layer client/server architecture is often supplemented by a portal layer designed to combine the various applications. This approach, however, does not consider that the switch to *service-oriented architecture* (SOA) incorporates all levels and in no way is limited to the user interface. The challenge lies in achieving genuine integration on all four levels: front end, information, processes, and applications. This is explained in more detail in the following section.

The Four Building Blocks of Service-Oriented Architectures

2.2.2 Components of SAP NetWeaver

The four building blocks of SAP NetWeaver comprise six software components.[2] A detailed introduction to these components can be found in

---

2 There are differing opinions about how to separate the components which together form SAP NetWeaver. For example, does Collaboration count as a separate component, or is it rather a part of the portal? To avoid unnecessary confusion, in this book we speak of six software components as integral parts of SAP NetWeaver. Regardless of this definition, we will, of course, also describe the individual subcomponents (such as Collaboration as part of the portal).

Chapter 9; the following paragraphs give a brief overview of their functions and tasks:

▶ **SAP Enterprise Portal** (with Knowledge Management and Collaboration)
The portal serves as the central point of access for the user to information, applications, and other content within and outside a company. A wide variety of role-based content is integrated and provided to the user via the intuitive browser interface. SAP Enterprise Portal (EP) includes software for *knowledge management*, that is, for the use of unstructured data such as logs, graphics, or presentations. Additional functions, collectively called *collaboration*, enable cooperation between companies so that they can, for example, work with vendors to draw up plans. The objective of using a portal is to provide the knowledge worker with an optimal, role-specific, and thus more efficient work environment.

▶ **SAP Mobile Infrastructure**
By using the Mobile Infrastructure (as an essential component of multi-channel access), various mobile terminals such as PDAs (personal digital assistants), laptops, and mobile telephones can be connected to one or more SAP systems. A constant online connection is not required for this; instead, the terminal can work independently and is synchronized with the back end only when necessary. Apart from existing applications such as *Mobile Sales* (sales connection for mobile terminals), new and tailored applications that use the MI can be created. The MI uses Java as its application platform, so the applications can be used across several platforms.

▶ **SAP Business Intelligence**
SAP Business Intelligence (BI) is used to create reports and analyses that can be displayed in various formats (especially in the portal) and different terminals. One of the major advantages of this SAP solution is that it can be easily connected to virtually any source system. Transparency across systems is achieved via the aggregation of information according to the greatest and most diverse multitude of needs, particularly in a heterogeneous system landscape consisting of SAP and non-SAP applications. The extensive possibilities of analyzing the data in depth are especially significant and critical to business.

▶ **SAP Master Data Management**
In the administration of master data, there is very often the problem that identical data is stored in several systems under different keys. If

this customer or product data cannot be retrieved in a unified manner and thus becomes unusable, business processes across systems become imprecise and prone to error. Reporting information is falsified, and data inconsistencies emerge. The costs for data maintenance increase. SAP Master Data Management (MDM) deals with this problem via the recognition and reconciliation of duplicates supported by the system and related entries.

▶ **SAP Exchange Infrastructure**
The SAP Exchange Infrastructure (XI) is the central integration broker, and it exchanges information and connects processes in a heterogeneous system landscape. It is the essential basis for Business Process Management (BPM). The communication between all connected systems is implemented using various formats (especially XML). With the help of XI, the hub structure significantly reduces the number of interfaces. This reduction, along with the use of open standards, significantly decreases the costs of integration.

▶ **SAP Web Application Server**
The proven reliability of SAP Web Application Server (SAP Web AS) has been the basis of almost all of SAP's products for years. Tools with a broad range of applications such as the transport system and the support connection show that this product has been designed for use in the company. Apart from its traditional areas of strength, which include the database and operating system abstraction, SAP Web AS stands out because of its extensive Internet capabilities, even for Web applications. Not only can it execute ABAP code, it can also be used as a J2EE server. All other six NetWeaver products described are based on SAP Web AS.

The SAP NetWeaver package includes only software that has no direct reference to processes, unlike applications such as CRM or SCM. The SAP Business Information Warehouse (SAP BW), for example, allows the creation of reports and evaluations important to making decisions, but there is no direct connection that would allow an order to be placed at the touch of a button. It is important to always remember that SAP NetWeaver has no direct correspondence to business processes. This is particularly important to the implementation strategy. If there are no processes, the software cannot be introduced into the process chain. You also need to consider this fact when examining the value of the NetWeaver components. Because the value is determined several times along process chains, it is important here also to revise your way of thinking.

Process Independence

SAP NetWeaver is a technological foundation that increases the value of the applications based on it. There are many ways in which it does this, for example, in the area of user interfaces or the integration of legacy systems. In comparison to its competitors, SAP NetWeaver places much more emphasis on the content that is delivered to its customers. SAP NetWeaver not only provides the customer with components, but it also provides them with ready-made content that can be used immediately. For example, this "business-ready content" includes portal elements that display the content from SAP R/3, and predefined queries for SAP BW.

Perhaps the most noticeable way in which SAP NetWeaver increases the value of the applications that are based on it is that it is the basis for the transition to a service-oriented architecture.

2.2.3 Architecture

Client/server architecture has had an impressive history full of successes; it has been able to solve many problems that mainframe architecture could not sufficiently handle. SAP's success with R/3 is probably the most visible sign of the assertiveness of three-layer architecture. The Internet wave of the '90s was also manageable with this architecture, but the Internet boom and the resulting diversity of systems created a major problem. The integration capability of function-oriented, non-service-oriented architectures is anything but optimal. It leads to high costs for setting up interfaces, and every update contributes to significant costs for their maintenance.

Weak Points of Non-Service-Oriented Architectures
Non-service-oriented architectures have the following weak points with regard to integration:

▶ Fixed linkage

▶ Functional orientation

▶ Rigidly defined interfaces (function modules and parameters)

▶ No set standards between systems

▶ Blending of user interfaces with functionality

Using Web Services

In reality this means that direct linkages between two systems have to be implemented using function modules. There are many ways in which to transfer large amounts of data between two systems. The oldest and most error-prone way is write data "flat" on the hard drive and make the second system read that data. Although we would not recommend that you use this solution, it is often chosen because of its easy implementation. The modern and recommended way of transferring data is the usage of Web services. Internet technology provides a solution to integration with Web services. Web services communicate with each other via Internet protocols and standards (XML, SOAP, and UDDI) and are self-descriptive, and thus establish an intelligent means of machine-to-machine communication. Because they allow a higher form of abstraction in comparison to function modules, they can be connected to one another more easily, and replaced, if necessary.

Web services are particularly attractive in that they can build on a client/server architecture. Existing function modules can be made available by using an application server as a Web service. This is therefore an evolutionary approach in which the previous architecture is kept, even with the introduction of SOA. Previous investments can continue to be used and leveraged with the new architecture. The database and service-oriented approaches are used in peaceful coexistence with each other. With the focus on enterprise applications, SAP has named the service-oriented architecture *Enterprise Services Architecture* (ESA).

Evolution to Service-Oriented Architecture (SOA)

Figure 2.6 shows how the individual elements of the IT architecture have changed during the transition from a client/server architecture to a service-oriented architecture. The functional orientation of the past (in which one application was responsible for database communication, processing and formatting, and the display and interaction with the end user) is supplanted by a division according to integration areas. Instead of functional "silos," the four blocks that comprise every SOA and communicate via Web services with each other are used. The user accesses the required content via a central portal, and from there can control all processes. Even though the company uses numerous systems from various manufacturers, the overall structure is transparent and easy to use.

Source systems are replaced by other systems as necessary without major integration expenditures. The clear separation into individual task blocks and the use of open standards such as XML make interfaces clearly defined and easy to handle. The linkage of the system using Web services is far less rigid than the linkage of the system using function modules.

Simple Replacement of Components

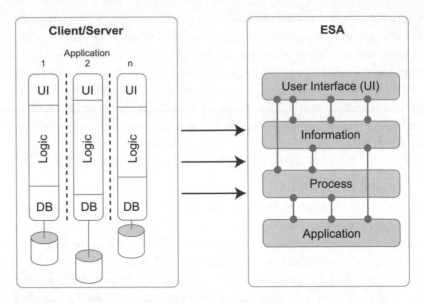

Figure 2.6 A Transition from the Functional Paradigm to Service Architecture

2.2.4 Supporting Standards

The discussion about the support of standards is often considered a purely technical debate. Of course there are major technical differences, for example, between transmission protocols, even if they serve the same purpose—TCP/IP and ISO/OSI are often cited as examples of these protocols. But on a certain level of abstraction, it appears to make little difference whether VHS or Video2000 is used as a video system. The decisive factor is whether there is a common denominator. An essential factor for the success of Web services is that they use certain standard protocols and other standards (XML, SOAP, and UDDI)—regardless of the platform they use. This ensures that a Web service can be used anywhere as long as it is compliant with a standard.

Influence of Standards

The significance of standards has another aspect that is far less inherently technical. Standards are integral to the IT industry in its struggle for customers and market share. Microsoft, for example, demonstrates mastery in optimizing the position of its products by using proprietary standards. Because of its dominance in the area of desktop operating systems, Microsoft was able to set standards for application programming interfaces (APIs) that could be used only with their own products. Thanks to the widespread use of the Microsoft Office applications, Word, Excel, and PowerPoint, the industry standard for the data exchange format for text, tables, and presentations has been set by these products. The products of competitors, which in some respects are superior, are somewhat incapable of communicating using the standard formats .doc, .xls, or .ppt, and thus have a significant disadvantage, since their content cannot be distributed as easily.

The effect of creating an additional advantage by spreading a standard is known as the *networking effect*. A typical example often used to explain the networking effect is the fax machine. An increase in the number of installed fax machines is an advantage for all fax machine owners, because the network of those who can be reached by fax has increased. This means that the very first fax machine was of no use, because there were no communication partners who could send or receive faxes. For SAP, this means that Java has a higher network value than ABAP, since there are more programmers who are familiar with the Java language.

The Networking Effect

The support of many (preferably open) standards is therefore important when selecting software, in order to avoid the risk of being able to communicate using only outmoded and less well known standards. SAP NetWeaver, for example, supports Web service protocols and XML (general XML standard and various dialects, for example, for integration using XI). Both J2EE and .NET are supported as architecture standards.

2.2.5 Costs

The discussion about IT costs is not really inspiring. TCO analyses are predominantly oriented towards the past, although they also make it possible to use benchmarks to recognize and address areas in which excessive amounts of money are spent. It is reasonable to make ROI analyses prior to an investment decision in order to avoid "unnecessary" investments, however, as previously mentioned, this carries with it the risk of investment backlog. At the time of the introduction of email systems, the demand for ROI was less frequent—today, however, the usefulness of email systems is unquestionable.

Of particular interest regarding costs is the question of how a budget can be used so that more is invested in real innovations rather than spending money only on maintenance.

SAP NetWeaver has proposed several ways to reduce maintenance costs:

Reduction of Maintenance Costs

▶ Consolidation by the standardization of IT landscapes and the integration of all systems

▶ Reducing the hardware requirements through the installment of several SAP components on one server

▶ Reduction of interface costs (a particularly significant cost pool) by switching from high-maintenance, manually created rigid interfaces to the modern hub architecture of XI with ready-made adapters for various systems

SAP contributes further to reducing costs in that NetWeaver licenses are already included in the licenses of new products such as mySAP ERP.

Cost Drivers of Integration Costs arise in three different areas in the integration of a company's IT landscape:

1. The integration of applications (for example, cross-company processes in the ERP and CRM systems)

2. The integration of technology (for example, a new BI report that is automatically available to the right users in the portal)

3. The integration of applications and technology (for example, portal content such as iViews for all integrated applications)

Integration of Applications and Technology SAP NetWeaver offers another essential cost advantage—SAP provides software both on the application side and on the technology side, and this software has already been integrated by SAP. Significant costs for customers who select different manufacturers arise in the integration of applications from manufacturer A to the technology of manufacturer B. SAP NetWeaver can therefore achieve cost advantages if a customer uses or plans to use SAP applications.

The discussion about the increased value of NetWeaver is continued in more detail in Chapter 3.

2.2.6 Innovations with SAP NetWeaver

From the point of view of IT, innovation means the enabling of new or improved processes (as discussed in Section 2.1.3). In this regard, SAP NetWeaver takes into account two perspectives: the short term (that is, solutions that can be immediately implemented) and the medium to long term (that is, solutions whose full potential will become apparent in two to three years).

The Short-Term Perspective Small applications can be set up quickly on the basis of the infrastructure provided by SAP NetWeaver, especially with SAP Enterprise Portal, SAP Web AS, and the development tools. If, for example, a query of data from several systems that allows the possibility of changing the data is required, the "GUI Machine" tool can be used to easily create such a query without requiring any programming.

The idea of providing an infrastructure that allows for new solutions with little expenditure within a short period of time is also the basis for the mobile infrastructure. A customer can, for example, simply connect mobile terminals to an ERP system and automate fill levels or counter readings using Java, regardless of the user's location. Error-prone and time-consuming paper forms are thus a problem of the past.

In the case studies (Chapters 4 to 7), several possible solutions for this scenario are introduced, and short-term optimization potential in particular is demonstrated.

Decisive innovations have come about because lateral thinkers did not shy away from what appeared to be unchangeable limits; instead, they asked, "What would happen if?" Hasso Plattner, one of the founders of SAP and Speaker of the Board for many years, is considered to have this quality (i.e., the desire to strive for new ideas and not be hampered by limits that seem to prohibit these ideas from becoming a reality), and many have said that it is one of his most important character traits. In the book *Realtime*, which was dedicated to him on the occasion of his 60th birthday, discussions with Hasso Plattner are described as a special intellectual challenge:

... and the Medium- and Long-Term Perspectives

> *"Those who have met Hasso Plattner have found the experience exhilarating. His mind produces a steady stream of questions, ideas, and probing analysis. Most conversations begin with an invitation to attack and challenge the ideas he is setting forth. Doing battle with Hasso is a unique pleasure."[3]*

What would happen if processes could suddenly be changed very easily? What if you could model process ideas with a graphic tool, resort to the existing function modules or Web services, and supplement the missing elements in Java? The ESA, and especially the Composite Application Framework (CAF) (as a component of SAP NetWeaver), fulfill these prerequisites precisely. They form the basis for SAP xApps, a new generation of business applications. xApps include the functionalities of large conventional applications, and, from these components, create a new process. They can be easily changed without necessary adjustments to the

Process Changes by the Click of a Mouse Button

---

3 Woods, Dan: *Realtime: A Tribute to Hasso Plattner*. John Wiley & Sons Australia, 2004, p. xxvii.

applications on which they are based. The way in which process innovations are made can be fundamentally changed with this new design paradigm. Instead of initiating a project that would take several months and consume a proportionate amount of a budget, a process could be adjusted or completely redesigned within a very short period of time.

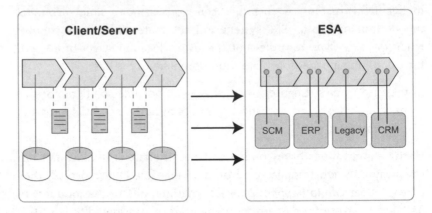

Figure 2.7 xApps As the Basis for Process Innovations

New software releases will of course continue to generate innovations that will be implemented within the functional orientation of the client/server architecture. But if a company previously wanted to be innovative by defining a new process, this inevitably meant high programming expenditure in order to implement it within the functional paradigm. xApps (or the CAF) moves this innovation upward in the level model. In this way, innovations that are to be integrated after shipment of the software can be implemented much more quickly and easily, and independently of the software version.

2.2.7 Strategic Significance

Because of its size and position in the market, SAP is at an advantage whenever companies select their software vendors. The closure of several dot coms at the time of the downturn of Internet hype made it painfully clear to many companies that investment security is a factor not to be underestimated when choosing software. Maintenance, service, and further development are, after all, ensured only as long as the provider exists.

SAP NetWeaver is a product of enormous strategic significance for SAP. It is *the* platform of all future SAP products, and it therefore establishes the essential general conditions for all SAP products. NetWeaver will become so relevant to all SAP customers that they should already start learning about it so they can benefit from its new possibilities as soon as possible.

SAP's decision to become a technology software provider with the introduction of NetWeaver (in contrast to its previous business as a vendor of only business software packages), has led to an inevitable change in the competitive relationship between SAP and other software manufacturers (middleware, platforms), as well as in its relationships with its customers. Since the task of integrating the company's IT systems has become a central problem, SAP NetWeaver has also taken on a strategic role. Companies are increasingly tending to limit the number of their software vendors. The architectural changes and the concurrent development toward a service-oriented architecture together are often the impetus for thinking about the general IT strategy. Although the gradual step-by-step transformation to SOA may lead to the impression that it is of minor significance, it is, on the contrary, of enormous significance. Hasso Plattner, who, as a founder of SAP, has been determined and has pressed ahead with the architecture of all SAP software of the past 30 years, puts it this way:

SAP As a Business Platform Provider

"We have our strengths, we maintain our strengths, and we add new capabilities. This is why I believe Enterprise Services Architecture is more important or probably at least as important as our invention in the early 1990s of the three-tier client/server architecture."[4]

The changes in SAP architecture and its product line that are currently underway are well-founded in SAP's strategic orientation. The market for technology and integration software determines to a large extent future access to customers. In other words, because customers usually decide to use just a few suppliers, if a company is chosen to be the integration software supplier, it is in a convenient position to cross-sell other products. Technological innovations have caused customers to focus on the question of integration. Because of its advantageous position, integration software vendors can use standards and supported products to influence how well applications function, and thus can hinder their development. A portal provider might, for example, no longer support all of the features of SAP applications in a new release, and instead provide the customer with features exclusive to its portal in order to gradually replace SAP. The discussion regarding integration software is therefore also a discussion about the use of standards, and by extension, market power.

The Strategic Significance of Integration Software

---

4 Woods, Dan: *Realtime: A Tribute to Hasso Plattner.* John Wiley & Sons Australia, 2004, p. 242.

Of course the struggle for market share also works the other way around. If SAP is represented in a company that uses components of SAP NetWeaver, SAP is put in a comfortable starting position. If, for example, a decision about a reporting tool is pending, there is a substantial argument for continued use of the existing software, that is, SAP BW, especially where (as in this case) a portion of the NetWeaver licenses are already available.

2.3   Paths to SAP NetWeaver

SAP NetWeaver can be described as a "toolbox for CIOs." It includes numerous tools suited to the widest variety of purposes. Just as you need only a hammer and a tape measure to hang a picture on the wall, only a portion of SAP NetWeaver's possibilities will be used for a particular task. It is important to make the right choice in individual situations since only a part of the whole is used and, in addition, the NetWeaver tools are a bit more complex than hammers and tape measures.

The objective is not to implement all NetWeaver components at once; first, you should hold a discussion regarding which steps a company should make, and which problems should be addressed when using SAP NetWeaver.

2.3.1   Project Procedures

SAP NetWeaver can be of importance in various projects: for reporting and user interface questions, the integration on diverse levels or, when deciding to change to a service-oriented architecture. A procedure that is determined openly by a wealth of diverse opinions can be implemented only step by step.

Step by Step to Success
Success can be achieved faster step by step, and if, for example, projects that are easy to implement are quickly dealt with, this has a positive effect on the economic result. Benefits from earlier projects can be used to the company's advantage while other projects are still in the implementation phase.

Of course, cross-project planning is reasonable in this case. Dependencies between projects can be managed with IT strategies and a planning period of three to five years. It is clear that a portal is required before reporting information within the scope of business intelligence can be presented in it.

2.3.2 Roadmaps

If the strategic decision is made in favor of SAP NetWeaver, that is, the choice has been made not only to solve individual problems with a NetWeaver component, but also to use NetWeaver as an infrastructure, the path to this goal has to be planned. Due to the magnitude and necessary time frame for such planning, the initial plans could be only a general roadmap that doesn't go into great detail.

Every demand a company makes is ultimately unique and requires close consideration. While company A may be considering the possibilities and opportunities of BPO, company B might be focusing on the integration of a new production location. Therefore, in this book, we have tried to examine as many different scenarios as possible. For this reason, the examples used refer to different industries, histories, and sizes of companies; this also applies to the software used and the specific problems.

In the following "Roadmaps to SAP NetWeaver," four scenarios are presented, and the individual roads taken—from the starting point to a NetWeaver implementation—are explained. These examples are based on real life consultation cases that have been made anonymous for use in this book.

1. **Global premium automobile manufacturer (Chapter 4)**
   Automotive Inc. is faced with the problem of having too little information about its customers and, because of this, it cannot provide them with optimal service. Therefore, the various data sources must be connected to the company, and the information gathered must be provided to the retailers.

2. **Manufacturing company (Chapter 5)**
   As a typical supplier, *Car Doors Inc.* has the problem of needing to grow faster than the market. Acquisitions that would necessitate large-scale integration projects are pending. Massive investments are made in research and development to boost organic growth. These constant changes in the organization must be able to be quickly and flexibly reflected and implemented in the IT systems.

3. **Medium-sized utilities provider (Chapter 6)**
   The liberalization of the supplier market increases the pressure on *United Gas* to provide optimal service to its customers and to develop new flexible solutions. The challenge lies in competing successfully while only having the limited resources of a medium-sized company. The IT landscape must therefore facilitate the implementation of inno-

vative solutions, and do so with as little expense to the company as possible.

4. **Bank (Chapter 7)**
   ABC Bank has a structure problem and must therefore closely check every part of its organization. Unprofitable areas must be cut, the IT landscape has to be simplified, and the remaining processes must be optimized.

Even if your company's situation does not fully match any of these descriptions, a combination of the aforementioned scenarios should answer the most important questions you might have about the possibilities with SAP NetWeaver.

3 Value Analysis

What are the benefits of SAP NetWeaver? How can they be determined and presented? What roles do flexibility, innovation, and cost reduction play within the framework of an IT infrastructure?

3.1 Market Requirements and Technology

Companies live off of their innovations. New products and services have to be developed constantly. The competition has to be outperformed, and the customers must be satisfied. In the daily struggle for market share, sales, and profits, aspirations are always with the product developers of a company. However, the best products don't help a company if no one wants to buy them.

Because market orientation is just as important as innovation, companies are forced to adapt their products and services to customer demands. And since the dynamics of markets are increasing, companies must behave dynamically, that is, they must adjust their products to the given situation. All of this works only if the processes of a company change. This is easier said than done. Automation and information technology play a central role in the handling of business processes. These processes receive considerable support from IT, but changes nevertheless require high expenditures. Clearly, IT landscapes must become much more flexible in the future so that innovative ideas can be successfully implemented.

Flexibility and Innovation

In times of tight budgets, IT departments are faced with the challenge of significantly lowering the costs of operation and maintenance of IT systems. A means of achieving this is the simplification of the infrastructure and the application landscape. One possibility is to outsource inefficient processes and functions by *Business Process Outsourcing* (BPO), or to bundle them using shared services and therefore handle them more efficiently. A prerequisite in any case is an IT architecture that supports the seamless migration of functions and services of the service provider. The IT platform must therefore accomplish the following:

Cost Reduction

▶ Make the changes of the company and its processes possible (flexibility)

▶ Serve as the basis for new products and services that must quickly achieve market maturity (innovation)

▶ Reduce the IT operating costs (Total Cost of Ownership, TCO)

In the past, there have always been new approaches to fulfilling these requirements, such as *Enterprise Application Integration* (EAI) tools. Lacking communication standards, however, led to failure in the effort to build a flexible system architecture. Web services use the manufacturer-independent standard XML, and they are defined and further developed by a large number of standardization groups.[1] The usage of Web services is a significant starting point to a Service Oriented Architecture (SOA).

SAP has developed the SOA approach to a new model of a service-based, company-wide solution—*Enterprise Services Architecture* (ESA). It forms the basis for service-based applications. The following features distinguish ESA:

▶ **Efficient upgrade or replacement of systems**
Web services makes information technology independent of the technical factors of individual systems. Individual components such as credit card validation or status displays can be upgraded or replaced without difficulty or effects on neighboring systems.

▶ **Flexible business**
Web services separate the business processes from the executing objects (for example, creating orders, canceling orders). In other words, process changes have no effect on the objects or systems. Changes can therefore be made more often and with less effort and costs. All this leads to more flexibility.

▶ **Quicker implementation**
Web services allow the isolated handling of software application functions (such as fulfillment or production scheduling). New functions can be introduced as necessary. The implementation of entire process chains is therefore no longer absolutely necessary.

▶ **Redundancy-free functions**
The reuse of Web services can help to reduce the number of similar redundant functions in a business application.

▶ **Outsourced functions**
The flexibility and openness of Web services enable the outsourcing of tasks (Business Process Outsourcing, BPO) and the implementation and automation of cross-company processes. Examples include payroll and credit card validation.

---

1 For example, by OASIS (Organization for the Advancement of Structured Information Standards), WS-I (Web Services Interoperability Organization), or UN/CEFACT (United Nations Centre for Trade Facilitation and Electronic Business)

- ▶ **Wider range of coverage**
  Companies can map entirely new business processes with partners and vendors by combining various Web services. For example, a distributor can provide the Web services of its vendor on his Internet platform.
- ▶ **Cost reduction**
  Costs can be reduced by reusing Web services when mapping business processes. This addresses one of core requirements of customers—the total cost of ownership reduction of software systems.

The aforementioned points clarify how important further development is to an Enterprise Services Architecture. SAP NetWeaver software is a technical platform that allows you to benefit from the advantages of this architecture. Today it is already possible to carry out the application developments with NetWeaver. SAP NetWeaver is the platform for all products from mySAP Business Suite[2] and the new SAP Composite Applications (xApps).

SAP NetWeaver

3.2 Description of the Value Analysis

In this section, we introduce ways to determine the usefulness of SAP NetWeaver on a *qualitative* basis.

Very recent value analyses focused heavily on the Return on Investment (ROI) approach. The ROI indicates the yield the company achieved with the total capital employed. It shows the profit objective or the percentage of profit based on total capital. The potential of the implementation of business processes can be determined with SAP NetWeaver in this *quantitative* manner. However, for the purpose of value analyses in Chapters 4 to 7, an initial *qualitative* estimate of the potential should be executed with SAP NetWeaver.

The ROI Approach

Every company considers the increasing of its value a central objective. In this context, however, it is not always easy to measure the total success of individual measures. To do this, a proven method is the *Economic Value Added* (EVA) approach. The EVA is calculated from the operative result after taxes minus capital investment. The process enables both a measurement of performance for a certain period of time as well as a future-oriented valuation. The EVA process measures to what extent a company's economic success can cover and exceed not only its operating

The EVA Approach

---

2 mySAP Business Suite contains process-specific products such as mySAP Customer Relationship Management (CRM) and mySAP Supplier Relationship Management (SRM).

costs, but also the costs for the capital invested. This approach is best suited for a company valuation; however, for an IT architecture, we need a more detailed methodology.

TCO Analysis   A *Total Cost of Ownership* (TCO) analysis takes into account the total costs of an IT infrastructure. With SAP NetWeaver, a comparison of only costs would neglect many fundamental advantages of an implementation. Therefore, this type of analysis involves an approach that valuates the installation of NetWeaver according to the criteria of innovation, flexibility, and cost-effectiveness. Whenever a company or an organization improves one of these criteria, the value of the company or organization increases. If one of the aspects is improved at the cost of another, this leads to a displacement of value. If the values develop negatively, the usefulness of an installation decreases.

Value Analysis Approach   The processes are considered in both an actual and target condition for the value analysis. To visualize the amount of value of the planned IT investments, a comparison is made exclusively with an IT reference value. This value is determined on the basis of a company's IT strategy (see also Section 3.2.4). Table 3.1 provides an overview of this approach.

			Customer				
			Reference value derived from the IT strategy of the company	Processes			
				Process 1		Process 2	
No.	Criterion	Valuation 0–5 (does not apply at all—fully applies)		Actual	Target	Actual	Target
Flexibility (IT)			0	0	0	0	0
1	System flexibility	Implementation time					
2	Process flexibility	Implementation costs					
3	Reaction speed / capability	Implementation time					
4	Outsourcing	Process costs					
5	Value chain	Implementation costs / process range					

Table 3.1 Value Analysis Matrix

			Customer				
			Reference value derived from the IT strategy of the company	Processes			
				Process 1		Process 2	
No.	Criterion	Valuation 0–5 (does not apply at all—fully applies)		Actual	Target	Actual	Target
Innovation			0	0	0	0	0
1	Value added	Profit increase					
2	Company value	EVA					
3	Innovation process	Time to market					
4	Communication	Development time					
5	Quality	Customer complaints, response rates					
Cost reduction (IT)			0	0	0	0	0
1	Infrastructure costs	Costs					
2	Initial costs	Costs					
3	Implementation costs	Costs					
4	Operating costs	Costs					
5	General costs	Costs					

Table 3.1 Value Analysis Matrix (cont.)

This structure allows the method to be used independently of both the specific industry and product, and it is suitable for:

▶ Determining the value of a NetWeaver installation
▶ Comparing the products of several different vendors

3.2.1 Flexibility

SAP NetWeaver provides a technology platform that makes flexible designing of business processes possible. The five criteria that enable a solid qualitative estimation of the flexibility of a company's IT infrastructure are as follows:

Criteria

▶ **System flexibility**
The essential question here is whether SAP NetWeaver can accelerate the integration of external systems. Integrating the applications of many manufacturers to map the processes required by the user departments poses a difficult challenge to the IT departments. System flexibility is qualitatively valuated within the scope of the required implementation time.

▶ **Process flexibility**
Here the focus is on the flexibility of adjusting the IT processes implemented in a company as required by the user departments. Often the implementation of creative ideas for products and services is, if at all affordable, very costly because the IT systems are too rigid and inflexible. The required implementation costs provide one way of valuating this criterion.

▶ **Reaction speed**
A company will be successful if it can quickly respond to the changes in the demands of the customers. SAP NetWeaver allows the IT department to make adjustments without large-scale development projects. A good example would be the interfaces between the individual application systems. They generally require a considerable amount of programming work whenever changes are made to business processes. This criterion is mapped in the analysis by the implementation time factor.

▶ **Outsourcing**
Market developments clearly show a trend toward the outsourcing of processes that don't belong to the core areas of a company's business. Web services allow the flexible integration of outsourced functions into the business process. For example, credit card validation in an online shop is, in most cases, handled by an external service provider. This ensures an improved quality of services as well as a reduction in process costs. The outsourcing criteria is valuated according to the cost savings potential.

▶ **Value chain**
Companies try to increase the range of their business processes. For example, individual Web services of equipment manufacturers could appear on the respective manufacturer's Web site. When examining this criterion, it is important to consider how an SAP NetWeaver installation would affect the optimization of the value chain.

3.2.2   Innovation

This section focuses on the criteria for a qualitative valuation of a company's innovation potential with SAP NetWeaver. An advantage of the SAP solution is the functionality of previously installed applications being made available via enterprise services, thus modeling cross-company business processes with the Composite Application Framework (CAF). These applications are called composite applications. Composite applications facilitate moving ahead with innovations in the area of information technology. Other starting points for the modeling of innovative processes with NetWeaver might include:

▶ *SAP Exchange Infrastructure* with the possibility of replacing hard-wired program components with flexible process integration

▶ *SAP Business Intelligence* for replacing non-transparent reporting structures with a flexible analysis platform

▶ *SAP Enterprise Portal,* which can replace the various user interfaces with a flexible, attractive interface to design innovative processes

The challenge lies in finding criteria that facilitate a realistic estimate of the potential of innovations. The following criteria are looked at when making this decision:

Criteria

▶ **Value creation**
Do the components of processes designed by SAP NetWeaver have a direct or indirect influence on the value creation in a company? In this case, a point of orientation could be a potential increase in turnover due to new products and services.

▶ **Company value**
To what level do processes like Composite Application built with SAP NetWeaver influence the value of a company? This criterion can also be seen as a follow-up criterion to value creation. One way of judging the value of a company is the aforementioned EVA method.

▶ **Innovation process**
Does the installation of SAP NetWeaver significantly accelerate or improve innovation management? A possible way of valuating the process would be by using the time period it takes for new products and services to achieve market maturity (time to market).

▶ **Communication**
This criterion focuses on communication processes. Do the components make improved communication possible between employees, customers, vendors, or partners (for example, with collaboration

tools)? The development time in the product design process could be used to valuate this criterion.

▶ **Quality**
Is the SAP NetWeaver software platform capable of improving the quality of the developed products and services, for example, by providing better documentation using knowledge management? Improvements to quality can be determined by analyses of customer complaints and response rates.

3.2.3 Cost Reduction

Why should a company be concerned with changes to its IT infrastructure? After the values "innovation" and "flexibility" have been discussed as important aspects of sustaining a company, the costs also need to be examined. Basically, it is quite simple: The profit of a company increases when the costs decrease. The demands on IT departments can be derived from this simple formula. It is a question of which parameters can be changed in order to achieve this objective.

Cost-Reducing
Potential

If you consider the situation today, the greatest opportunities for reducing costs in the IT infrastructure area can be summarized as follows:

▶ Elimination of heterogeneity of technological platforms and systems that need to be licensed, operated, and supported.

The analysis of the license costs for the SAP software used plays an important role here. According to an AMR Research[3] report, companies invest an average of 10% to 13% of their annual IT budget in infrastructure technology.

In most cases, approximately 25% of the employees of a company per SAP installation are named users who require licenses. These named users are in a position to offer the cost-reducing potential. If a company is using a product from mySAP Business Suite, for example, Enterprise Resource Planning (mySAP ERP), the usage rights for SAP NetWeaver are already included in the price of the corresponding mySAP licenses. In other words, there are no additional license fees for the named users of SAP NetWeaver.

Since SAP NetWeaver replaces the operation of a wide range of individual basic applications, the management of the individual applications is simplified. This becomes noticeable with the reduced amount of work required on system upgrades and system monitoring.

---

3 Austvold, Eric; Shepherd, Jim: *SAP NetWeaver 2004*. AMR Research Report.

▶ The use of *adaptive computing* with SAP NetWeaver makes a flexible assignment of processor capacity possible.

Adaptive computing systems can be adjusted independently of conventional programming to the requirements of the current application in software and hardware-related aspects. In contrast to this, the flexibility of the application for standard processors is defined entirely by the software. In many cases, this forces an oversizing of the processor to make effective program handling possible. This process, however, negatively impacts the development of hardware costs, which includes the following effects:

▶ Reduction of expenditures that arise from the on-site programming of application systems. There is potential for reducing costs in the area of development if a standard IT basic platform is used. There is also cost reduction potential in the reuse of previously existing components and accelerated knowledge transfer.

▶ Reduction of interfaces necessary for data exchange between individual systems. Room for savings is offered by both the accelerated implementation of system interfaces via a hub component (such as the Exchange Infrastructure) as well as the resulting decrease in maintenance work.

▶ The option of outsourcing individual services of a company to reduce the costs for business processes

▶ Reusability of SAP skills in the development and integration of application components

The most important criteria for valuating the cost-reducing potential are discussed in the following sections. The details are based on published TCO models and publications on the calculation of total IT costs by leading analyst firms such as *Gartner* and *Meta Group*.

Criteria

▶ **Infrastructure**
Depending on the type of cost, the allocation of financial expenditures on an IT infrastructure can be determined only to a certain degree. The costs for IT purchasing, inventory management, IT support, software and server administration, service, training for support employees and communication costs (WAN/LAN environment) are typical kinds of indirect costs. The allocation can be determined only with the help of the corresponding compensation keys or if it is ensured that the departments responsible view tasks only in the context of the IT structure.

▶ **Initial costs**
These costs arise whenever studies on value or cost analyses are carried out for an IT infrastructure in the evaluation phase. The setup of the technical infrastructure is also part of the initial costs.

▶ **Implementation costs**
The financial expenditures for an SAP NetWeaver installation can be allocated to the project activities as direct costs. Process design, technical structure, process implementation, testing, training, and the setup of a support organization are typical tasks necessary for software implementation.

▶ **Operating costs**
The operation of SAP NetWeaver involves direct costs for application management, the data center, projects, software upgrades, and maintenance fees.

▶ **General costs**
These include costs for employees, property, and work centers. In certain cases these costs could be considerable when taking the total costs into account if, for example, special safety measures need to be taken for an IT server landscape.

Indirect costs such as training or employee support are not considered when looking at total costs.

3.2.4   Reference Value

Reference Value Based on the IT Strategy Which IT investments are worthwhile depends on both the strategic objectives of a company as well as its competitive position in the market. Whether it is a question of improving the situation with regard to cost or achieving growth and expansion objectives with IT, ultimately, the IT strategy must support the company's strategy.

The IT strategy considers the chances of increasing the turnover and revenue of a company, for example, the setup of an Internet Web site as an integrated marketing and sales instrument. The IT strategy also has basic requirements with regard to business operation, for example, the task of modeling business processes more efficiently via IT— for instance, purchasing, production, or sales. Therefore, a good IT strategy specifies the general conditions for the IT management of a company. It indicates the scope and direction of future action towards reaching long-term company objectives.

The description of value analysis discussed in this chapter determines the usefulness of SAP NetWeaver with regard to the strategic IT objectives of a company. It specifies an objective with reference values for flexibility, innovation, and cost reduction in a target scenario to be achieved by installing SAP NetWeaver. The creation of a complete IT strategy would not fulfill the purpose of this qualitative method of determining the usefulness of an installation. Rather, the goal is to introduce you to the typical components of an IT strategy. You can use them as a basis for your own valuation.

An IT strategy can comprise five essential components, depending on the business strategy:

Components of an IT strategy

▶ The *infrastructure strategy* considers the basic components. They include hardware, operating systems, and networks.

▶ The *application strategy* focuses on the use of software to support the business processes of a company.

▶ The *innovation strategy* deals with new technologies that need to be valuated for use in a company.

▶ The *sourcing strategy* focuses on the IT value chain of a company to establish which existing IT services it will adopt and which services outside the company it will purchase.

▶ The *investment strategy* examines the IT investment decisions of a company.

3.3   The Value Analysis Process

The IT strategy of a company, the valuation of the actual situation, and the valuation of a possible target architecture are all phases that are part of the value analysis. The complete approach consists of the following individual procedures (see also Figure 3.1):

The Value Analysis Process

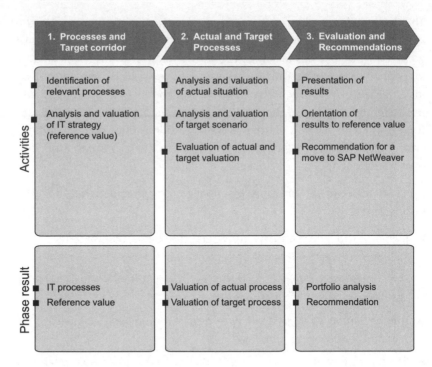

Figure 3.1 The Value Analysis Process

▶ **IT processes and target corridor**
The identification of the IT infrastructure processes of the company is first focused on in this phase. As soon as this is known and, if necessary, prioritized, the IT strategy is considered in the second step. The reference value is determined via a valuation using the previously mentioned criteria *flexibility*, *innovation*, and *cost reduction* on a scale of 0 (does not apply at all) to 5 (fully applies). The reference value works like a target that IT-relevant processes of the company should try to emulate.

▶ **Actual and target processes**
In the second step of the value analysis, the identified processes are analyzed and valuated in the actual situation. A possible target system architecture is analyzed and evaluated with NetWeaver components to show value-added IT potential. A graphic presentation of the individual criteria should be used to show the change.

▶ **Evaluation and recommendations**
In this phase, the qualitative total estimate of the actual and target processes are evaluated. The results are presented via a portfolio diagram in respect of the criteria's flexibility and innovation. The size of

the circles entered corresponds to the estimated costs of a NetWeaver solution. It is critical that the evaluation is oriented toward the IT strategy of the company. The reference value is calculated for this purpose. The results can then be entered in the portfolio matrix, providing a target scenario. Specific measures for introducing SAP NetWeaver are shown at the end of the analysis.

In this chapter, the basics of value analysis were explained based on the advantages of SAP NetWeaver. The criteria of flexibility, innovation, and cost reduction are essential to carrying out a valuation of the identified processes. A reference value derived from an IT strategy is used to define a target scenario. This procedure is used in value analyses in the following chapters. Companies can now carry out a qualitative, yet subjective value analysis of implementing SAP NetWeaver.

Conclusion

4 Roadmap to SAP NetWeaver at Automotive Inc.

The industrial world is changing, and nowhere is this metamorphosis occurring as rapidly as it is in the automotive industry. Where manufacturers were once responsible for only production and shipping, today these same manufacturers make up multinational companies that must fulfill every customer's wish—from financing, to marketing, to sales, and from production to disposal.

4.1 Scenario Description

As the automotive industry is changing, so, too, is the world of the carmaker. Today *the* carmaker no longer exists; instead, the market is divided into mass producers and premium producers. These two types of companies differ substantially in terms of product portfolios and the different ways in which they foster customer relationships. *Automotive Inc.*, a premium producer, wants to do more than simply produce cars; it wants to bring lifestyle products into the market that the customer can identify with and remain faithful to for a lifetime. In addition, Automotive Inc., like other premium producers and sporting goods manufacturers such as *Nike*, intends to focus more on marketing and coordination, and outsource technical aspects of the original business—namely, the development and production of cars—to other companies.

In this regard, there has been much discussion of a shift in focus among carmakers from internal processes (product focus) to the customer (customer focus), which requires a restructuring of the entire organization. A study from Roland Berger[1] reported on this trend years ago. The study described nine main trends in the automotive supply industry, all of which are derived from the strategy of the carmakers. The two most important of these trends are:

▶ The restructuring of all internal processes with the goal of greater customer focus

▶ The outsourcing of development and production to tier-1 suppliers (suppliers with direct connection to the manufacturers)

---

1 Berger, Roland: *Nine Mega-Trends Re-Shape the Automotive Supplier Industry.* Roland Berger & Partner GmbH, Munich 2000.

Carmakers have also undergone internal structural changes. Ten years ago, Automotive Inc. (the company we are using to illustrate this scenario) had only two production sites; today it has six production sites worldwide. The company's relationship to its suppliers has also shifted. In the past, it independently developed and manufactured almost everything, which contributed to a great production depth (i.e., Automotive Inc. produced most of the car). Today, Automotive Inc. Involves its system suppliers in both development and production (see Figure 4.1 and Figure 4.2). Where earlier, precise numbers of units were ordered and the actual development occurred at Automotive Inc., today entire components are developed and produced by the supplier.

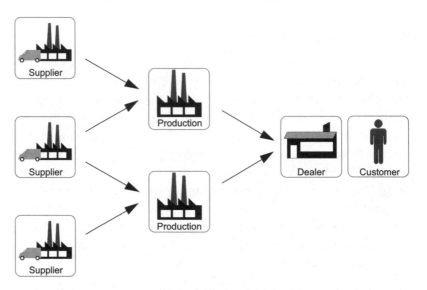

Figure 4.1 Development and Manufacturing in the Automobile Industry (Yesterday)

One of the great challenges facing premium producers is their inexperience with interacting with customers to having direct contact with customers. Previously, they were active in the fields of marketing and advertising, but did not maintain direct contact with customers. For this reason, they often lacked data to precisely describe their customers and their requirements (such information did stay in the cardealers' heads however). Such customer data was not accessible because it was either spread across dealer networks (and therefore not consolidated or comprehensive enough to be useful) or kept under lock and key at foreign subsidiaries, and protected as though it were a formidable state secret (and therefore not shared).

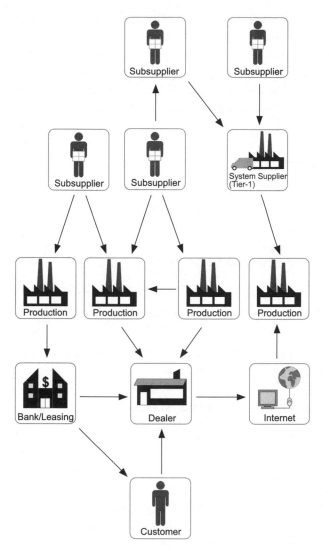

Figure 4.2 Development and Manufacturing in the Automobile Industry (Today)

The financing business has developed into another field that carmakers have become active in. Customers are offered classical products such as leasing and financing, and lately, investment funds and credit cards as well. Fringe fields such as travel agencies and event management will not be considered in the following discussion. However, it will be made clear that individual manufacturers are becoming active in an ever wider array of fields, with the goal of offering the customer more comprehensive service.

Products from Different Fields Supply Customer Data

In the past, the primary consideration was that all systems should first have a uniform data model, so that they could be connected to one another. However, this could not be implemented due to IT difficulties. Another consideration was integrating customers' and suppliers' systems via interfaces and electronic data interchange (EDI) techniques. This was technically possible, but contributed to immense maintenance expenditures.

4.2 The Challenge

The CIO of Automotive Inc. is responsible for restructuring the existing IT landscape to meet the requirements of the future. His long-term goal is to integrate all important processes into one landscape (not one system) and to significantly reduce operating costs using economical user interfaces. This poses the following secondary challenges for the company:

▶ Connection of all customer data sources to one analytical CRM system

▶ Assignment of a single, uniform customer number for all customers worldwide

▶ Integration of the most important suppliers into the production management system of Automotive Inc.

4.2.1 Building an Analytical CRM System

The most important goal in restructuring the system landscape is building an analytical Customer Relationship Management (CRM) system. Customer data is currently collected at many points, but unfortunately, a network between the systems is lacking. This is why Automotive Inc. is starting with the process that is most important to it, the customer process. The first goal of Automotive Inc. is the introduction of a worldwide CRM system, with the primary challenge being collecting information.

The goal of Automotive Inc. is to set up a CRM reporting system that makes it possible to observe and capture the behaviors and likes and dislikes of their direct customers and to determine what actions influence and promote buying decisions. It is also important to maintain customer relationships, even through sales companies. This is all the more important if the buyer obtains information in Germany and then buys the vehicle in a neighboring foreign country.

The idea is to give each customer a unique customer number in order to identify him for the long term as a "permanent customer" and to keep him . Therefore, every customer in every business relationship should be uniquely identifiable. Examples of different customer relationships that are currently not transparent to Automotive Inc. would be:

▶ As a used car buyer

▶ As an interested party

▶ As a new car buyer

▶ As a service customer

▶ As a rental car customer

▶ As a finance customer

▶ As an employee of a large customer

▶ As a foreign customer

This idea is not new, but previously the assumption was that for problem-free implementation, all data would have to first be stored in one system. This was the starting point for many *company data models* (CDM). However, this approach could never be completed at Automotive Inc.—as with many other companies as well—because all involved parties (dealers and sales subsidiaries) often used different systems and an integration of the dealers and sales companies is almost impossible. This integration is particularly important when the involved parties are legally independent companies that have little motivation to cooperate in these processes.

No CDM for Uniform Customer Number Possible

For a long time, uniform data models were a big topic in IT. However, they could be implemented only when the companies using them acted passively, that is, when the companies did not change. However, the automobile industry in particular is in a constant state of change. Smaller manufacturers are constantly being bought up; production and sales sites worldwide are being expanded; and new fields of business are constantly being opened up with new niche models.

In addition to a uniform database, another goal is to make the success of individual marketing measures measurable. How long does it take from the first point of contact at a dealership until the customer makes a decision? Currently, the success of individual measures can be determined only by juxtaposing sales success with the measures carried out. Unfortunately, it is almost impossible to follow customer behavior based on actual patterns. It would also be useful to know which individual measures were particularly successful. The company could then recognize patterns and use them to gain long-term customer loyalty, so that all of the customer's expenditures in the automobile field benefit the company.

Measurement of Individual Marketing Measures and Benchmarking

In Germany, the ZDK (Zentralverband der Automobilindustrie—Central Association of the Automotive Industry) has determined that between the ages of 18 and 72, a car buyer pays 394,395 USD for new purchases and additional costs, i.e., maintenance, insurance, and so on. A large portion of this amount is for new purchases. If a carmaker succeeds in binding a customer to a brand early and comprehensively, it will make a lot of sales with the customer. If the company acquires the customer when the customer is 60 or older, proportionally more expensive vehicles will be sold, but the total sales per customer will be less.

One way of building this customer loyalty is to secure the customer as a used car buyer before the purchase of a new car. In addition, customer contact can be built up by using comprehensive financing offerings (financing, fund savings plans). These customers are then emotionally connected to the brand through constant information and promotion.

Unused Data from the Dealer Side A huge amount of data on the customer is also collected on the dealer side. Unfortunately, this data often remains in the dealer's database system, which typically consists of information that would be kept on a rolodex, instead of a CRM solution.

4.2.2 Supplier Integration

In the future, customer loyalty will not be the only factor that determines the success of the company; the connection with the dealer will also be increasingly important. As a second step (the first step was building an analytical CRM system), the CIO therefore must focus on his relationship with the dealers. Interfaces for data exchange already exist (EDI), however, when collaborating with suppliers, the only existing interface is the mail system.

Integration of Suppliers Is "The" Future Success Factor The demands on suppliers have changed considerably in recent years. Where it used to be sufficient to supply parts at an economical price, requirements today look like this:

▶ Delivery of self-designed components

▶ Worldwide production in the direct proximity of Automotive Inc.

▶ Acceptance of product risk

▶ Delivery based on just-in-time delivery schedules

To ensure that all of these requirements are met, it is necessary to involve the suppliers early on in the development process. The supplier must assume the task of developing individual components until it can achieve mass production. This is done in close collaboration with the internal development department. The supplier also requires a lot of information in advance of the delivery schedule. For example, which vehicles are selling particularly well, and which vehicles are not? Often the marketing department of Automotive Inc. can determine whether the supplier's components will be in demand in the future. Also, how does the planning of the model cycle look? Can components be used in the next generation of a vehicle, reducing high development and testing costs?

Another viewpoint is becoming equally important. The supplier is increasingly responsible for the quality of the brand and has an intense interest in making components that cause as few errors as possible. This requirement for "zero errors" was recently renewed by a large carmaker that had received heavy criticism for problems with its electronic components.

"Zero Error" Becomes the New Standard of Quality

Here, in particular, the system supplier can have a decisive influence on the brand image if he or she develops and delivers his or her parts with "zero errors." However, this requires a high level of coordination between the manufacturer and the individual system suppliers. This coordination often occurs too late in the development process. But an IT department that establishes a platform across all systems can recognize most weak points at an early stage.

4.3   The Points of Focus

In this section and Section 4.4, we'll look at the requirements and demands described in the previous sectionand the ways to meet these challenges with software solutions. We have chosen to focus on theoretical solutions; therefore, no precise specification of the technical implementation is provided here. Instead, the actual implementation is discussed in Section 4.5.

To achieve a division of tasks that have to be addressed in different fields, we will differentiate between systems that are in contact with the customer and those that are in contact with the supplier. Both fields have great significance for our company. As described in Section 4.2.1, the company's primary goal is to create a uniform platform in the field of customer relations. We will describe this in greater detail later. The second important field, supplier relations (supply chain), will be described in more detail in Section 4.3.2.

4.3.1 Integrating All Customer Relations in One Platform

The Achilles' heel of the customer processes in Automotive Inc. is the collection of all relevant data generated in the customer process. Here the previous focus, collecting data from the ordering and invoice process, is expanded and reorganized.

Next, we won't elaborate on the uniform CRM system, because we'll assume that our company has not agreed on one CRM system, but rather that various CRM systems are used at different levels. Therefore, we'll focus on the integration of the CRM systems.

One aspect is the corporate business. Automotive Inc. sells approximately 56% of its new vehicles to corporate customers rather than to private individuals. You should note that in recent years company cars are increasingly being used as incentives and therefore form part of employee compensation. As a result, employees are becoming freer to decide what company car they drive, and the company maintains multiple business relationships with multiple premium automobile manufacturers.

Because the employees have the freedom of choice and are subject only to budget restrictions, the employee must be seen as an end customer and his or her loyalty must be won. This can be achieved only when the large customer (corporate customer) and its employees are each seen as independent customers, and the employees can be connected with the company customers. The data model has to create a link between the corporate customer and a single end customer that happens to be an employee of the company.

The goal is to collect information on all existing and potential customers. Collectively, these customers fall into the following categories, which are each of strategic importance:

▶ Integration of all data collected via Internet traffic into one CRM/data warehouse system

▶ Integration of all information collected on the dealer side into one CRM/data warehouse system

▶ Integration of the European dealers into one CRM/data warehouse system

As you can see, a separation already exists between the individual systems. Entering the data in a pure CRM system, that is, in a system required for direct customer contact only, makes little sense. It is necessary to have the data in an aggregated form in order to evaluate it, in short, to perform analytical CRM. These evaluations, in particular, generate the added value of the CRM solution.

Not only evaluations of past data can be initiated; you can now create data forecasts. This can be performed using data mining as well as classical planning, whether rolling or integrated.

Data Mining Supports the Analysis Process

Integrating All Information Collected Via Internet Traffic into One Information System Architecture

As our first point of focus, we will look at the integration of all customer relations that take place over the Internet. The first challenge is that currently no one system—but various different systems—exists that is in contact with the customer.

For example, there is a system in which the customer as an interested party can configure a vehicle and must identify himself as a user. In addition, the customer can also request information directly. Unfortunately, various platforms exist for the vehicle configurer because, as part of the quick introduction of the European sales companies, the company has given itself a great amount of space with which to work. These customer relations must now be integrated, because, for legal reasons, it is now very difficult to impose a solution on the now partly independent importers.

We also still face the challenge of getting the user to provide his or her true identity on the Internet. This can be done only with an interesting bonus program, so that the user sees an added value as compared to logging on anonymously.

True Identity of the User

It would also be interesting to know which vehicles are configured on the Internet and whether these vehicles are then purchased. Here it is extremely important to make a unique connection between configuration and order.

It is also important to recognize when the user leaves the Internet platform without completing actions already in progress. For example, it is interesting to evaluate why users don't continue on to save their configuration and thereby leave a unique profile.

For the Internet user on the platform, how the individual steps look and where important data can be attained can be seen in Figure 4.3.

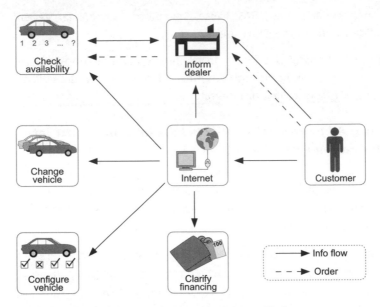

Figure 4.3 The Ordering Process Using the Internet Platform

When we now look at these steps in detail, we see that the customer can configure a complete vehicle on the Internet, or actually does so, but cannot complete the most important step—ordering a car. This step is reserved exclusively for the support point dealer.

Customer Information from the Internet

However, the customer does answer many questions:

▶ What base model is he interested in?

▶ What equipment does he find interesting?

▶ How does he imagine the financing?

▶ How many miles does he plan to drive a year?

▶ How will the car be used?

▶ When does he plan to drive the vehicle?

All of this information is available directly or indirectly and can be transmitted from the Web site to the CRM/data warehouse system. The goal of the company is to expand the Web site with Web services that deliver this information to the data warehouse. The main use of Web services here is the integration of data.

Corporate Customer Portals

The goal in this area is to expand the existing portal so that there is a separate area for each corporate customer. Individual prices and equipment packages can be stored in these areas. It is also possible that the company will already focus primarily on the user, allowing him to access company-specific rules during configuration.

This lets Automotive Inc. precisely analyze, for 56% of its customers, the relationship between the selections made over the Internet and orders actually carried out. This is possible because these buyers can be accurately analyzed as company car buyers.

Integrating All Information Collected by Dealers into One Information System Architecture

Among dealers as well, there is currently too little information collected. This is partly because the dealers enter and maintain their customer data on their own IT systems, and partly because the dealers have not yet recognized the necessity of comparing their data with that of the manufacturers. They are also often afraid of the competition and that data will be misused. However, data exchange as part of the inherent cooperation that must exist between partners is not a one-way street; dealers profit from it as well.

As far as data volume and data quality is concerned, the dealer is success factor number one when one wishes to redefine the customer process. The customer usually has very good relations with him, and during the sales process, the dealer learns the most about the customer. However, sometimes dealers don't keep this database current due to the expense of doing so.

Problem: Data Volumes

To view what information can be collected via this channel, see Figure 4.4.

The figure shows that the dealer usually knows the wishes of the customer best. He knows what the customer's dream car looks like, and he also knows the financing options. He knows where the customer has had problems with the technology in the past, and the extent to which these things have been changed in newer models.

However, the dealer has no information on the customer's relationhips with other dealers, what vehicles he has rented recently, and what the general motivating factors are for a buying decision in this target group. This information is usually not collected, and when it is, it has a certain market research quality to it.

Lack of Additional Customer Data

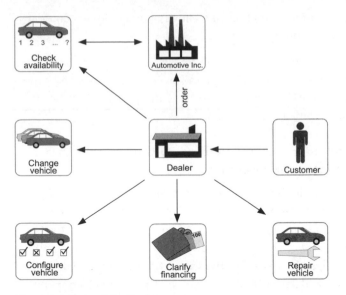

Figure 4.4 Tasks of the Dealer

The most important task for the dealer is to get a uniform customer number for the customer in order to be able to offer him targeted service over the long term. However, it is imperative that this number not be assigned individually by the dealer, but rather by Automotive Inc. This is the only way to ensure that each customer is eventually assigned to a company or corporate group and that the data is still available in uniform form after mergers between manufacturers or the next regional structure reform.

This also ensures that each customer is openly addressed only once in the same context. Nothing is more embarrassing than when a carmaker sends a customer the same mail several times or when a customer is courted simultaneously by several dealerships.

Local and Global CRM Complement Each Other Perfectly A unique assignment can be performed only if the existing CRM system at the dealership is expanded by interfaces to the CRM system of the carmaker. In this context, it must be considered whether the dealer's CRM system, which was most likely introduced as a pure invoice system, can really be expanded. In this case, one should think about Web services. Web services enable the dealer to access a CRM system at the manufacturer and avoid the purchase and maintenance of such a system.

The interesting question here is how the dealers can be motivated to take part in such a system. To summarize, cooperation can only take place as part of a partner relationship. The technical advantages for the dealers are explained in Section 4.5.2.

As you can see in Figure 4.4, the dealer often deals with financing for the customer or learns of the details of possible financing via the customer's bank. Here it is also very important that this information be passed from the dealer to Automotive Inc. Only this information makes it possible to adapt the conditions of the company's own bank so they can make offers at attractive conditions. For example, in Germany, all car manufacturers also own banks that focus on financing car deals. However, they are in competition with normal banks. The dealer usually knows what kind of financial offering a customer received.

In recent years, another topic has also become increasingly important. The quality of premium vehicles as perceived by customers is decreasing continuously, and this is primarily due to problems with car electronics and the repair visits associated with them.[2] So far, communication between the customer and the manufacturer on this topic has been carried out through the dealers. The manufacturer only rarely learns how dissatisfied a customer is with a certain car or even whether he is considering changing brands. It would be helpful if this data, which the customer leaves with the dealer, could also be collected so that it is available to Automotive Inc. Because the dealer usually does not have a complaint management system, here as well, a Web service should be considered in which the dealer can enter this data.

There is great potential for optimization in another field as well, namely, troubleshooting.

Web-Based Issue Management

The process in this area is still not uniform, and the usefulness for Automotive Inc. is very slight. Faults are found and corrected individually at each dealership. The dealers only communicate safety-related faults and recurring faults with Automotive Inc. But, because Automotive Inc. only acts as a marketer for many components and passes on production and development to first-tier suppliers, an information flow between the first-tier supplier and the dealers and customers is actually required. This process, however, has not yet been installed.

Figure 4.5 shows how this process would run ideally. It is derived from the software industry, which has used Web-based services for issue management.

---

2 According to a German newspaper of May 22, 2004, DaimlerChrysler has now started a zero error initiative that explicitly includes electronics. This shows that the problem of reclamations is being taken very seriously.

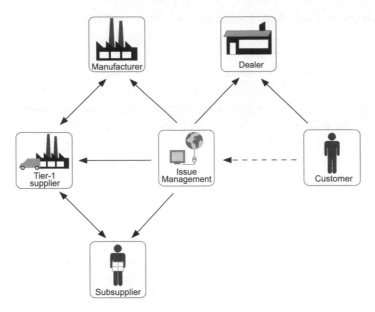

Figure 4.5 Web-Based Issue Management via the Dealer

The process runs as follows:

1. The customer raises an issue with the dealer.

2. The dealer assigns the issue to a component and enters it in the issue management system.

3. Automotive Inc., the customer, the tier-one supplier, and any subsuppliers can track and process the issue.

4. The dealer can now access all issues raised in this regard or for this component and initiate fast and economical error correction.

Advantages The advantages of the process are as follows:

▶ The dealers access the knowledge from other problem cases.

▶ The customer can follow the progress of problem-solving at any time.

▶ The suppliers learn more about the problems with their components and can actively help in fault correction.

▶ Automotive Inc. increases the advantage to the customer and prevents dissatisfied customers from leaving.

However, there are also disadvantages—quality problems of the individual suppliers or Automotive Inc. quickly become apparent, for example. A good authorization and role concept that regulates access can help to correct this ability of other suppliers to look at (overall) quality information.

Integrating the European Dealers into Analytical CRM

Integrating the data of European dealers is interesting in two respects:

▶ Reduction of the sales effects caused by new car purchasing abroad

▶ Expansion of customer service and supply throughout Europe

Reducing the Negative Effects

Long before the development of the Internet, profit margins at Automotive Inc. were under pressure. The opening of the European common market in 1993 and the eastward expansion in 2004 brought with them a great demand in the retail market for new cars, and this demand became even more acute the closer one got to the national border. Because car prices differ significantly in the European countries (depending on the economic output per head, taxes, etc.), many people in Germany buy their new car in Denmark where they can save up to 30%. Therefore, it is imperative for Automotive Inc. to know how these buyers act or react to what's happening on the (European) market look and how they can be correctly directed in the company's interest.

Figure 4.6 shows the relationships between the individual contract parties. It is apparent that the European dealers get only a piece of the action, because there is a significant price difference between the list price at home and the price abroad.

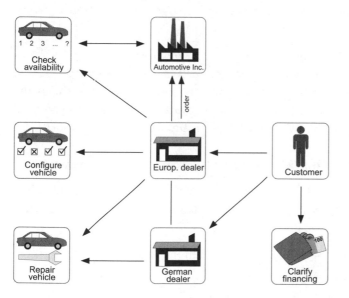

Figure 4.6 The Ordering Process in the European Context

The goal must now be to research the exact reasons for this movement (i.e., Automotive Inc.'s response to how customers react to the different prices on the European market) with the available data and to stop this movement with appropriate offers. Ideally, Automotive Inc. will be able to have vehicles cost the same in all countries so no movement will be necessary. Yet another parameter must be observed with regard to car buying abroad in Europe. Many customers from other countries would like to order the newest model as soon as it is available and not wait months for it. This creates a movement toward markets in which the models are introduced first. These movements must be analyzed so that during the next market introduction, the model becomes available in other countries at the same time it becomes available on the domestic market.

Expanding customer service is another aspect that must be considered when performing this integration task. Relations to corporate customers are particularly important here because corporate customers usually active in several countries and require comprehensive, full-coverage service in those other countries as well. In this way, all concepts that are already used by German dealers can be expanded to offer the maximum service to foreign dealers as well.

This will be done primarily using a portal, because we can simply expand the existing concept to account for the language and the regional circumstances.

We have now thoroughly investigated the requirements and possibilities of the customer process. However, as we have seen at several points, the suppliers must also be integrated into this process, because this is the only way to ensure that the customer is 100% satisfied with the process. The following sections describe what this supplier integration looks like.

4.3.2 Integrating All Supplier Relations in One Platform

Integrating all supplier relations in one infrastructure architecture is second in priority to customer relations at Automotive Inc. The goals in this area are:

- Joint development of components with the supplier
- Reduction of the number of suppliers to a few top suppliers
- Production of the components by the suppliers
- Quality assurance and issue management by the suppliers
- Joint market research/market evaluation with the supplier

The area of delivery schedules and just-in-time (JIT) delivery, which already works well today, will not be considered in the following. This field has been pushed forward since the beginning of the '90s, both by Automotive Inc. and its suppliers, and will be placed on a new technical platform as part of the new IS architecture in order to minimize the adaptation effort for future interface changes.

Joint Project Development Platform

So far we have focused only on cooperation with the sales side, the dealers. But cooperation with the suppliers is becoming increasingly important for Automotive Inc. Here we can distinguish between two types of suppliers:

▶ Tier-1 suppliers (all system suppliers)

▶ Tier-n or subsuppliers (all component and parts suppliers)

In the following, we will deal with the tier-1 suppliers, because these suppliers play an important role in the future value-added chain of Automotive Inc. These suppliers are responsible for developing and producing complex systems and delivering them "just in time" to the production conveyor belts of Automotive Inc.

The most important step in achieving cooperation with the suppliers is creating a joint IS architecture on which joint development projects can take place. To see how a joint platform of this kind looks, see Figure 4.7.

The main advantage of such a uniform platform is that everyone involved in the process—even the smallest subsuppliers—is informed on the current state of development at all times. The tier-1 suppliers work to integrate the smaller subsuppliers; Automotive Inc. has access to the data, however. In such an environment, it is also possible to ensure via a role concept that every participant sees only the information intended for him or her.

Automotive Inc. has the advantage that it can observe all development steps, even after it has turned development over completely to tier-1 suppliers. Even in this kind of networked environment, you can still implement simple changes to previous developments without risking not meeting final deadlines.

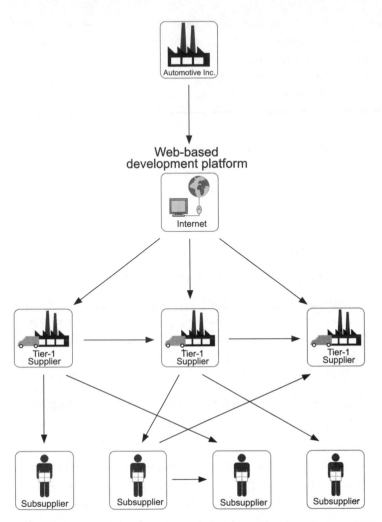

Figure 4.7 Web-Based Development Platform As an Interface Between All Participants

In order to build a development portal, let's first look at the participants in a portal. We'll consider all departments that are used as part of "simultaneous engineering":[3]

▶ Development department

▶ Purchasing

▶ Testing and materials testing

---

3 "Simultaneous engineering" is the acceleration of the development process of a new product achieved by parallel development employed by the manufacturer and the supplier. All available resources (employees and capital) are invested concurrently to push forward real-time development projects.

- ▶ Cost accounting
- ▶ Marketing and sales department
- ▶ Quality assurance
- ▶ Production planning
- ▶ Work preparation
- ▶ Finance department

Figure 4.8 shows how the development progresses through time.

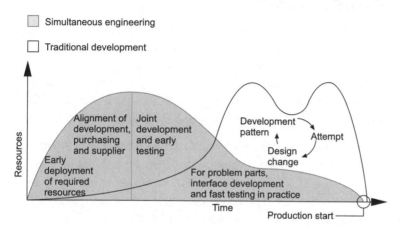

Figure 4.8 Simultaneous Engineering

You should note that this development process is running today between Automotive Inc. and tier-1 suppliers, however, there is currently no joint IS architecture.

Joint Fault Evaluation Platform

A change in the way faults are documented and corrected is an important step toward reliability, even for complex vehicle systems. As we saw in Section 4.3.1, Automotive Inc. lacks a central tool that can be used to enter, monitor, and solve all faults. However, only if all suppliers participate in the system can such a tool be successfully introduced.

What form can this participation take? As a first step, suppliers require information on where exactly problems have occurred with their components, how these problems were corrected, and whether they were quality or design faults.

The area of design faults is particularly important when the supplier is also responsible for developing the components. In this case, it is important

Real-time Integration of the Suppliers

that the designer be informed quickly (in realtime!) of these faults so that he or she can suggest a solution as soon as possible.

Such a platform is also important for Automotive Inc., because the tier-1 suppliers supply the same components to several manufacturers, and problems that appear at one manufacturer can be corrected at several manufacturers simultaneously. Such a measure increases the quality of the individual supplier, and that supplier gains a competitive advantage.

Joint Marketing Studies/Presales Platform

Lastly, we must look at the increasing variety of vehicles in planning at Automotive Inc. The company wants to bring evermore variants of a platform (for example, variants of an existing model such as the Ford Mustang Convertible is a variant of the Ford Mustang) to market in an ever shorter period of time. This is the only way Automotive Inc. can expand its market share, or simply maintain it in several areas.

Joint Marketing Studies on Niche Models

However, these variants can only be brought to market after marketing studies, which are often extensive in scope. Then it must still be ensured that the model meets the sales expectation. This is where the joint marketing platform with the suppliers comes in (tier-1 suppliers). Information from the following fields can be shared on this platform:

▶ The configuration wishes of the customers for similar models (predecessor models)

▶ The supplier's own market research data

▶ The market research data of Automotive Inc.

The features that the customers would like to see and which are not yet available, which are listed on the Internet and at the dealership, are particularly important for future model design and are critical for getting just the right specification in the future series of models.

This data is important for estimating future requirements, and is included as part of the continuous planning for the suppliers.

4.4   Fast Project Successes

In Section 4.3, we saw where Automotive Inc. is going. All necessary steps are known and correctly prioritized. Now we must implement these steps so that we can achieve an IS architecture that does not rely on one huge "big bang project," but instead integrates and optimizes old applications and processes in steps.

Various approaches exist for attacking such a large project. In our example, Automotive Inc. has decided to address the goals in the customer process field first. Therefore, Automotive Inc.'s project procedure looks like this:

Project Procedure

▶ Setting up a data warehouse landscape

▶ Setting up Web services for the dealers

▶ Collaboration portal for the suppliers during development

These projects can be started immediately, with each of them requiring a certain running time (time 'til the project ends); furthermore, they can be organized productively into partial steps.

In general, when designing a roadmap toward SAP NetWeaver, one should always start with the areas where internal know-how already exists in the company. This is the only way to ensure that the knowledge that is brought from the outside to Automotive Inc. can be developed further internally. Figure 4.9 shows how the course of this project looks. There are two processes: the customer process and the development process. It is interesting to note that parts of the customer process cannot be implemented while the supplier process is running (for example, the issue management portal).

Think Big, Start Small

Setting up the data warehouse landscape requires the simplest project procedure. First, a certain level of knowledge already exists in-house in this field; secondly, the technology is already very mature and a lot can be implemented in the existing standard from the very beginning. We'll discuss which of the individual components will be used for the implementation in more detail in Section 4.5.1.

Data Warehouse

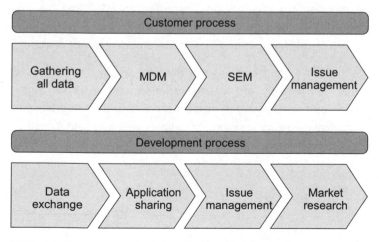

Figure 4.9 Course of the Project for the Two Core Processes

Next, setting up Web services for the dealers can begin. These include all those services intended to strengthen the dealer's connection to Automotive Inc., and those services employed to supply the dealer(s) with more and better information. All these services are provided via a portal, and each dealer can call them up or integrate them in his or her application there. In particular, these Web services allow Automotive Inc. to bind the dealers more closely to itself, and to collect missing information about the customers and their buying behavior.

The individual Web services are:

▶ Central master data management via SAP Master Data Management (SAP MDM)

▶ Campaign support by mySAP Customer Relationship Management (CRM)

▶ Planning platform by SAP Business Intelligence (SAP BI)

▶ Issue management portal with suppliers by SAP Knowledge Warehouse (SAP KW)

All of these Web services can be implemented by the individual dealer at only very great cost, or sometimes cannot be implemented at all. Because Automotive Inc. has so far had no extensive experience with Web services, it will start with a small test group—the large dealers in one metropolitan area. These dealers are connected to the central master data management system, and their master data is adjusted via this interface.

Automotive Inc. sees setting up a development platform along with the tier-1 suppliers as the third component of an integrated project procedure. These suppliers already develop components for Automotive Inc., and this process has to be lifted to a new level using a collaboration portal, and then successively expanded into an issue management portal.

Automotive Inc. see a great challenge in this process. In the future, the tier-1 suppliers will perform most of the development work for a new vehicle. Therefore, it is necessary to install a substantially more intelligent platform than pure data exchange on the delivery schedule and exchange with a groupware solution (email, etc.) during the delivery process.

4.5 Integrated Project Procedure

Now that we know the precise requirements of Automotive Inc. for a future IS architecture and have created an initial project plan to implement the customer and development processes, we can deal with implementation using a software component. After a preliminary investigation, Automotive Inc. has decided on the SAP product, SAP NetWeaver, as a platform for the implementation of the new IS architecture. The main reasons for the decision were:

▶ Excellent integration of the existing ERP landscape, which is currently at SAP 4.6C

▶ Good integration into the CRM solution from SAP

▶ Extensive functionality in the field of data warehousing and planning

▶ Clear product strategy for the fields of SAP MDM and SAP Exchange Infrastructure (SAP XI)

▶ The wide distribution of SAP solutions among suppliers

▶ The option of integrating the dealers economically into the SAP world using SAP Business One

Reasons for NetWeaver

Automotive Inc. can now begin to implement the planned project and build the new IS architecture on the flexible SAP NetWeaver solution.

4.5.1 Setting Up the BW and BPS Solution

The first task in implementing SAP NetWeaver is setting up an integrated SAP Business Information Warehouse (SAP BW) and Business Planning and Simulation (BPS) solution. These components are the most fully developed on the SAP NetWeaver platform, and sufficient knowledge from previous projects at Automotive Inc. exists to implement a comprehensive solution.

BW and Planning As a Basis

Automotive Inc. requires this integrated solution with all customer data and all possible derivations of purchase and do-not-purchase decisions in order to better plan and control the following aspects in the future:

▶ Sales

▶ Market introduction of new models

▶ Price policy

Figure 4.10 and Figure 4.11 show how such a landscape looks in detail:

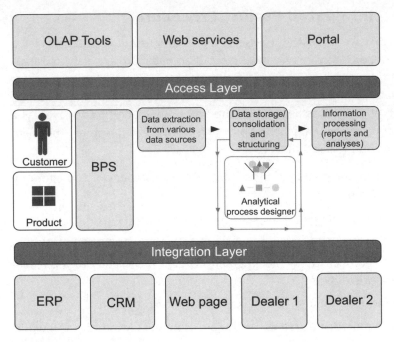

Figure 4.10 Architecture of SAP BW

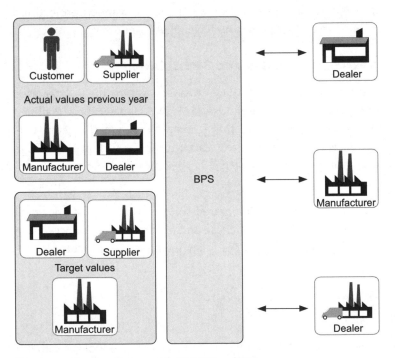

Figure 4.11 Planning Process with SAP BW and BPS

In the first step, a data warehouse platform that fulfills the following criteria is implemented: Services

▶ Flexible connection of any number of subsystems

▶ Access to the information either directly or in the form of Web services

▶ Uniform master data model for customers and products

▶ Extensive data mining tools

Flexible Connection of Any Number of Subsystems

The goal here is to extract data from subsystems using standard interfaces without exerting an implementation effort. This applies primarily to data extraction the dealers' customer systems at a later point in time. Here it is important to have tools and interfaces that can be used via the Internet (via XML) or other interfaces. The goal is to reduce the data collection and preparation effort so as to be able to connect to any data sources. SAP XI is a tool for very flexibly connecting to the most varied data. It is described in detail in Section 9.4. Standard Interfaces

Only as part of an SAP solution does the XI application enable you to connect all existing systems so that data exchange can occur among the systems. This data exchange is necessary so that all process steps in a process are provided with the same information and the same current version of the data.

This solution consists primarily of two parts: a definition environment in which the most important business objects and the processes resulting from them are created, and a runtime environment, which allows interaction among the systems using a number of adapters (connections).

As part of business process modeling, SAP XI takes on a central role, because in the future it will allow the mapping, implementation, and monitoring of company-wide and intercompany business processes as part of business process management (BPM). **BPM**

Access to the Information Either Directly or in the Form of Web Services

When the information is in SAP BW of Automotive Inc., the first part of the work is finished. The part in which the information is provided again to all participants is far more important. This can be done either via a Web interface (portal) or by providing the information again in a form that is easy to process via Web services so that they are available in the subsystems of the dealers and other participants directly and without a break in medium. The overall goal is to make the information available to end users. This is done in two steps: 1) Gathering the information into SAP BW (done at that point in time) 2) Offering the information a) either as Web reporting (using the portal) or b) as (technical) via a Web service that can be integrated into the (sub)systems of dealers, etc. The use of Web services is more elegant, because it avoids media disruptions.

Master Data Model for Customers and Products

Data Model As Key for Successful Data Mining

The greatest challenge is the master data model for customers and products. The goal is to find a data model in which all necessary relations are mapped and precise derivations and predictions can be made concerning why a certain customer decides on a certain product to buy. The model should be flexible enough so that any subsequent changes don't lead to excessively high costs.

After the homework is completed, the actual work can begin using data mining. Extensive data mining tools are used for this purpose. These tools enable you to make evaluations on buying decisions at the Headquarters of the company Automotive Inc. or, on-site at the dealer. This is the first application, in addition to master data management, for which the dealer and Automotive Inc. have a real use.

Data Mining Results Determine Sales Planning

The results of data mining, together with the normal planning scenarios, can then offer the starting base for sales and equipment planning for the next sales year. Another advantage comes into play here, because the dealers receive their target figures directly and can adapt them directly. This means that comprehensive cooperation takes place. The dealers can also specify initial trends for equipment lines, which then flow into price formation. These planning applications are ideally provided as a Web service so that smooth integration on the part of the dealer is possible. This process was illustrated in Figure 4.11.

4.5.2 Master Data Management for Dealers

As we mentioned in Section 4.1, the greatest potential lies in the utilization of previously unused data sources. This includes the data that comes from the dealer side. However, the dealer group is the most difficult to integrate. This is primarily because the dealers are independent companies that don't want to reveal their customer base. Another reason this group is difficult to integrate is that the dealers don't have extensive IT knowledge, because they have mostly grown from small independent garages that got bigger and now are also selling new cars.

Therefore, the primary impetus for dealers to want a master data project is that it poses more advantages for them than disadvantages. How the data flow looks and how the dealer becomes "master" of his/her data can be seen in Figure 4.12.

Creating Advantages Creates Acceptance

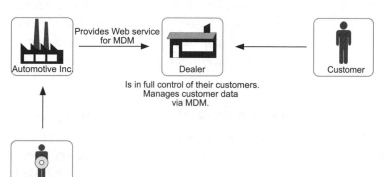

Figure 4.12 MDM at the Dealer

This advantage can be achieved if the dealer has more and better customer data so he/she can plan and execute marketing and campaigns in a more targeted way. To see the advantages here, we must get a more detailed view of how the CRM system is set up at the dealer. The dealer usually has only an invoice system and a system that lets him/her store addresses in order to send advertising mailings. Often the system for shipping informational material is PC-based (i.e., Word or Excel). These systems are usually several years old and rarely offer the option of creating partner relationships, that is, storing how the individual persons (physical customers) and the companies (logical customers) stand in relation to one another. This lack of mapping means that the customer is not perceived correctly and key customers are not serviced as they should be.

SAP Master Data Management (MDM) can be used here for the following:

Services

▶ Comparing the data with that of Automotive Inc.

▶ Eliminating duplication of information and correcting address errors

▶ Qualifying the addresses and assigning them to any partner role

▶ Supplementing the addresses with geofeatures and sociographic market data

▶ Expanding the stock of addresses with new contact data

Comparing the Data with That of Automotive Inc.

VPN and XML The customer master data such as Name, Address, Preferences, Company, and so forth are compared with the data of Automotive Inc. This comparison decisively improves the database. It can take place in many ways. Automotive Inc. and its dealers want to perform the comparison over the Internet and use XML as the technique. This saves them installation costs. Data security is ensured via a VPN connection, so that the data cannot be misused by third parties. It must also be ensured that the dealers' data can be viewed only by them and is not provided to competing dealers. This is done using the concept of role assignment—that of the dealers to the customers.

Eliminating Duplication and Correcting Address Errors

Increasing Data Quality Nothing is more annoying than a customer database that has not been maintained. But the process of address maintenance requires great effort and setting it up is both time-consuming and labor-intensive. Therefore, it is imperative to maintain and correct the data at a central point and not at each individual dealership. This is the only way to rid the system of duplication and assign the customers uniquely.

Qualifying the Addresses

Assigning the Contacts Partner Roles As we mentioned in Section 4.1, Automotive Inc. makes 56% of its sales with corporate customers. Unfortunately, most dealers lack an assignment between customer and company and therefore also a way to determine what buying habits and preferences individual companies have. A central comparison at Automotive Inc. is another plus point. This means that the customers can be assigned to the various companies and it will be clearer which customers have purchased which vehicles for which companies and what the preferences of the various companies are.

Supplementing the Addresses with Geofeatures and Sociographic Market Data

GFK Data for Dealers As Well Geofeatures and sociographic market data is currently only used by the central marketing department of Automotive Inc. in the field of market research and advertisement placement. This data is often difficult to obtain and provides precise knowledge of existing buying power and buying wishes according to regional (geospecific) and sociographic features. The main supplier for this data in Germany is the Consumer Research Association (GFK) in Nuremberg. This data can now be assigned to existing customer data as part of an analysis process, and then be provided to the dealer as additional information. This allows the dealer to better plan their campaigns and gives them access to more comprehensive information in sales discussions.

Expanding the Stock of Addresses with New Contact Data

Expanding the stock of addresses is clearly the greatest advantage of the new system to dealers. The dealer receives the addresses of customers that they don't currently have in their database from Automotive Inc. These addresses come from:

New Addresses Increase Sales Chances

▶ The Automotive Inc.'s Web site

▶ Conventions

▶ Third-party providers

▶ Customers who have moved

These addresses are provided to the dealer without additional charge and help them to expand their market share.

4.5.3 Development Portal with Suppliers

Automotive Inc. would not only like to improve the sales process and the service process, it would also like to improve and accelerate the development process.

The goal is to create an integration platform on the basis of SAP NetWeaver in which all participants (Automotive Inc., tier-1 suppliers, and subsuppliers) can work together. The main components of this platform are SAP Enterprise Portal and SAP Knowledge Management. However, SAP BW also performs a large part of the work. The basic goal is to map the following partial processes:

▶ Accessing information on the state of development (specification booklets and requirements)

Requirements of the Development Process

▶ Providing information on the state of development (drawings, calculations, test results)

▶ Interaction/cooperation on joint processes

The first two points have already been implemented at Automotive Inc. Most information is provided to the suppliers via email. Some documents are also exchanged via a portal server. The focus here is the pure distribution of information. The distribution of information on the development process is usually not sufficient to make the process faster and more economical. Automotive Inc. requires a portal that acts as a uniform platform for the following processes (the same ones that are also participating in the simultaneous engineering project).

What do the integration scenarios between the tier-1 suppliers and Automotive Inc. look like? We'll look at three processes during development as examples:

▶ The design process

▶ The calculation process

▶ The production/work preparation process

The Design Process

The design process contains all steps from the creation of the requirements booklet to the first prototype. This process is characterized by a very strong interaction between all participants, because here, in particular, there is a great need for comparison and adaptation. This process can now be performed on the basis of SAP NetWeaver by representing the following contents with SAP NetWeaver:

▶ Information on the cost structure of the previous model delivers an extensive analysis of the existing data using SAP BW.

▶ Information on buyer wishes for new models can be collected using data mining within SAP BW and the mySAP CRM solution.

▶ Requirements from the point of view of quality are only available unstructured. This information can be evaluated using SAP KM.

Cost Structure for the Previous Model
The information on the cost structure for the previous model can be collected using SAP BW and can be distributed into the following areas:

▶ Development costs

▶ Production costs

▶ Quality costs

These costs are then provided to the individual participants depending on role and serve to minimize cost factors during new development.

Buyer Wishes for a New Model
The information on buyer wishes for a new model are extremely important for the development of a new model. Success is ensured only when the buyer's wishes are taken into account and an attractive model that reflects the buyer's wishes is found. That's why an analysis of the CRM databases using data mining techniques is absolutely necessary to deter-

mine buyer wishes for newly developed models and for the analysis of the requirement for the current model. In this way, Automotive Inc. and the supplier can determine where the customer would like changes and innovations. The NetWeaver solution with SAP offers exactly these options.

The requirements from the point of view of quality have a decisive influence on the long-term market success of Automotive Inc. Only with excellent quality is it possible to survive as a premium manufacturer. Therefore, it is necessary that all information that pertains to quality be collected centrally and be provided via a portal. Requirements for product quality are usually available as only unstructured information (i.e., PowerPoint slides, feedback texts, etc.) but not as actual percentages on customer satisfaction and are stored at various locations. Many of the customers' suggestions and criticisms are reported via letters and email, and dealers deliver their statistics on defective parts. In addition, questions on quality can also be answered via evaluations in SAP BW at Automotive Inc.

<aside>Requirements from the Point of View of Quality</aside>

With NetWeaver, SAP offers the appropriate integration options for these requirements as well. Within NetWeaver, you can realize these requirements consisting of structured SAP BW figures and search for additional information that resides in SAP KM and SAP Portal.

The Calculation Process

After the development process, the second process looked at in detail is the calculation process. This process runs parallel to the development process and is run both by Automotive Inc. (What does the new model cost?) and by the supplier (What does the component cost?). This is a very critical process, because the supplier does not want to reveal their price structure and calculation base, despite tight cooperation. However, to achieve fast development, it is necessary to perform a new calculation after (or even before) each change.

This calculation process can be offered as a Web service both by suppliers and by Automotive Inc. To do so, place the corresponding Web services at the application level. Changing the input values yields new calculation values, which are immediately visible to all participants.

<aside>Web Services</aside>

The Production/Work Preparation Process

The next process, which is represented via a development portal, is the production and work preparation process. This process usually begins as a prototype and focuses on which components are installed in which sequence. The system supplier plays an important role here, because he delivers his components just in time, after which they're installed. However, the larger the individual components, the more production must be adapted to them. This adaptation is performed prior to the decision on which components are to be used in which way, and has a crucial influence on production costs.

Ideally, the supplier performs the installation of the components, so that Automotive Inc. pays an *all-included* price for the components.

The production process is supported primarily by SAP Exchange Infrastructure (XI). The goal is to create all business objects and relations between process steps and systems that are necessary for the later production process in XI. The more this setup can be performed with flexibility, the faster and more economical the later production process will be.

4.5.4 Issue Management

Automotive Inc. is setting up an issue management system as another part of the IS architecture. The goal of the issue management system is to give the customers, dealers, and suppliers a uniform platform for information exchange and fault analysis. So far, all information is collected centrally at Automotive Inc. and then distributed further. Whether the information is distributed further depends on the know-how of the particular dealer or developer. To remove this bottleneck, it is necessary to have a superimposed platform on which all information can be collected and provided. Using a comprehensive role concept, you can protect the information in such a way that only those who have an authorization for the particular process can access it. Figure 4.13 shows the process.

Individual Processes

The individual processes for issue management look like this:

▶ Issue Management by the customer

▶ Issue Management by the dealer

▶ Issue Management by the supplier

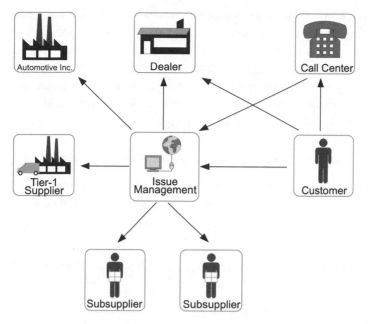

Figure 4.13 Web-Based Issue Management by Customers, Dealers, and Suppliers

Issue Management by the Customer

A fault is entered by the customer via the customer portal, a dealer, or a call center. This issue receives a unique number and is assigned to a component. If the issue is not yet known, it is made accessible immediately to all participants up to the relevant subsupplier via a role concept, and a solution is introduced. During the process, the customer can access their issue at any time and track the progress. The issue management system is mapped using the collaboration function of SAP Enterprise Portal, and is also supported by Knowledge Management.

Issue Management by the Dealer

The dealer also has the option of opening an issue for any atypical problems or cases that fall under general servicing. As soon as the dealer has opened an issue, they can search for similar errors in an issue database. This gives them access to a comprehensive database based on SAP Knowledge Management, which allows them to correct the errors faster.

Issue Management by the Supplier

Issue management by the supplier must be understood in such a way that the supplier can see all issues affecting them and must guarantee their processing. This is the only way they can learn of faults in their components. In addition to this issue management, the supplier can also open issues independently if they determine that their components were delivered in faulty condition or when one of their suppliers informs them of an issue. This information then goes to Automotive Inc., which can compare it with its production system to easily determine which vehicles are affected. This makes it possible to trace errors easily and avoid laborious recalls, which also damage the company image.

4.5.5 Overview of the SAP NetWeaver Components Used

Automotive Inc. has decided on SAP NetWeaver for the restructuring of its IT landscape. It now has a comprehensive platform for reaching its IT goals. This section provides an overview of which NetWeaver components will be used.

The following components are used within SAP NetWeaver in the field of analytical CRM:

▶ SAP Business Information Warehouse

▶ SAP Web Application Server

▶ SAP Master Data Management

▶ SAP Exchange Infrastructure

▶ SAP Enterprise Portal

▶ SAP xApps

The following components are used within SAP NetWeaver in the field of supplier integration:

▶ SAP Web Application Server

▶ SAP Exchange Infrastructure

▶ SAP xApps

▶ SAP Enterprise Portal

4.6 Automotive Inc. — Value Consideration

IT Core Processes of Automotive Inc. Automotive Inc. works in an environment characterized by stiff competition, extreme cost pressures, and technological change. According to a study of changes in the automotive industry,[4] by 2010 only eight independent manufacturers will exist, each having average sales of 2.8 million vehicles. To be among the winners in these predictions, it is very impor-

---

4 Berger, Roland: *Nine Mega-Trends...*

tant for Automotive Inc. to fiercely attack the goals of sales maximization and process optimization. To achieve this, the company concentrates on two important processes in our example:

▶ Better management of customer relations

▶ Optimized integration of the suppliers

The IT infrastructure plays a decisive role here. Because Automotive Inc. usually supports its business processes with a heterogeneous application landscape that has grown throughout history, installing SAP NetWeaver promises great potential advantages. To depict this potential objectively, during the course of the process, the actual and target situations of the identified processes are evaluated according to the criteria of *flexibility*, *innovation*, and *cost reduction*. This approach was described abstractly in Chapter 3 and is being applied here.

4.6.1 Management of Customer Relations

Automotive Inc. has set the goal of using an analytical CRM/BW system to increase customer loyalty in order to achieve a significant sales increase. The key to this goal is information on the customer, arising along the entire process chain, which is stored centrally in one system and is unique throughout the whole IT landscape.

Customer Relations Using CRM/BW

The evaluation of the current situation is determined by a low level of networking of the individual data sources. Figure 4.14 shows this networking using the weakly distinguished criteria for system and process flexibility. In other words, due to its structure, the actual system landscape at Automotive Inc. cannot perform an integration of the information already available, and therefore cannot increase reaction speed.

The Current IT Situation at Automotive Inc.

If you look at a possible target scenario with SAP NetWeaver, the focus is on technical integration via an exchange infrastructure (SAP XI). This is to be ensured by a flexible connection of any number of subsystems—the data sources. Another advantage is the shortened implementation time of the processes that have been set up. To improve the data quality for the evaluation using SAP BW, a master data management system (SAP MDM) is used. These measures serve to improve customer management through flexibility and faster process execution.

Target Scenario with X1 and MDM

The evaluation of this scenario with the criteria mentioned shows a substantial cost-savings potential. The most important points are:

Cost Potential

▶ **Reduction of development and maintenance costs for system inter-faces**
This savings effect can be achieved with a standard EAI application, however, with SAP XI, the existing, predefined templates come into effect (for example, SAP process models for Business Process Management (BPM) or SAP templates for interface description). These reduce the development costs substantially.

▶ **Reducing the costs through setup and maintenance of a central master data system**
The SAP MDM program allows central storage of a company's master data. This makes it possible to eliminate inconsistencies in the data and to achieve savings through a consolidation of existing project solutions.

▶ **Reduction of costs for monitoring and support**
The consolidation of existing EAI systems into a platform offers more potential because SAP XI substantially simplifies operation and maintenance.

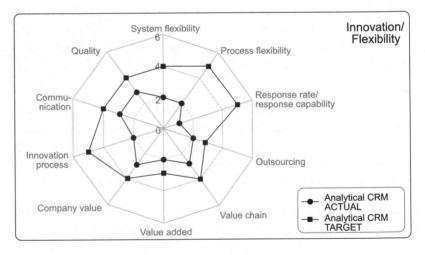

Figure 4.14 Evaluating Analytical CRM

4.6.2 Integrating the Suppliers

Integrating the Suppliers Using SAP XI

Optimization of supplier loyalty is an important step for Automotive Inc. The actual situation is characterized by intensive cooperation in the field of supply by the suppliers (for example, just-in-time delivery). This can also be seen in the well distinguished Outsourcing criterion in the actual evaluation. On the other hand, joint development, production, and quality management with the suppliers offers substantial new potential. Automotive Inc. would like to improve in this area in particular. For these considerations, the innovation criteria *Quality*, *Communication*, and *Innovation process* are of great significance. Expansion of the *System* and *Process flexibility* offers further potential for achieving successful supplier integration (see Figure 4.14).

The scenario described places these points in the center. A joint development platform can be implemented on the NetWeaver platform with the appropriate SAP Enterprise Portal collaboration tools. The goal is to optimize cooperation with the suppliers by allowing improved communication. Here the quality of the development and the constant improvement process plays a special role, of course. The management of quality problems by a portal platform represents a great added value in the with the supplier as well as the customer.

Target Processes with the Company Portal

If you look at the cost side, a large savings potential is apparent in the area of operation and implementation. The most important points are:

Cost Reduction Potential

▶ Cost reduction through a joint development platform, that is, the shortening of development time. This can be implemented through the already described collaboration applications or with the support of business packages for the SAP Enterprise Portal. These are functions that are specially preconfigured for product development.

Portal with Collaboration

The graphics tools installed with the Enterprise Portal for developing and changing user interfaces mean shorter development times and lower costs.

▶ The costs for quality management are reduced with a joint information platform such as SAP Knowledge Management, because everyone involved in the process has access to the essential data.

SAP Knowledge Management

▶ In the supplier integration scenario, the advantages from SAP XI for connecting development partners come into play. This means that all features mentioned find unrestricted use in order to lower costs here as well.

SAP Exchange Infrastructure

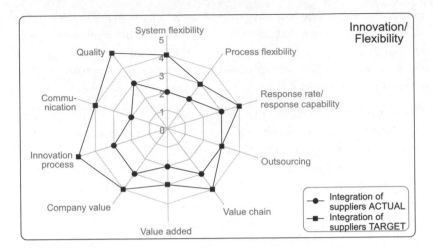

Figure 4.15 Evaluation of Supplier Integration

4.6.3 Evaluation and Recommendation

Comparison with the Reference Value from the IT Strategy

It is important for Automotive Inc. to avoid faulty investments in IT projects. The main reason for IT project failure is usually the inability to select and implement the initiatives that have measurable advantages for the company. Therefore it is necessary to compare the identified "Analytical CRM" and "Supplier Integration" projects with the IT strategy. For this purpose, the reference value was also included as part of the evaluation (see Section 4.6). Figure 4.16 shows a comparison of the two scenarios. The criteria of flexibility and innovation as well as cost reduction (as a circular value) were used for the total view.

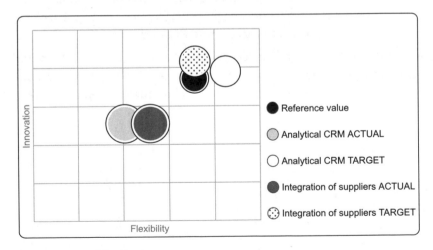

Figure 4.16 Portfolio Matrix

A comparison with the reference value yields an interesting picture. Both target processes modeled with SAP NetWeaver achieve better values in the portfolio matrix than the evaluations derived from the IT strategy. This means that the IT system architecture of Automotive Inc. with NetWeaver is optimally prepared for the changes and new developments of the future. If one views the picture from the point of view of total strategy, you can see that:

Evaluation of the
Portfolio Matrix

▶ Analytical CRM primarily supports the process flexibility.

▶ Supplier integration primarily supports innovation.

Viewed together, the planned NetWeaver processes implement the IT strategy of Automotive Inc. optimally. If you add the already demonstrated savings potential, you'll see that SAP NetWeaver meets the company's demands by reducing total IT costs.

5 Roadmap to SAP NetWeaver in an Automotive Supplier Company

This chapter describes how an automotive supplier can create DP structures (electronic data processing structures) in order to remain competitive in the automotive market. Using Car Doors Inc. as an example, the developments in the automotive supplier industry are highlighted along with the consequences of these developments. Using SAP NetWeaver, a concept for Car Doors Inc. is developed that will enable it to maintain its position in the tough environment of consolidation and growth in the industry.

5.1 Scenario Description

5.1.1 Developments in the Automotive Supplier Industry

Developments in the automobile manufacturing industry are having a decisive influence on trends in the automotive supplier industry. Automobile manufacturers (Original Equipment Manufacturers—OEMs) have been able to strengthen their market position through takeovers and mergers. By buying and selling strategic business units in recent years, OEMs have been able to concentrate on their core competencies. One such example is the sale of *debis IT Services* (a European IT service provider, part of *T-Systems*) by *DaimlerChrysler* to *Deutsche Telekom*.

This growth in the consolidation of OEMs can be illustrated using the S-curve concept (see Figure 5.1). This focus on core competencies is still underway or already completed. DaimlerChrysler has managed to optimize its product and market portfolios by revising its marginal business activities (sale of *debis IT Services*). It has thus been able to strengthen its market position in known markets. Selling marginal business activities is synonymous with concentrating on the company's core competency: automotive engineering. However, nowadays, automotive engineering generally tends to mean the final assembly of prefabricated modules by suppliers, as already described in the case of Automobile Inc. in Chapter 4.

Increasing Concentration of OEMs

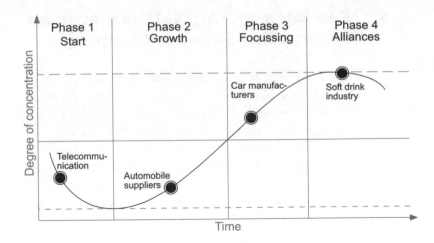

Figure 5.1 S-Curve Concept[1]

In addition to this process of consolidation, we also see an increased globalization of the OEMs. Worldwide, production facilities are being set up to serve customers locally. For instance, due to the high rate of growth in China and the more dynamic nature of other regions in Asia, the global share of production facilities in Asia will continue to increase in the next few years. Since the OEMs are pursuing the strategy of just-in-time (JIT) production, suppliers are being forced to participate in this process of globalization. The consequence of this increase in globalization is that OEMs are establishing operations in proximity to the new production facilities around the globe.

Outsourcing by OEMs As a Result of Reduction to Core Competencies

A consequence of this concentration on core competencies is the gradual contracting out or *outsourcing* of production processes. The OEMs outsource the assembly of individual components (modules) with exactly defined interfaces to their suppliers. This modularization offers the OEM further advantages over component and system supply. Due to this modularization, assembly and delivery times, and therefore the entire product development cycle, can be shortened, because the suppliers must assemble the new technologies in the modules. In 2000, the lead time for a new car in terms of production and distribution was 28 to 32 days. Today, the lead time is only 10 days, with customer specifications being attended to a full six days before outbound delivery.

Figure 5.2 shows how vertical integration has been reduced in the last 20 years.

---

1 Kearney, A.T.: *Management Consultants*. Munich 2001.

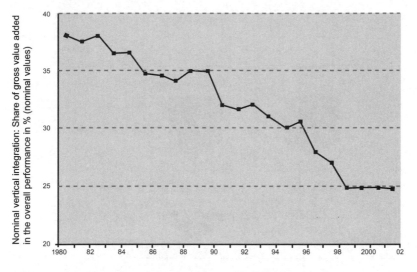

Figure 5.2 Vertical Integration for German Car Manufacturers[2]

The result of this development is that an increasing amount of responsibility is being passed from the value-added process of the OEMs to the automotive suppliers. For example, in recent years, the number of tasks from the area of research and development (R&D) that have been outsourced to suppliers has grown steadily.

Another element in this trend is the development of new business models, in which the suppliers have a stronger tie to the OEMs in terms of investments. An example of this is the pay-on-production system. The suppliers are paid on the basis of the vehicles produced. If fewer vehicles are produced than forecast, the suppliers bear the risk.

Added-Value Share of Suppliers

This trend in the automotive industry illustrates the consequences and potential for change in the automotive supplier industry.

The supplier industry has been under immense pressure to grow for some time now (see Figure 5.1, S-curve concept). In the next 10 years, the supplier industry is expected to grow by 40%.

Outsourcing As a Catalyst for Growth Among Suppliers

The main reason for this growth is the continued reduction in vertical integration of the production processes of the OEMs. In addition, the competencies of the individual companies involved in the production process will change in the future.

---

2   Source: German Association of the Automobile Industry (VDA).

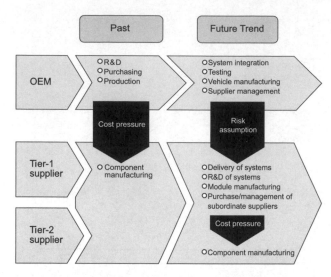

Figure 5.3 Trends in the Development of the Supplier Industry

Until now, price policy has had top priority in the competition strategy of automobile suppliers who fall into the range of tier-1 to tier-n suppliers. Tier-1 suppliers supply the OEMs directly, while tier-n suppliers act as intermediate suppliers for the tier-1 suppliers.

Due to their great dependency on the OEMs, who drive the market, the tier-1 to tier-n suppliers were placed under great cost pressure. Added to this is a profit-sales ratio of 4.2%, which is below average compared to other companies in the production industry. This cost pressure narrowed profit margins, and investment in research and development tended to be low.

In the future, OEMs will focus on their core business and therefore transfer an even greater share of risk to the tier-1 suppliers. These suppliers must now position themselves as module manufacturers in order to be able to remain competitive on the automobile market. This, however, can only be realized through greater R&D investment in module development. It is expected that the cost pressure will be passed on to the subordinate intermediate suppliers.

Survival Strategy: Developing Module Competence The trend toward modularization will continue. An "End Game Scenario for Significant Module Segments" by A.T. Kearney in 2001 describes 10 segments in which the tier-1 suppliers will operate in the future, ranging from the cockpit module through the front-end module to the door module. According to estimates from PricewaterhouseCoopers, the number of tier-1 suppliers is expected to drop from the current level of 800 to 35 by the end of the decade. These 35 tier-1 suppliers will then share the 10 module segments. Among tier-2 suppliers, a drop from 10,000 to 800 is expected.

Despite low profit margins, the tier-1 suppliers, including Car Doors Inc., will be forced to grow even more and develop additional expertise.

Next, you'll see how Car Doors Inc., a supplier of components, turned itself into a successful module supplier, and the role an effective DP infrastructure played in this fundamental change.

5.1.2 Growth and Situation of Car Doors Inc.

Car Doors Inc. has grown to become one of the largest global manufacturers of components for vehicle doors. As a result of the globalization of the OEMs, Car Doors Inc. owns more than 35 facilities worldwide where more than 12,000 employees produce window regulators and door and locking systems for more than 30 automotive brands. In 2003, Car Doors Inc. achieved sales estimated at $4.9 billion.

Due to the constantly increasing number of subsidiaries of Car Doors Inc. worldwide, a very heterogeneous DP infrastructure has developed over time, which has greatly impeded data exchange between the facilities. Worldwide joint ventures with majority interests and the addition of licensees working for Car Doors Inc. have brought all kinds of DP systems into the Car Doors group.

Incompatibility of the IT Infrastructure

With a considerable investment in finance and resources, the proper requirements must now be met in order to bring business processes that extend beyond the company limits of Car Doors Inc. into line.

For this reason, Car Doors Inc. began introducing SAP R/3 in 1997, in order to consolidate the heterogeneous landscape of software systems that had developed. The area of logistics was mapped in R/3 at individual locations. At the company headquarters in Detroit, the various threads of Car Doors Inc. were woven together again to form a central SAP system for all branches.

Necessity for Integration of Systems

It soon became apparent to everyone involved that simply implementing logistics functionality in individual facilities of the Car Doors group would not suffice in the future.

Purchasing has a major influence on achieving the company objectives of Car Doors Inc., since material costs comprise almost 70% of production costs. The tier-n suppliers receive up to 3,000 order requests a year, including orders for punched parts, electrical parts, and engines. Car Doors Inc. is pursuing the strategy of allocating delivery orders per production run.

Inefficient Purchasing Process

At Car Doors Inc., the request process and the concomitant selection of suppliers falls into three purchasing areas, with different roles assigned to each area:

1. The *Customer Team Purchaser* handles the specifications of customers and is responsible for the purchasing of materials for the project.
2. The *Plant Purchasing Department* is responsible for all production facilities of the Car Doors group and primarily handles local suppliers in the request process.
3. The *Central Purchasing Department* coordinates procurement beyond existing projects and heads up supplier management.

All three areas collectively decide on which suppliers to select.

Until now, this request process has been relatively inefficient. The Customer Team Purchaser sent requests via email with relevant documents as attachments to Car Doors Inc.'s suppliers. Similarly, the two remaining areas received information about this request by email. Once the quotations had been received from the suppliers, a quotation price comparison list was created manually in Excel, to serve as the basis for selecting the suppliers in question. A final selection was then made by the three purchasing areas in various meetings. In this process, there could be considerable delays if new information arose from the other two areas that initiated another round of selection. The conflicts of objectives that ensued between the purchasers could not be properly channeled by the decision-making process, which resulted in the process taking at least six weeks to as long as six months.

Evaluation of Options

To optimize the purchasing process, exploration of alternative ways of structuring an electronic request process for tier-n suppliers began at the end of 2002.

Together with the tier-n suppliers of Car Doors Inc., electronic marketplaces such as *SupplyOn* were also explored at that time. However, these marketplaces did not meet the requirements because only standard processes could be mapped, and because integration of a request process into the SAP system of Car Doors Inc. was not possible at that time. Additionally, operation and administration of electronic marketplaces was too complicated for the tier-n suppliers.

At the beginning of 2003, the SAP solution *mySAP Product Lifecycle Management* (mySAP PLM) was implemented at Car Doors Inc., with the functions applied for intercompany data exchange and document management. Thus, the request process can now be linked to other internal processes, as shown in Figure 5.4.

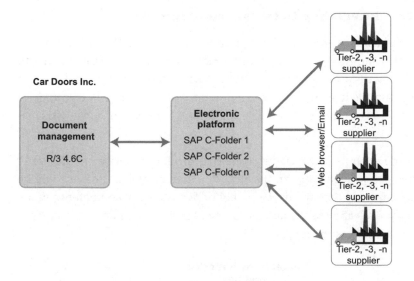

Figure 5.4 Request Process in Purchasing at Car Doors Inc.

To keep the investment risk in this project relatively small, an electronic platform was chosen on which so-called *Collaboration Folders (C-folders)* are provided for the suppliers. Via these collaboration folders, the suppliers can communicate with Car Doors Inc. and provide quotations and important documents. With SAP R/3, all request documents for all internal areas involved in the process can be made centrally available in the most up-to-date version. Changes in status trigger defined workflows, for example, the sending of messages to the suppliers involved.

With this semiautomatic support of the collaborative purchasing process, Car Doors Inc. was effectively able to reduce the amount of time and resources spent on processing by 30%.

Additional developments are planned for the future. One area of focus will be the effective integration of the existing DP systems and closer cooperation with the development partners of Car Doors Inc. In doing so, the goal will be to realize the concept of cooperative, shared product development (Collaborative Product Development) in terms of feasible solutions.

5.2   Challenges

What challenges and dangers does Car Doors Inc. face considering both intra-company developments and developments in the automotive industry?

5.2.1   Integrating Heterogeneous Systems

51% growth

As you can see from the S-curve concept (Figure 5.1), the automotive supplier industry is currently in the midst of a period of growth. Due to the growth in outsourcing by OEMs, the trend toward modularization will continue to increase. In the door module area alone, a drastic jump of over 51% is forecast for development and production in the next ten years.

This development will lead to increased product requirements for tier-1 supplier Car Doors Inc. In the future, a greater global presence will be needed, along with the development of technological competence in the area of R&D and the absolute necessity of building up integration competence in the entire process chain.

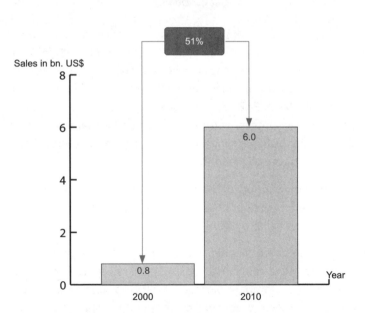

Figure 5.5 Market Growth for Door Modules[3]

3   see Kearney: *Management Consultants.*

How will Car Doors Inc. have to position and align itself in the future in order to maintain relative independence and flexibility in the automotive market?

Strong growth is required to meet this challenge. Car Doors Inc. must further develop the strategy of merging with other strategic partners in order to be able to build up the necessary competence required as a module supplier. The company can hardly manage this on its own, since it is impossible to get adequate financing due to the relatively small profit-sales ratios in this industry.

Development of Module Competence Through Mergers and Acquisitions

Merging with or acquiring international companies with different systems and mentalities represents an integration approach that was frequently underestimated in the past. The proportion of renewed outside contracting to outsourcing to new locations abroad increased considerably in recent years in the industry.

However, with the help of consolidation in the form of mergers and joint ventures, Car Doors Inc. can succeed in making the step from component to module supplier in the industry.

From Component to Module Supplier

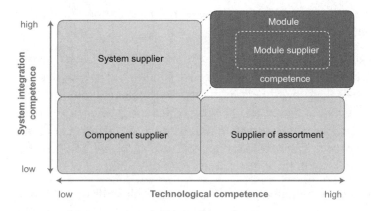

Figure 5.6 Position Portfolio of Automotive Suppliers[4]

Due to the increasing pressure to grow and the fact that new subsidiaries and business partners must be integrated into this growth, rapid and cost-effective networking of business processes beyond the limits of the company itself is required. The integration of heterogeneous DP infrastructures is becoming increasingly important within this context.

---

4 Kearney: *Management Consultants.*

Integration Costs A great impediment to rapid implementation of networking processes is the fact that standardized interfaces for data exchange have been lacking until now. The incompatibility of both the systems within the Car Doors group and those of its business partners has therefore meant a time-consuming and resource-intensive problem for Car Doors Inc. The maintenance and administration costs of its own systems and the costs of adapting the external systems of its business partners must be reduced in the future.

Therefore, the continued development of e-business is a decisive factor for Car Doors Inc. The increased electronic linkage of the companies to one another (from electronic request to electronic forecast delivery schedule) must be standardized, since presently the company has to deal with all the different systems used by the market participants.

For example, the OEMs set up electronic business process integration with their own supplier portals. Thus the OEMs have made the suppliers come to them instead of vice versa. In the past, quality, stock, and delivery reports were transmitted directly from the OEMs to the suppliers. Today, the suppliers must retrieve this information from all kinds of portals. Usually, this is done with a great deal of manual effort, because of the different technologies.

Investment in Technology Despite savings being made in the DP sector in the last few years, investment must be made in the company's own DP infrastructure. For this reason, forward-looking investment in the right technology is required. This kind of investment in the future will bring with it a high level of flexibility so that Car Doors Inc. can integrate into its own DP infrastructure new DP systems with a multitude of technologies, and furthermore, so that communication within the entire supply chain is ensured.

A consequence of the heterogeneous build-up of all kinds of systems in the Car Doors group is the requirement for harmonization among similar company objects. The relatively simple requirement of working with a standard intercompany supplier number at all locations can become a very costly challenge for Car Doors Inc.

5.2.2 Optimizing the Supply Chain

Despite a relatively low profit-to-business volume ratio compared with the average in the production industry, the tier-1 suppliers must, along with Car Doors Inc., invest more in R&D in the future to meet the demands of their role as module suppliers. This also increases the risk.

What is required is intercompany, collaborative product development with partners.

Here, the development departments of the OEMs must work very closely with those of the module suppliers. Similarly, this development can also be found in the relationship between the module suppliers and the tier-n suppliers. Constant contact among the individual parties within the entire production process must be automated to a certain extent. One of the main arguments for collaborative product development is the reduction of development costs and time-to-market.

Lowering the Development Costs Through SCM

If Car Doors Inc. is to optimize and direct the current production process via feasible measure systems (Supply Chain Operational Reference model—SCOR), strategic cost management and controlling is unavoidable. In this respect, the concept of supply chain management gains an increasing importance for Car Doors Inc.

In the production process, individual companies no longer compete with one another individually; instead, the competitive forces are now entire supply chains—groups of companies within the automotive industry. With collective optimization of the supply chain beyond the existing company boundaries, the need for a standardized procedure and description of the supply chain management processes grows.

Integrated, intercompany planning and management of the flow of material, and information across the entire value-added process and beyond, with the objective of structuring the entire vehicle door production process optimally in terms of time and costs, will be one of the greatest challenges for Car Doors Inc.

SCOR Model

Using the SCOR model, which was developed as a standard process reference model for information exchange between different supply chains, as a basis, intercompany, standardized description can be ensured. If all relevant data from the supply chain is brought together in one Car Doors Inc. information system, then, using the SCOR model, a framework with common key figures can be used, and benchmarking can also be carried out concurrently. Using the results from benchmarking, Car Doors Inc. can identify the potential for improvement in the production process and then take the appropriate measures.

The use of modern controlling instruments gives rise to new challenges for Car Doors Inc. in terms of its own information and DP system. Contribution margin, activity-based cost calculation, or target costing will be possible only if comprehensive information is made available from many different levels in the supply chain.

5.2.3 Optimizing Intercompany Process Flows

Purchasing Material costs for Car Doors Inc. comprise almost 70% of product costs. For this reason, the purchasing process was improved with the suppliers from the second and third tier by the introduction of a portal. With the portal, it was possible to develop a collaborative request process with the tier-n suppliers in the first step and to partially automate the purchasing process.

The standalone solution used with selected Car Doors Inc. suppliers was—at that time—favored over a solution with electronic marketplaces, since these online shops did not yet meet technical or functional requirements. However, for Car Doors Inc., only a complete integration of trading platforms (such as SupplyOn) into its own retailing system will ensure greater savings on process costs in the future.

Integrating Intercompany Business Processes The decisive added value for Car Doors Inc. is achieved by complete integration of all purchasing, sales, and distribution processes with the marketplaces of the OEMs and automotive suppliers. If, for example, a changeover is made from a standalone solution to an electronic marketplace, in which many more market participants can exchange information with one another, requirement forecasts for various tier-1 suppliers can be combined to create one cross-company scheduling agreement.

Marketplaces for the entire automotive supplier industry—as compared with individual solutions or with the company portal of Car Doors Inc.—have even more advantages:

▶ A common, industry-wide approach for meeting the special requirements of tier-n suppliers

▶ Distribution of risks and costs for system development and operation

▶ Development of uniform standards for processes, contents, documents, and interfaces

With a process lead time of 10 days for an automobile, and the buyer's option to make changes to specifications up to six days before the completion of the transaction, the OEMs' sales order system must be very closely integrated with the suppliers' systems so that the latter can respond immediately to such modifications to orders. The reduction of the production time for an automobile also demands closer integration with the subsuppliers from the tier-2 to tier-n supplier levels in order to make just-in-time delivery of the required modules possible.

5.3 The Supply Chain As a Future Success Factor

Because of the current situation and the challenges that will face Car Doors Inc. in the future, managing the supply chain will be of the greatest importance in the medium term. In addition to mastering its own production processes, mastering the entire value chain from tier-n suppliers right through to customers will be key for Car Doors Inc.

This is supported by a survey of 82 suppliers. The survey established the following criteria:

The Supply Chain As a Challenge to Suppliers

▶ Mastering the entire production process will be the central focus. In addition to the internal production processes that can be described by the value chain,[5] the external processes must be considered along with the internal ones. Interoperability is required between customers, retailers, OEMs, tier-2 to tier-n suppliers and the electronic marketplaces.

▶ The great challenge for the automotive supplier industry will be to achieve optimized interaction between the internal value chain and the supply chain overall. In addition to optimization and taking into account the most important physical processes within the supply chain, a main focus will be the concomitant DP infrastructure, which first and foremost must deliver the required information from the entire supply chain and provide this information at the right time and at the right place within the supplier production process.

5.3.1 The Car Doors Inc. Supply Chain

The supply chain of Car Doors Inc. is shown in Figure 5.7, along with its internal processes.

The Car Doors Inc. value chain falls into primary and secondary activities. Primary activities cover the actual production process of Car Doors Inc., which is divided into five areas. Additionally, the company has four secondary activities. The main task of these four branches of the company is that of supporting and optimizing the production process so that the main objectives of Car Doors Inc. can be achieved.

Value Chain

---

5 Porter, M.; Millar, V.: "How information gives you competitive advantage." In: Harvard Business Review (HBR), 7/8 1985.

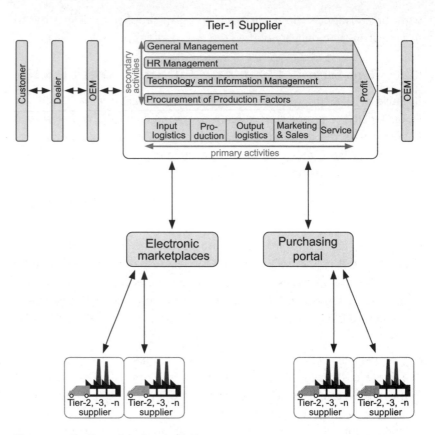

Figure 5.7 Car Doors Inc. Supply Chain

The *General Management* branch defines the company strategy and specifies the company's strategic objectives. In *HR Management*, planning and allocation of employees within Car Doors Inc. is managed and defined.

A main focus is the *Procurement* of production factors. Since material costs comprise up to 70% of production costs, purchasing in Car Doors Inc. must be automated and optimized within the production process. With the help of the company's own portal, the first step toward this has been made.

The *Technology and Information Management* branch covers both the development of networks within the Car Doors group and the storage and management of knowledge and data. Another focus area for Car Doors Inc. will be the integration and standardization of the entire DP infrastructure.

In *HR Management*, planning and allocation of employees within the company is managed and defined. The focus area is that of further education and training of employees in order to meet company objectives in the medium to long term.

As you can see in Figure 5.7, the OEMs are at the entry and exit points of the Car Doors Inc. value chain. After placement of orders by the OEMs, production takes place within the individual areas of the value chain of Car Doors Inc. The final result is just-in-time delivery of the finished products in the form of vehicle doors to the OEM location. The customer is positioned at the start of the supply chain. It is the customer who ultimately triggers this value chain with everyone involved, by ordering a vehicle from the car dealer.

Car Doors Inc. communicates with its own subsuppliers regarding product manufacturing via its own purchasing portal. Using this portal, as already described, quotations can be solicited and the purchasing process carried out in a semiautomated manner. In addition, there are the electronic marketplaces in which Car Doors Inc. can also place orders in the future. In addition to the integration of procurement, close cooperation with its subsuppliers in the area of R&D will play a large role in the future for Car Doors Inc. Under the heading of *Collaborative Product Development*, Car Doors Inc. will develop new products together with its partners.

5.3.2 Objectives of Car Doors Inc.

Due to the developments in the automotive supplier market, the *General Management* branch of Car Doors Inc. has drawn up the following strategic objectives for the *Technology and Information Management* branch to ensure future success in this market:

Technology and Information Management

1. Introduction of a uniform, integrated DP platform to standardize the heterogeneous DP landscape
2. Extension of the internal controlling system
3. Company-wide harmonization of business objects
4. Improvement of process integration with external business partners

Before Car Doors Inc. begins improving the integration of external systems, it will first optimize the internal infrastructure. This will lay the foundation for the successful implementation of Step 4. By creating a uniform, standardized DP infrastructure, high maintenance costs can be

Optimization of Internal DP infrastructure

reduced and a flexible foundation for dynamic, rapid growth of the Car Doors group can be laid.

Development of a Controlling System

In a second stage, using the consolidated DP infrastructure as a basis, an effective controlling system will be developed with which the supply chain can be managed and optimized. It is critical to Car Doors Inc. that company-wide access to information be made available from the entire supply chain, that the data be consistent, and that the forms of evaluation be flexible, so that the production process can be managed optimally. In addition to illustrating the current situation with current data, an effective planning system must be developed that can respond immediately to demand changes and problems arising across the entire supply chain.

Company-Wide Harmonization of Business Objects

A uniform, company-wide set of business objects (for example, business partners in the form of suppliers) is connected to an effective information system. A standardized view covering all suppliers to the company ensures optimal control over purchasing.

Business Process Integration

Once the aforementioned internal requirements have been met successfully, the company must push ahead with the integration of business processes and the necessary data integrity. Therefore, the entire business process—ranging from the OEMs to the tier-1 suppliers to the subsuppliers—can be further optimized and thus ensure the required quality improvements and cost reduction measures in the industry.

5.4 Integrated Project Planning Procedure

Integrated Procedure with SAP NetWeaver

Using an integrated procedure with SAP NetWeaver, the following sections show how the *Technology and Information Management* branch of the company can meet this challenge successfully. We show how the Car Doors Inc. supply chain can be optimized in coordinated steps using SAP NetWeaver functions, and also point to future potentials.

5.4.1 Integrating a Standardized DP Integration Platform

The current allocation of the IT budget of Car Doors Inc. is similar to the one shown in Figure 5.8.

Maintenance As Cost Driver

Almost 70% of the available budget must be used for the maintenance and repair of the current system landscape. This leaves little room for investment in new systems or modification of existing ones, although such systems are mandatory for future development.

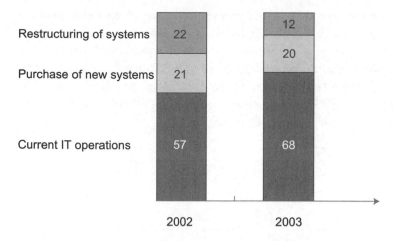

Restructuring of systems   22   12

                                      20

Purchase of new systems   21

Current IT operations   57   68

              2002   2003

Figure 5.8 Allocation of IT Budgets in Europe[6] by Percentage

In the already heterogeneous DP structure, new systems can be integrated only with a great expense of time and money. Many different systems in the Car Doors group are linked to one another via direct interfaces. With these point-to-point connections, the integration information is, in most cases, hard-wired into the application components. These individual interfaces are the result of a home-grown DP infrastructure.

Figure 5.9 depicts such a heterogeneous system landscape with different systems via direct point-to-point interfaces.

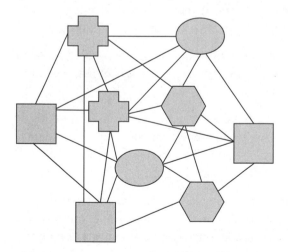

Figure 5.9 Heterogeneous System Landscape with Point-to-Point Interfaces

---

6   Giga International Group; Forrester Meta Group, 2003.

To reduce the maintenance and care requirements of the heterogeneous system landscape of Car Doors Inc. to a reasonable level, Central Interface Administration of the required integration knowledge is needed. The role of SAP Exchange Infrastructure (XI) in this landscape is that it offers cross-company integration services on the basis of the SAP Web Application Server (Web AS). By using these services, the different Car Doors Inc. systems can be connected to one another.

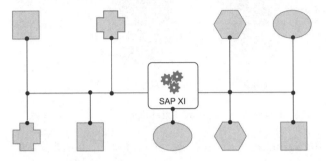

Figure 5.10 Standardized System Landscape with Central Interface Administration

As you can see in Figure 5.10, the interfaces are centrally managed and controlled at exactly one point. Thus rapid integration of any systems in the Car Doors group is possible.

SAP XI is a message-oriented solution based on generally recognized standards such as Hyper Text Transfer Protocol (HTTP) and Extensible Markup Language (XML). Therefore, it remains open to integration of external systems. Figure 5.11 shows the main elements of SAP XI.

The system landscape at Car Doors Inc. is defined in the *System Landscape Directory* as the basis for the description of the cross-system business processes.

In the *Integration Repository*, the interfaces are stored independently of system and platform in the design environment and are generally described with the help of Web Services Description Language (WSDL). Different interfaces are defined and mapped onto one another here.

In the configuration environment, the relevant objects are selected from the Integration Repository according to the specific system and business process. These objects are then assigned to one another via *logical routing* and stored in the *Integration Directory*. The message flow between the logical systems of the Car Doors group is clearly described. At this level of abstraction, the logical receivers are linked to a technical system using end points (*technical routing*).

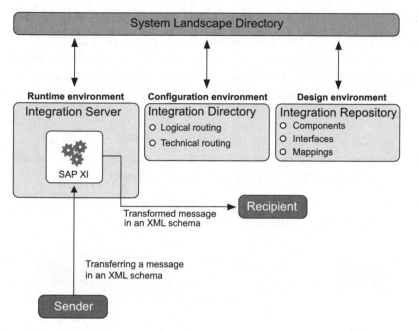

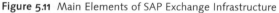

Figure 5.11 Main Elements of SAP Exchange Infrastructure

The information required during runtime is retrieved from the Integration Directory and evaluated in the *Integration Server*, which is the central communication and distribution engine in the Car Doors group.

Adapters, which are additional components of SAP XI, are also supplied for connecting interfaces from external systems.

Adapters

All processes running between the communicating systems can be monitored and controlled via the *Integration Monitor*.

Using SAP XI as an integration and distribution system, the basis for standardized, central administration of interfaces and the concomitant communication of different systems within and beyond the Car Doors group has been established. With standards such as HTTP and XML, and using the transformations described above, information from many different systems can be retrieved, exchanged, and processed.

The fact that abstraction levels separate the interface descriptions from the technical details of access makes rapid integration of new systems and optimization of the current DP infrastructure possible.

5.4.2 Integrating a Supply Chain Controlling Solution

To optimize the process flows within the supply chain, Car Doors Inc. requires an effective planning and analysis tool with which all information that plays a role within the supply chain can be gathered, analyzed, and made available in all different kinds of ways to everyone involved in the production process.

Access to Internal Data Having company-wide access to information, consistency of data and flexible forms of evaluation is vital for the production process to be optimally managed and company objectives to be achieved.

Figure 5.12 shows the process of data integration necessary for information analysis for Car Doors Inc.

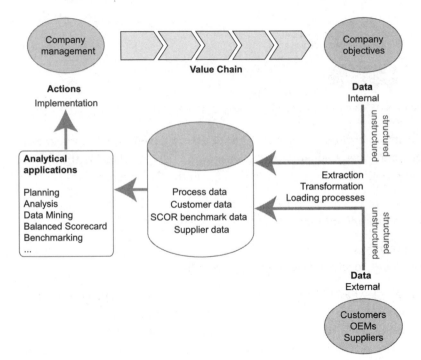

Figure 5.12 Business Intelligence for Managing the Supply Chain

ETL By utilizing extraction, transformation, and loading (ETL) tools, data can be extracted from the entire value-added process and stored as analysis-capable information. This process is further complicated by heterogeneous and non-conforming external systems. In the case of Car Doors Inc., there are more than 35 locations, each with different kinds of systems from which data must be aggregated in one central controlling system.

In addition to internal data that primarily comes from the individual areas of the Car Doors group, external data from all different kinds of data sources is also stored centrally and used for additional comparisons. The data in question is data from the automobile customer, the OEM, and the subsuppliers of Car Doors Inc.

External Data

As an example, we should mention the car buyer, who is ultimately the person who requests the produced subsystems and modules. The car buyer's desire for innovation is a very important factor for tier-1 suppliers when they're developing new modules. Without this customer information, components and modules that don't meet customer requests and specifications would be developed and produced.

To complete the spectrum comprising an adequate information system for Car Doors Inc., a planning system that improves planning quality and facilitates early intervention in the event of plan deviations in the entire production process must be integrated. With integrated planning based on current central data, medium- to long-term planning—along with market share, sales revenue, and demand planning at the product level and detailed planning from profit center to cost center levels—can be coordinated and accelerated.

Integrated Planning

The individual business units of Car Doors Inc. are therefore more intrinsically involved in the planning process, and the process itself becomes more transparent because of this integrated approach.

Information is generally stored in specifically dedicated systems, since it must be ensured that large amounts of data can be processed and that this data can be accessed rapidly and specially processed. SAP BW meets the requirements for Car Doors Inc. to implement an efficient supply chain controlling solution. In addition to facilitating the integration of internal and external data, the Car Doors Inc. production process can be planned integratively with SAP BW 3.5.

Distribution and the accompanying access to actual and planned data take place via a central medium. The user (purchaser, production manager, managing director) does not log on to different systems to retrieve the important information that he is seeking, but instead logs on via Single Sign-On (SSO) to only one system. SAP Enterprise Portal (SAP EP) offers all users a standardized interface where they must log on only once. This user interface enables users to call up all relevant functions and information they need for their activities. The functions and information they require are stored in user roles that ensure that the users are provided with all the necessary information (structured and unstructured). The SAP BW functions can be automatically integrated into SAP EP. This results in a completely integrated solution.

Integrated Solution for Purchasing

Request Process As an example of an integrated solution, we'll use the Car Doors Inc. purchaser request process. Using the role concept, the relevant information is made available to purchasers via SAP Enterprise Portal so that the areas can be coordinated optimally. In this way, the current quotation price comparison list can be made available to all purchasers, while at the same time, a selection of suppliers can be accelerated.

In addition to the quotation price comparison list, the C-folders from mySAP Product Lifecycle Management (mySAP PLM) are integrated into the portal and made available to the purchaser roles so that the quotation information from the suppliers can be accessed directly. Therefore, it is possible to continue using the solution via mySAP PLM immediately.

In addition to this central information, all supplier information can be made available in the purchaser roles via the portal. Consequently, these roles are gradually provided with all the information necessary for purchasers to be able to buy. For example, this information could be reports from SAP BW that provide the following data for purchasers:

▶ Top 10 suppliers according to location

▶ Volume of posted quantities per supplier

Supply Chain Controlling with the SCOR Model

By integrating the actual and planned data from the areas of procurement, production, and delivery in SAP BW, Car Doors Inc. has laid the foundation for managing the supply chain on the basis of the SCOR model. In the case of Car Doors Inc., the term *supply chain management* pertains to intercompany supply chain networking with its business partners (OEMs and subsuppliers) and cooperation between its various branches.

SCM Focus Areas The Supply Chain Management (SCM) focus areas are those areas founded on close intercompany and intracompany cooperation, joint planning of the core areas of procurement, production, and sales, and the immediate forwarding of relevant information to all those in the supply chain in order to be able to respond immediately to any changes to the environment (modifications to orders).

In the SCOR model, the processes from the supplier through to the customer are mapped on four levels of detail using the core areas of planning, procurement, production, and delivery as a basis:

SCOR Model with Four Levels of Detail

1. On level 1, the processes of a company are described.

2. On level 2, the supply chain of a company can be configured in core process categories.

3. On level 3, the individual process elements of the process categories are defined. This level is also called the *model level*.

4. On level 4, the process elements are defined in detail. This level is also called the *implementation level*.

Within these levels of detail, different objectives are pursued. In addition to strategic competition objectives and overall evaluations, which are defined on the first two levels, the focus for levels 3 and 4 is on smaller, more detailed aspects of the production process.

The decisive factor with the SCOR model is the standardization of the process descriptions on the first three levels. This is not possible on the fourth level because the processes are too individualized. Therefore, Car Doors Inc. can determine its current situation on the initial levels using a defined schema of key figures, and compare these figures with the same key figures from other supply chains in the industry.

For example, level 1 offers the following key figures:

Key Figures on Level 1

▶ Delivery time

▶ Delivery capacity for products kept in stock

▶ Delivery reliability for order-related products

▶ Production flexibility

▶ Correct order performance

This key figure schema forms the basis for Car Doors Inc. for constant assessment and optimization of the entire value chain. The company can regularly monitor its own objectives to determine the efficiency of its supply chain—by importing comparable reference values from the industry into SAP BW as an exercise in benchmarking—and compare these reference values with its own values.

This important information can be made available in a clearly laid out form and distributed to the key positions in the supply chain via the portal. The information on supply relationships is also accessible to purchasers and can be used to optimize the purchasing process.

5.4.3 Integration and Harmonization of Business Objects

After central management of the interfaces within the Car Doors group with SAP Exchange Infrastructure (SAP XI), SAP BW was integrated into this group. In Figure 5.13, SAP BW is represented by the data cube. In this data warehouse, all relevant information from the supply chain is aggregated and made available to a certain number of users for optimizing and managing the supply chain.

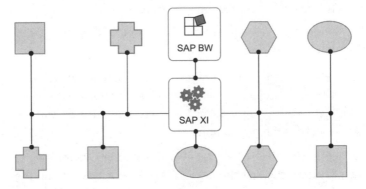

Figure 5.13 System Landscape of the Car Doors Group with SAP BW

One of the most important business objects for Car Doors Inc. within SAP BW is the business partner or, more precisely, the supplier. With the initial analyses, which provided an overall view of Car Doors Inc. across all locations, the inconsistent definition of the business object of supplier across all locations was identified. In order to be able to structure and optimize the purchasing process more effectively, a global, uniform view of the supplier is critical for Car Doors Inc.

Standardized, Groupwide Master Data Using SAP MDM

By introducing SAP Master Data Management (SAP MDM), Car Doors Inc. can consolidate, harmonize, and centrally manage its most important master data objects in three steps. For example, in the first step, supplier master data from all different kinds of systems are brought together, and identical or similar master data are identified. After this process of consolidation, the master data of the supplier can be harmonized (this is the second step). During this process, the generally applicable master data is saved again in the local system of the relevant location and enhanced with special information. In the last and third step, Car Doors Inc. can store its master data centrally in SAP MDM and manage it for the rest of the group.

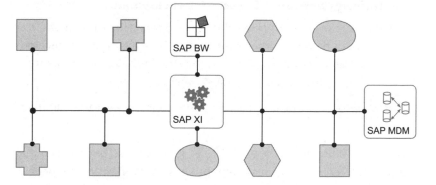

Figure 5.14 System Landscape of the Car Doors Group with SAP BW and SAP MDM

The best way to integrate SAP MDM into the Car Doors group is to use SAP XI. By doing so, several advantages can be exploited: On the one hand, the streamlined data can be forwarded directly via SAP XI to SAP BW, to ensure a standardized, intercompany view of the master data in reporting. On the other hand, with regard to changes to the external systems, messages can be sent to SAP XI and, using the push procedure, automatically forwarded to SAP MDM.

Integration Using SAP XI

Figure 5.14 shows the now standardized system landscape of Car Doors Inc. SAP XI is at the center with the function of central interface administration. Communication of the various systems within the Car Doors group takes place via SAP XI. SAP BW and SAP MDM are similarly integrated into this infrastructure.

5.4.4 Integrating Business Partners from the Automotive Supplier Market

Due to the current situation of the automotive supplier market, collaboration of the individual business partners involved in the supply chain will keep increasing. It is particularly in the area of R&D that Car Doors Inc. must create new structures so that the new products to be developed can be created together with the subsuppliers relatively rapidly.

In addition, Car Doors Inc. plans to integrate electronic marketplaces into the value-added process. The tendency was once to view these marketplaces rather skeptically, but today they have reached a level of technological sophistication that means integration is possible. They also offer other interesting business possibilities. Real added value can be attained only if the sales and distribution processes of Car Doors Inc. have been completely integrated with the marketplaces of the OEMs and the automotive suppliers.

Electronic Marketplaces

Cooperatively Distributed Product Development

To reduce the risk inherent in product development to a minimum, Car Doors Inc. has no choice other than to distribute the product development process among several parties in the supply chain. One of its main objectives is to reduce costs and time-to-market.

So which options are open to Car Doors Inc. with the existing DP infrastructure?

SAP Enterprise Portal

Using SAP EP, a user interface with the key functions can be provided that all those involved in the development process can work with, irrespective of their location. Role-based provision of information and working in *Collaboration Rooms*—chat rooms in the portal that a certain user group can access via the Internet—provide the technical basis for cross-company collaboration. The CAD drawings stored in the C-folders of the local portal solution can also be integrated into the portal. In the collaboration rooms, there is a calendar manager that is used to plan meetings. In this way, the full integration into the development process is achieved.

SAP Knowledge Management

Users can also access additional unstructured information via SAP Knowledge Management (SAP KM). On the portal interface, they can search for important information using the search and classification features. For example, profit and loss reports from SAP BW can be adopted in SAP KM as documents. Consequently, employees can search for information on figures that will support decision-making.

With this platform, Car Doors Inc. can provide a communication system for implementing cooperative, shared product development to all those involved in developing the required products (see Figure 5.14).

Integrating Business Partners and Markets

The advantages of an electronic market in comparison to an individual solution have already been illustrated. Figure 5.15 shows, in simplified form, the possibilities of this DP infrastructure once it has been implemented.

With the SAP XI functions, communication between all different kinds of systems has been enabled using standards such as HTTP and XML. These systems can also exchange data which, in turn, can be used and processed in a multitude of applications.

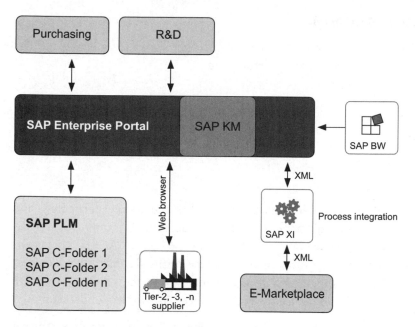

Figure 5.15 Integrating Business Partners

Because of these functions offered by the electronic marketplace, the process steps for initiating contracts can be executed all the more efficiently. With the electronic marketplace, extended support of the existing local portal is possible, in the form of an extended search. Moreover, electronic invitations to tender requests (creating and sending requests) and compare bids are supported. In addition, the electronic marketplace offers the following functions for optimizing the purchasing process:

▶ Special request formats for a structured request

▶ Automatic distribution of the request with all attachments to the suppliers

▶ Standard evaluation reports for comparison of quotations

▶ Use of a Buyer Cockpit for managing all submitted quotations and covering all requests

▶ Standardized request structures

Of course, quotations can also be auctioned in the electronic marketplace via e-bidding according to known auction rules.

5.4.5 Conclusion

The following NetWeaver components were used to integrate the Car Doors Inc. project planning procedure:

► SAP XI

► SAP BW with SAP BW-BPS

► SAP EP

► SAP MDM

► SAP KM

With these components, Car Doors Inc. has equipped its technology and information management system for the successful integration of applications in heterogeneous system landscapes. By using SAP XI with its central interface administration and because of the flexibility this provides, Car Doors Inc. should be able to integrate new systems rapidly into its DP infrastructure and reduce the maintenance costs for this undertaking.

SAP BW provides the foundation for efficiently managing and optimizing the supply chain due to analysis of defined key figure systems and detailed scheduling functions.

With SAP Enterprise Portal, all internal and external users involved in the supply chain can access the information they require, in the form of data and documents, using a role concept via an access point. With this overall solution, Car Doors Inc. is able to meet the requirements of a close collaboration with its business partners.

Web Services As the Platform of the Future In addition to the developments taking place at Car Doors Inc. in the business and technical areas, there are also similar changes occurring in the company processes, from those in Enterprise Resource Planning (ERP), to intercompany collaboration, to Collaborative Business. On the technical level, this covers the development of mainframe architectures to client/server architectures to Web services.

Web services represent a new technology for facilitating intercompany provision of business logic on the basis of existing systems. Business processes are encapsulated and made available to the other business partners as Web services. The searching for, locating of, and use of other Web services that can be provided—not only within the Car Doors group but also made available by other business partners—makes it possible to exchange information beyond company boundaries, and offers unprecedented efficiency in interacting with electronic marketplaces between system applications.

SAP NetWeaver meets the technical requirements for this future technology for Car Doors Inc. However, meeting the technical requirements alone will not be enough to ensure the successful use of the Web service technology in the future. The business partners' organizational structures must also be changed. As long as companies adamantly continue to seal off their systems from the outside world and prevent external business partners from automatically processing business transactions that are already underway in their own systems, there can be no real system-supported, interoperable, intercompany cooperation.

The restructuring of internal organizations, along with the development of fully integrated DP systems and collaborative networks that are seamless and built on mutual trust takes time. Therefore, the introduction of and familiarization with this new kind of interaction between business partners will occur gradually.

The sooner a company acknowledges the signs of the times, the more time it has to prepare for the new organizational and technical challenges ahead. Car Doors Inc. has acknowledged these requirements and will be able to face the future challenges successfully using SAP NetWeaver.

5.5 Car Doors Inc.—Value Consideration

Like so many other companies in the automotive supplier industry, Car Doors Inc. finds itself in a challenging position—between the demands of providing greater performance and, at the same time, continuously providing lower prices. Previously, the delivery of components was the central focus, whereas now entire assemblies (e.g., the whole door and not just parts of the door) are produced and delivered to the car manufacturers. This trend will grow even stronger according to leading market research institutes. To be successful in the face of this trend, Car Doors Inc. has decided to adopt a growth strategy based on its optimization of the supply chain. To realize this in terms of operational measures, the company is concentrating on the following processes:

► Standardized integration platform for IT systems

► Improved data integration for the supply chain controlling

► Improved supplier integration via electronic marketplaces

By introducing SAP R/3, Car Doors Inc. has already begun optimizing internal processes and consolidating IT systems. As another extension level, mySAP PLM was then implemented to optimize the purchasing process. Savings of approximately 25% were made due to the use of this solution. However, to remain competitive in the market, the company must take further measures to push ahead the optimization of its supply chain.

As we already stated, the company is pursuing a strategy of integration. In this section, the potentials of the SAP NetWeaver integration platform will be considered. The approach already described in Chapter 3 focuses on the criteria of *flexibility*, *innovation*, and *cost reduction*.

5.5.1 Standardized Integration Platform

Car Doors Inc. is currently in a period of growth. A global presence is therefore crucial for its survival to supply its large OEM customers. Mergers and acquisitions are a tried-and-tested means of meeting the market requirements. The challenge now is in consolidating the heterogeneous IT landscape that has grown up over the years. Also of importance is the need to build up technological competence in the area of research and development. Since the OEMs are passing on increasingly more tasks to tier-1 suppliers, the suppliers are being forced to build up their own expertise, or to integrate with other partner companies.

The current IT situation only partially meets these requirements. Inconsistencies between different systems and the lack of standards when creating system interfaces have resulted in a disproportionately large expenditure of time and money and have also made the systems very inflexible. This is illustrated in Figure 5.16, which shows the low rating for the criteria of system and process flexibility.

Implementing the objective of a standardized IT integration platform is therefore particularly important. SAP NetWeaver supports these endeavors toward integration and thus represents one step in the direction of a fully integrated supply chain. An overall architecture that builds upon SAP Exchange Infrastructure (XI) makes it possible to eliminate weak points in system integration using a standardized interface concept. In addition, XI can map and monitor cross-system business processes. This scenario is supported by the evaluation of the flexibility and innovation criteria for a possible future scenario (see Figure 5.16).

In terms of costs, the greatest potentials can be found in the following areas:

▶ Simplified development, maintenance, and monitoring of the system interfaces

▶ Fewer resources spent on operating the integration software

▶ Shorter implementation time for cross-application business processes, for example, via graphical process modeling

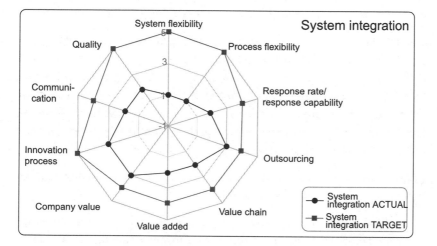

Figure 5.16 Evaluating the System Integration

5.5.2 Data Integration for Supply Chain Controlling

The optimization of the supply chain is critical for Car Doors Inc. To push this ahead, planning and analysis tools should provide valid information about the business processes. However, the current IT landscape is characterized by heterogeneous systems and data structures that offer only limited opportunities for carrying out controlling along the entire supply chain. A further disadvantage of the current system architecture is that the companies involved have no standardized view of the underlying IT systems. A multitude of user interfaces makes things more difficult for users and therefore contributes to the intransparency of the overall process. If you compare this with what is shown in Figure 5.17, you can see that the lack of integration affects primarily the value-added and flexibility criteria.

Data Integration with SAP BI and SAP MDM	To this end, Car Doors Inc. is concentrating on integrating the existing information along the length of the supply chain. Using SAP Business Intelligence (SAP BI), the necessary data can be made available to optimize the process. Additionally, with valid information, the company's production process can be supported because of improved planning.

The quality of the master data plays a significant role in improving supply chain controlling. With an SAP MDM system, the supplier data can be consolidated and any duplication eliminated. With a centralized storage of master data, data management and monitoring are improved.

Controlling with SAP EP

Good data quality is important, but data processing and display are equally important. The implementation of an enterprise portal is planned within the framework of the future architecture. With SAP Enterprise Portal (EP), the consolidated data from the BI system can be displayed in an adequate form according to the various user groups. Figure 5.17 underlines this picture of improved data integration with SAP NetWeaver, with higher values in the areas of communication and added value.

Potentials for Cost Reduction

Considering the costs of the planned solutions, the following savings potentials can be realized with SAP NetWeaver:

▶ With the Business Intelligence system, the resources spent on creating, carrying out, and managing reporting can be reduced. Furthermore, with this application, planning potentials and data quality can be improved and therefore the costs of manual activities can also be reduced, for example.

▶ The cost reduction potentials of SAP Master Data Management lie primarily in the development and management of company-wide master data. Instead of connecting all kinds of different database solutions, using an integrated application means savings potentials can be exploited in the areas of operation and support.

▶ With the portal solution outlined in this chapter, considerable savings can be made in the field of supply chain controlling. With role-specific display of report data, information can be retrieved faster and operational activities initiated more rapidly. This contributes considerably to creating transparency along the entire supply chain.

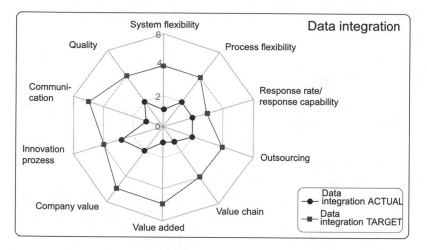

Figure 5.17 Evaluating the Data Integration

5.5.3 Supplier Integration

Integrating its own suppliers is critical for Car Doors Inc. To this end, the existing functions of mySAP Product Lifecycle Management (mySAP PLM) and of the collaboration folders (C-folders) are to be used and developed to create an intercompany scenario. The goal for Car Doors Inc. is to integrate its own suppliers more closely into the area of research and development. In addition, supplier integration via electronic marketplaces plays a major role. For this, the current technical restrictions of the existing system must be addressed. The current situation can be seen in Figure 5.18, with the low rating for flexibility and the communication that is important for an integrated scenario.

Developing the Supplier Integration

In order to make improvements, an architecture that includes SAP NetWeaver focuses on integrating the supplier IT systems. The benefit achieved is implementing an enterprise portal that is integrated with the existing collaboration folder function. In this way, Car Doors Inc. can work together with its suppliers on development projects. In this context, building up a knowledge management system such as SAP KM is critical. Existing knowledge creates added value only if all individuals involved have access to this knowledge and long search times are eliminated.

Integration with SAP Enterprise Portal, SAP KM, and SAP XI

To achieve the integration with a marketplace, the initial technical requirements must first be met. With the implementation of SAP XI, Car Doors Inc. wants to create a foundation for standardized data exchange to exploit the potential of an electronic marketplace. This is confirmed by comparing the evaluations in Figure 5.18: Improved cooperation means higher quality and flexibility, and results in a more successful innovation process.

In terms of costs, savings can be made in the following areas with the NetWeaver solution:

▶ The partners involved in a development process generally have many different applications installed for communication purposes. Consolidating these systems within the context of the collaboration platform has cost-saving potential.

▶ With SAP KM, this potential can be found in two areas: Considerable development costs can be saved by using already predefined content, and consolidating existing systems into a standardized knowledge management system has cost reduction potential.

▶ Other cost-saving possibilities that can emerge from implementing the XI platform are found in the areas of development, maintenance, management, and monitoring of the system interfaces.

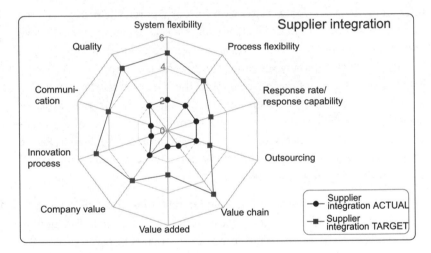

Figure 5.18 Evaluating the Supplier Integration

5.5.4 Evaluation and Recommendation

Becoming a module supplier is strategically important to Car Doors Inc. The processes discussed in this chapter represent the operational measures that should be taken to reach this goal. But how do these measures compare with the company's IT strategy?

The reference value represents a qualitative evaluation of the IT strategy according to the criteria of flexibility, innovation, and cost reduction. For the sake of simplification, we have depicted these three processes in a diagram.

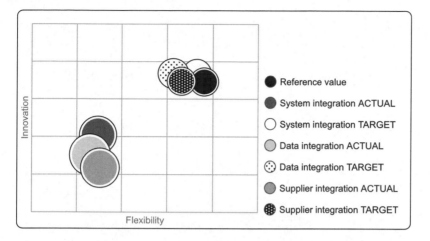

Figure 5.19 Portfolio Matrix

A comparison with the reference value shows a good positioning in relation to the processes modeled with SAP NetWeaver. The cost reduction potential can be realized despite the growth strategy of Car Doors Inc., as represented by the size of the circles. Since the optimization of the supply chain is crucial, system flexibility is also significant. Given this set of circumstances, it is therefore important for the company to thoroughly and rigorously restructure its IT landscape within a relatively short time frame. This is undoubtedly a basic requirement for remaining competitive in the future.

6 Roadmap to SAP NetWeaver for United Gas

Due to the reorganization of the gas supply industry, existing oligopolies are being put to the test. The following scenario looks at a regional purchasing company for natural gas that views competition after the liberalization of the gas market as both a challenge and an opportunity.

6.1 Scenario Description

The gas supply situation could have been described as precarious even as far back as three decades ago. Geographically isolated gas generating plants based on coal and the depleting of stock from regional natural gas storage facilities were typical. The amount of natural gas available was insufficient. Also, transportation to the consumer was not guaranteed, as there was no comprehensive network of gas pipelines.

Thus regional gas supply companies came into being. It was their task to look after local supply interests. This constituted the main objectives of organizing long-distance transportation of gas and procuring additional quantities of natural gas.

Whereas today, thanks to effective energy-saving measures, the heat market is slowly reaching its limits of growth, new rules are coming into play with the liberalization of the gas market and there is now movement in the hitherto highly profitable area occupied by these supply companies. These changes to the regulatory framework are also increasing the cost pressure from the competition.

United Gas operates solely in the US market, as a regional purchaser of natural gas. The majority of the partners are municipal energy supply companies with varying stakes in the company. They are using the expert's specialist knowledge and by acquiring an interest have dissolved or outsourced their own internal departments for managing the gas business.

Because United Gas exclusively meets the demands of municipal energy suppliers and some smaller regional gas suppliers and is constantly developing its customer relationships, it has become the market leader in its region. United Gas has also strengthened its position even further and now supplies its industrial customers directly.

Background

Upheaval in the Gas Market

Local Provider

The uneven distribution of the gas sales of United Gas can be seen clearly from Figure 6.1. Sixty-six percent of gas sales are accounted for by municipal gas providers; however, this segment makes up only 10% of customers. By contrast, 85% of customers are industrial customers; however, these make up only 14% of gas sales. Whereas the regional and municipal gas providers are resellers, the industrial customers are supplied directly. Thus this particular customer relationship is by comparison disproportionately more profitable.

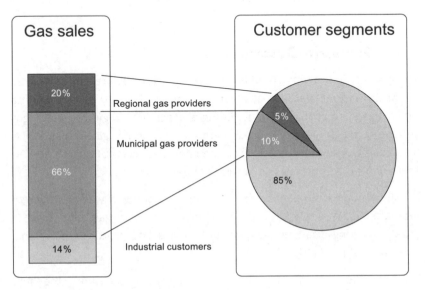

Figure 6.1 Share of Gas Sales By Comparison with the Customer Segment

Task and Day-to-Day Activities

Generally speaking, United Gas's job is to procure and transport natural gas, with both the optimization of procurement and security of supply being its highest priorities.

The transportation of gas through its own natural gas network—with a distribution system supported by storage facilities that stretches more than 1,000 miles—ensures constant supply and bridges peaks in consumption.

There is diversified procurement of gas from a base comprising various suppliers and contracts with varying validity periods. This minimizes supply dependency and optimizes the procurement portfolio.

Gas is stored in the company's own storage facilities, which helps buffer price peaks by offering the greatest possible flexibility. This is therefore a tried and tested means for risk minimization in terms of securing supply and optimizing gas procurement.

United Gas is subdivided into several subsidiaries that perform different tasks. Its own trading company was established to optimize gas procurement and minimize risk. One subsidiary specializes in short-term trade. Additionally, one service subsidiary is responsible for transmission management and new products. Sales inclusive of all subsidiaries of United Gas amount to over 1 billion dollars.

A total of some 140 employees work in the company, distributed among the said subsidiaries. The members of staff either come from the special departments concerned or have been employed from elsewhere. This means that they're distributed among various locations, but all access the same systems that are centrally managed.

This company structure, which is partly due to the way the company has evolved, together with the strong influence of the municipal partners, creates a compartmentalization of functions, which is similarly reflected in the United Gas system architecture. The departments incorporated from the purchasing companies brought IT systems into the company or made requirements to the functionality of the software. Because in the past United Gas had no standardized software for the industry, there were diverse systems that arose due to the creation of customized, self-developed solutions. The majority of these systems now use their own types of software, which can be managed only separately.

These systems are connected via self-developed interfaces. There is both synchronous and asynchronous data exchange,[1] for which there are various interface formats.

United Gas has recognized that it is important to present its services in an up-to-date manner, particularly to industrial customers. This profitable group of customers is seen as offering great potential for future growth. Various measures will be used to expand and optimize the company's Web site. In doing so, the Internet and intranet interfaces will be restructured in terms of content and technical requirements.

It is important to the local partners to make timely decisions. In doing so, they want to rely on significant company figures. For this purpose, an

---

1   Asynchronous data transfer is manually planned and then executed automatically at a particular time (e.g., once a day or week), while synchronous data transfer is executed by the system "as it happens."

employee is designated as being solely responsible for consolidating data from all the different kinds of systems and reporting his findings directly to management.

The entire IT system is overseen by two people. One employee concentrates on *basic and interface support*, while the other is responsible for *system and applications support*.

The management has already decided to replace the company's self-developed systems with standard software. Implementation is not yet complete, however. In an analysis of requirements, future challenges have been outlined and shortfalls identified.

6.2   Challenges

United Gas is operating in a growth market. The market share of natural gas is rising steadily, but the competition is becoming increasingly more demanding. For this reason, management is not content to simply maintain the status quo.

It sees great potential in particular in the industrial customers as profitable direct customers, who in 2002 met 32% of their planned independent energy requirement with natural gas. However, these companies are also being wooed by other gas suppliers. Systematic development of the range of products and services offered to purchasers of natural gas is therefore planned. This direct strategy will be supported by portfolio management measures. Existing customer relationships will be made more transparent via more comprehensive reporting, so that customer requirements can be identified and satisfied faster.

Objective: Constant or Reduced Operating Costs

It has been recognized that the product portfolio can be extended and intensively managed only if there is strong IT support. Apart from this, future process and personnel costs should at least remain constant. General cost-saving programs in the area of personnel led to the decision to keep, among other things, the number of IT employees constant, that is, on no account to increase the number. The management is not prepared to continue to bear the rising operating costs of the old systems; in this area too, all efficiency potentials will be systematically exhausted.

6.2.1 Self-Developed Solutions versus Standard Software

The IT based on self-developed solutions in the past resulted in a heterogeneous system landscape. Creating a homogeneous system landscape
represents a first step toward containing costs. This has already begun
with the introduction of a content management system and will be pursued further. The conscious choice made was for an almost infinitely scalable system based on open standards and with a very wide range of functionality. These measures are still being applied and the plan is to
continue to implement them systematically.

The IT department intends to implement a completely integrated group
of systems that permits external systems to be connected via standardized interfaces. The decision to use standard software provides a starting
point for discussing the next steps. The SAP solution mySAP ERP with
NetWeaver components offers possibilities for mapping as many process
areas as possible.

By using SAP NetWeaver, it is therefore possible to not only replace the
non-standardized system landscape but also to realize additional optimization objectives. Therefore, it is hoped that the following disadvantages
of self-developed systems will be eliminated:

▶ Heterogeneous system landscape
▶ No open standards
▶ Non-scalable systems
▶ Restricted functionality
▶ No support of standard formats
▶ Self-developed interfaces
▶ Complex dependencies when changing versions

6.2.2 IT Infrastructure

As a general rule, no additional personnel costs are to arise in any department. A particular objective of the management is to keep administration
and maintenance costs either constant or to reduce them after modern-
izing and expanding the IT infrastructure.

Furthermore, IT is viewed as tried and tested and the sole means of
achieving these objectives. This means however that the portfolio of
products used must be expanded and new functions must be implemented in some systems. Cost savings together with the expansion of IT

support are to be achieved by introducing a cost-effective IT infrastructure that can ensure future competitiveness.

United Gas must also consider the idea of exploiting opportunities for future growth by making strategic acquisitions. To be a safe investment for the future, the IT infrastructure must also afford maximum flexibility.

Standards The desire to increase sales with industrial customers brings with it the requirement for data exchange with these customers via interfaces. Self-developed systems offer no standard data formats for data exchange. Therefore self-designed interfaces had to be developed to enable a connection of the customer systems, although customers to some degree supported standard formats. Changes of version and release on the customers' side required additional adaptation of the self-developed, non-standardized interface formats.

Interfaces To achieve this, external expertise had to be bought in, since the IT department did not offer this expertise in terms of quantity or quality. This knowledge could not be built up due to time and cost restrictions. Because the software was set up by external consultants, a dependency situation resulted. Additionally, management of the interfaces increased expenditure of resources on maintenance and operation.

Despite the fact that the individual systems were connected to one another, no consolidation of data storage was ultimately possible. Thus evaluations and analyses provide no overall picture and have to be brought together manually. The idea of developing further interfaces between the systems to improve the consistency and consolidation of data was rejected for cost reasons.

With the system updates of the self-developed systems, some interface adaptations are also needed, which is additionally time-consuming. On top of this, changes to the interface specification often bring more adaptations with them. Any change (e.g., in mapping) must be designed, executed, and tested. The expertise this requires can hardly be provided by two IT employees.

Very few interfaces use the XML (Extensible Markup Language) standard. Since the introduction of an XML-capable connector, all new and newly-adapted interfaces have been created using this standard. Harmonization is also the objective here.

Operation and Maintenance Operation and maintenance of the systems and servers is becoming increasingly difficult, since the number of legacy systems that can be maintained by two employees has reached a critical limit. Not only are operating system and database updates along with system support required, but increasingly more complex rules of compatibility and restrictions must be taken into account also.

With the last system introduction, the attempt was made to accommodate the differing objectives with an infinitely scalable content management system based on open standards. It currently manages the data published on the intranet and extranet. With the introduction of the content management system, two legacy systems were eliminated as part of a system consolidation.

There was a self-developed quality assurance software existing that was to be used for scheduling and managing maintenance work on the systems. This approach failed due to the expenditure of resources on system maintenance and to the extremely complex nature of the system; now, however, there are still guidelines and work and quality instructions. These are managed in the document management part of the content management system and can be called up over the intranet.

The second system was to make the basic tasks of a knowledge management system available. The specialist departments decided to forego the overdimensioned functions and to transfer to the document management system those tasks that essentially consisted in managing the previously stored documents. Overall, however, this infrastructure has shortcomings:

▶ No consolidated data storage

▶ Maintenance and operation are time-consuming

▶ Rigid, hard-to-adapt structure

▶ Updates and changes of release are subject to restrictions and complex rules

▶ Expansion of human resources required

▶ Dependency on external consultants

▶ Costly maintenance of the interface landscape

▶ Ambitious spectrum of tasks at the same cost

Disadvantages of an Old Infrastructure

6.2.3   Collaborative Business and the Intranet

A modern company should have a Web site. United Gas began using this platform for showcasing its company early on. The company has now gone one step further by introducing a content management system. The objective was to expand and manage content efficiently.

Customer-Specific Data Provision

The traditional, standardized presentation of company information to all customers no longer suffices, however: Independent marketing and reorientation toward existing and potential customers is required. On the Web site of the purchasing company of United Gas, customers will find all kinds of information about the range of services offered, contact persons, and the usual Web site structure overview. Industrial customers should also be able to call up specific information rapidly about products and services offered by United Gas. The presentation of this information should be customer-specific. For example, for private customers of the regional providers, calculations based on tariff entries and meter readings should be simulated. Additionally, the user should be able to create a profile so that direct conclusions can be drawn about his interests. Even if the primary goal of dissemination of information were solved with this method, it would still not suffice. Not only must customers be able to find information on the Internet, but employees must be able to access information and documents on an intranet. Also, it should be possible to call up applications and services via this medium. Employees should be able to access work documents (particularly contracts) on the intranet. All documents are managed and maintained via a structured buffer with a version management feature.

Standardized Data View

The management no longer wants to use the Internet and intranet simply for presenting information. The standardized data view for all employees is one shortcoming. It should be possible to have a certain perspective toward contents. Moreover, access to certain data should be possible for only defined groups of people. Among other things, these measures should facilitate and promote the cooperation of work groups.

Not least, user management with these diverse systems is a complex task. Continuous support and operations are also being made more difficult and incurring extra costs.

While the display of information is to be tailored for specific users, standardized, central access is the objective for logging in. Ultimately, this means integrating the various applications via a common access. In the past, the introduction of new systems slowed down the productivity due to the recurrent need for training in the operation of the user interface. Daily operations are also made more difficult because of the use of various interfaces.

To increase added value in general, the management is striving to create a standardized interface for displaying information and operating all IT systems. On the customer side, the hitherto "organized" system, which in fact comprised the mere presentation of information, is also to be extended. There is to be intercompany integration of employees and process owners on the customer side. Here, data is not only to be exchanged, but, in particular, there is to be intercompany integration of processes. The management's vision is that of a common execution of processes and automated data exchange. The common interface is viewed as the first step toward collaborative business; it should facilitate common processing of business transactions and eliminate the problems listed below.

Inflexible Internet and intranet structures have the following negative aspects in particular:

▶ Mere presentation of information

▶ No standardized data view for all employees

▶ Increased need for training on user interfaces

▶ More difficult operation due to inconsistent user interfaces

▶ No selective access to information for groups of persons

▶ Use by temporary work groups not possible

▶ Complex user management due to heterogeneous system landscape

▶ No standardized system access and interface

▶ Collaborative execution of processes not possible

Disadvantages of an Inflexible Internet and intranet

6.2.4 Key Figures and Reporting

The management wants to be able to make decisions based on consolidated key company figures. While access to functions and applications is being centralized, operational information is not centrally available but this information is distributed among several points. Key figures should no longer be compiled manually but instead this process should be automated. The objective is to introduce automated reporting. Figure 6.2 illustrates how, previously, data had to be entered and consolidated manually in order to obtain the desired figures.

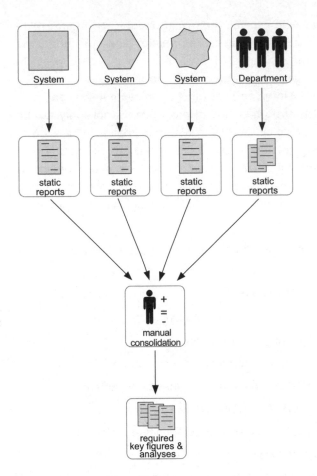

Figure 6.2 Manual Reporting

Manual Reporting Currently, it is difficult to obtain meaningful evaluations. As shown in Figure 6.2, some data had to be compiled manually. Many systems also have inadequate reporting functions. Ultimately, the quality is also unsatisfactory. Non-harmonized systems provide differing databases and thus to a certain extent inconsistent analysis results.

Overall, analysis and reporting is made up of a patchwork of different applications. One employee appointed by the management for this purpose creates the desired analyses and key figures manually. He adjusts inconsistent results and adds missing data after researching these inconsistent results. The reports cannot be created as they are required, but must be asked for in advance. The evaluations are therefore not as up-to-date as would be desired.

The management requires current data on selected operational processes. The efficiency of the company and the productivity of employees is to be managed on an individual basis. The management is of the opinion that sound company decisions can be made only with real-time, current analyses. Typically, these key figures should be created in real time using a common data basis and this process should be automated in order to ensure rapid responses to changes in consumer behavior or in the market.

By pinpointing dependencies rapidly and reliably, the diversification of natural gas purchasing in particular should be advanced. Portfolio management should be monitored via targeted analyses and planned, structured procurement should be facilitated. Overall, the following weak points can be eliminated by central reporting:

▶ Limited reporting functions

▶ Questionable quality of analyses

▶ Inconsistent analyses

▶ Key figures are not current

▶ Manual consolidation of data and creation of evaluations

▶ No common database

▶ Manual creation of analyses and evaluations

6.3 Approaches

In Section 6.1, the current situation of United Gas in respect of the industry, market, processes, and partners, and IT in general was examined. The objectives of United Gas have been formulated. The management has created a plan that should prepare the company optimally for achieving its goals. Finally, in Section 6.2, the disadvantages of the current IT solutions were highlighted.

The task is now to formulate IT strategies that optimize the planning and execution processes and ensure that objectives are realized both in the short and the long term. To do so, decisions already made should be considered and restructuring measures currently underway should be integrated, continued, and further developed.

Implementation of the measures below should be continued:

▶ Restructuring of the standard software

▶ Use of the content management system

▶ XML as preferred interface standard

6.3.1 Introducing a Cost-Effective Infrastructure

The decision to use standard software as an all-purpose measure can solve several infrastructure problems simultaneously. There are implicit advantages for United Gas in three key features of standard software:

▶ High level of integration

▶ Open standard interfaces

▶ Uniform version cycles

SAP NetWeaver together with mySAP ERP offer great potential for optimization in terms of each of the preceding advantages.

High Level of Integration

The systems that have already been distributed among various servers can be brought together physically. Monitoring and maintenance of the systems is thus made much easier and this can still be administered by only two employees in the IT department. The high level of integration offered by standard software automatically optimizes the previous interface and database landscape. The easier it is to manage a common database also makes all data available in consolidated form. While the self-developed systems are currently connected to one another by self-developed interfaces, this will no longer be required. Only external systems will have to be connected via interfaces. The IT department already has the expertise required for connection via XML in particular, so that external expertise is no longer necessary.

The individual applications of mySAP ERP are already fully integrated. Using SAP NetWeaver as an integration platform means that other systems can also be connected.

Open Standard Interface Formats

Open standard interface formats for data transfer are available for these connections, and the content management system already introduced will utilize them. Here, XML will be used primarily as the data format. The IT department already has the required expertise for this, having built up this expertise early on and having used it in the context of possible implementation of XML. Thus the management and maintenance of the interfaces will be the exclusive responsibility of the company's own IT employees. By focusing on a single format, the dependency on external consultants will be reduced, and therefore expertise will remain in-house along with the resulting cost savings. Furthermore, because the standard formats are now so widespread, connecting customers and integrating external systems will be far easier.

With the J2EE Engine of the SAP Web Application Server (Web AS) and, in particular, the SAP Exchange Infrastructure (XI), SAP NetWeaver offers diverse standard interfaces and data formats.

Standard software is subject to its own version cycles, which follow simple rules. There are version dependencies of components, but these are manageable and documented by the manufacturer. If system modifications are necessary, for example, due to new legal requirements, or if new functions are desired, these can be added via a system upgrade, without the need to create a self-developed system. Finally, support is also provided by the manufacturer. If it is still not possible for the company's own IT staff to create an upgrade, external providers must be used. The market for such providers is, however, transparent. Locating and selecting these providers and negotiating a price are therefore easy tasks. This is usually more cost-effective than expanding a self-developed system, since the analysis phases, development costs, and "monopolistic knowledge" relating to the self-developed software are eliminated.

Uniform Version Cycles

The version cycles of mySAP ERP and SAP NetWeaver are harmonized with each other. The downtime during a change of release is therefore minimized and administrative preparations can be bundled.

6.3.2 Collaborative Business

The United Gas Web site is supposed to be expanded massively. Implementation of collaborative business can be supported by a portal solution. The advantages of this approach include:

▶ User-specific info views

▶ Standardized login

▶ Common execution of processes

Customers of United Gas will be able to call up more comprehensive and specifically defined information. The breadth of information can also be managed by the existing content management system. Since the information presented will include gas tariffs, the service tariffs shown must be up-to-date, relevant to the customer in question, and complete. This is ensured by a centralized management and maintenance of all contents.

User-Specific Info Views

Document management is already used within the intranet for managing work and quality instructions. It is important for United Gas that the documents are available independently of an employee's location. These documents are used constantly, particularly for maintenance and repair of

Document Management

gas storage facilities. Current information can be called up by employees due to continuous updates. The procedure and responsibilities for maintenance work are given in detail here and are supported by checklists and forms (e. g., for acceptance). With a portal solution, access to this sometimes sensitive data can also be restricted to only the relevant group of employees.

Team Rooms The information distribution feature—team rooms—can be used internally in a much more intensive manner. Employees should organize themselves via special areas, only accessible to them, mostly on a per project basis. In addition to the setting up of these special team rooms, company information ranging from internal job advertisements to the cafeteria's menu can be stored. Conference room bookings and pool vehicle reservations will be made only via the portal in the future. Administrative processes will become simpler and more transparent.

Project organization is particularly important for United Gas. The following projects are planned or have already been initiated:

▶ Industrial customer acquisition

▶ The development of new service offerings

▶ An "Autogas" campaign

▶ Strategic company acquisitions

The team rooms are important for exchanging information; for example, project directories can be created here. This is particularly important when developing new services, for example, since findings of customer surveys on the attractiveness of future services can be viewed and any changes to the concept are documented. In developing the service concept, United Gas included employees with their contact information and roles, and also contact persons from the customer side are managed here. Deadlines, milestones and other key dates are made known to the team. When developing new services, the team room acts as a virtual workspace.

Standardized Login The standardized "Single Sign-On" will also simplify the management of user data. Using role-based profiles, all employees can obtain information selectively and perform activities. With some team rooms (e.g., those for strategic company acquisitions), access is permitted on the basis of the employee profile assigned, thus protecting sensitive information. The interface becomes a "collaborative desk." The need for training is reduced, since only one interface must be used.

While the information level is being used by customers and employees, employees can also operate all systems at all locations via a common interface, and handle all processes relating to daily activities. Customer inquiries (e.g., about gas tariffs) can be forwarded electronically by customer service to the relevant customer adviser and be processed directly by the latter. In the customer service area in particular, processing times should be minimized and the principle of "one face to the customer" implemented. Customer requirements and the potential for new services are recognized more rapidly.

Common
Execution of
Processes

This "collaborative desk" thus stretches across all business processes. Customers and business partners can be integrated into the process, participating via the portal with a restricted access entitlement. Industrial customers are to be given an "exclusive customer status," providing them with access to special areas on the Intranet, which will make it possible to call up statistics on their consumption, consumption peaks, and other evaluations. This should increase the rate of customer retention at United Gas.

This kind of portal can be realized using SAP Enterprise Portal (EP). The aforementioned evaluations and reports are made available using SAP Business Information Warehouse (SAP BW).

6.3.3 Decisions Based on Key Company Figures

The management requires sound analyses in the future, based on which business decisions can be made. For example, it should be possible to call up gas sales to individual customers at the push of a button. This type of analysis is currently created manually using the data in the self-developed systems. Similarly, the current database is heterogeneous.

In the future, analyses will be current for the day in question and it should be possible for these up-to-the-minute analyses to be retrieved automatically upon request. A homogenous database is expected from the implementation of a central entity that gathers and processes all data from all systems. Inconsistent results will therefore be eliminated. The expenditure of resources on these evaluations will be greatly reduced.

Up-to-the-Minute
Analyses

The management expects evaluations to support company decisions. To this end, key figures provide the greatest possible amount of aggregated information. These should provide the basis for decision-making in the areas of purchasing, stockholding, sales and cost (controlling) in particular. For example, it should be possible to determine the average stock-holding costs in the various storage facilities per cubic meter.

To increase the transparency of key figures or identify interdependencies where this is necessary, the analyses can be shown in relation to one another. Reciprocal dependencies can thus be made apparent or clearer. It should also be possible to answer questions regarding profitability in the customer segments.

Currently, these options are not available. The IT department has tried to provide these features using the existing system as a basis by integrating various systems. The "n:n integration" approach failed. This failed attempt and the fact that its limitations became clear when presented with this task provided the main catalyst for rethinking the existing system structure.

Ultimately, the management questioned an IT landscape that had performed its task in individual areas but that overall could not deliver consistent company information and therefore could be used in only limited respects as a basis for decision-making.

Reports and evaluations can be created using SAP BW. If the reports provided don't suffice, they can either be extended or new analyses can be developed.

6.3.4 Changeover to Standard Software

United Gas has relied on self-developed software in the past. The individual partners had their own special systems designed and developed, since there was no industry-specific software available. When merging the areas, the need to harmonize the system and process landscape was neglected. This will now be implemented systematically.

With the changeover to standard software, core functions must remain available. These include, for example:

Checking Management of Gas Contracts Contracts with suppliers must be monitored with regard to time and quantities. The delivery capacity must be ensured and the price optimized; conversely, the dependency on one supplier must be kept small. Not least, the key figure models should support United Gas in this.

In terms of gas sales, the contracts must be concluded for a specific time. Sales forecasts are also important. However, at United Gas a large part of the overall sales from contracts with the local authorities exhibits only marginal volatility.

The gas stock serves to buffer peaks in consumption and additional demand. The industrial customers, who are supplied directly, play the largest role here. Their peaks in demand must be met directly. The automated reports should support this additional demand and make forecasts based on historical values.

Monitoring the Gas Stock

Maintenance of the facilities is to be ensured via maintenance and work plans. Safety requirements are to be met. This results in actual schedules that must be adhered to. Spare parts and consumables must be provided and procured in good time.

Maintenance of Gas Supply Pipes and Storage Facilities

The allocation of costs is important for every company. Cost drivers are to be identified. In this case, cost-saving potentials are to be determined with the aid of the controlling system. Up to now, this has only been possible to a limited degree. Controlling, the analyses already mentioned, and the key company figures are viewed by the management as possible bases for supporting decision-making and reasoning and as a success indicator that can be presented to the shareholders.

Controlling of Operational Areas

Process optimization potential can be exhausted using automated document creation, for example. The open standards provided in the future for document creation should also ensure automated invoice transfer.

Automated Creation and Issuing of Invoices

Automated creation and dispatch of documents in a standard format has cost-saving potential in all areas in which documents were previously issued manually or only semi-automatically to customers, suppliers, and other business partners.

Accounting acts as a substitute for functions that are subject to external business standards. In general terms, it should be possible to support these standards with unmodified standard software. Up until now this was only possible by programming the systems.

Standardized and Certified Accounting

When considering the advantages of standard software, the disadvantages should not be overlooked, however. For one, the cost-saving aspects are to be viewed against the license costs, which are not incurred with a self-developed systems. These costs must be taken into account.

The functionality available must also be determined. It was not without reason that companies in the past opted for tailored, self-developed systems offering all desired functions. Savings from harmonization and standardization are ultimately achieved at a cost to the individuality of the product.

However, in the final analysis, an individual system does result, in terms of customer-specific business process settings. Furthermore, customer-specific system enhancements are also possible. These should be avoided in relation to standard software, however.

6.4 Rapid Project Success

mySAP ERP generally meets the requirement of achieving an integrated group of systems with a homogeneous database that permits external systems to be connected using standardized interfaces. The advantage of this solution in terms of integration and optimization is that SAP NetWeaver is already included in the software as its technical basis and thus no further license costs are incurred. However, the problems stated here can be solved by other standard software packages as well. In addition to consideration of the known risks when making a selection (e.g., future existence of the manufacturer), the decision is ultimately based on two criteria:

▶ Whether the required functionalities are covered

▶ Whether there is support in developing further troubleshooting approaches

mySAP ERP provides various functionalities that are already used by or are attractive to United Gas. In this case, the analysis of costs is often a central focus.

Attractive Functions of mySAP ERP

The gas storage facilities can be monitored via inventory controlling, which provides qualitative and quantitative data on stockholding. Typical fluctuations in the past can be tracked and analyzed. The storage facility stock can be evaluated using various procedures. The proper maintenance and care of the gas storage facilities and pipelines is ensured using the Asset Lifecycle Management component together with a sophisticated inspection scheduling system. Maintenance dates and tasks are managed and any auxiliary materials required are itemized in advance.

The functional versatility of mySAP ERP is certainly indisputable. It solves some general problems encountered by United Gas, but we will only mention it marginally as it is not supposed to be the focus of this book. Despite this, it must be verified for each individual case whether requirements can be met completely. In case of any doubt, SAP NetWeaver offers the possibility of developing flexible solutions beyond the limits of the standard version.

SAP NetWeaver is supplied along with mySAP ERP, and its components are thus also available for use. Because SAP NetWeaver and mySAP ERP are supplied together, you should check company requirements to determine which solutions can be offered using mySAP ERP along with the SAP NetWeaver components. We should point out the synergies of SAP NetWeaver and mySAP ERP here.

6.5 Integrated Project Planning Procedure

The introduction of mySAP ERP alone does not meet all the IT requirements of United Gas. The SAP NetWeaver components however indicate that specific additions can be made. Four areas should be addressed consecutively. This step-by-step implementation ensures gradual but continuous introduction.

1. **Development of a modern infrastructure**
   SAP Web Application Server (Web AS) forms the basis for SAP NetWeaver, which, in turn, forms the basis for all other components. As a core component, it offers the required function of central administration and can thus be used immediately.

2. **Key figure models**
   SAP Business Information Warehouse (BW) brings together all data from all connected systems. It integrates, analyzes, and processes this data automatically as required. The urgency of the requirement for meaningful figures and the fact that the solution is well-tested led to the decision to introduce these additional system components.

3. **Optimization of customer relationships**
   SAP Enterprise Portal (EP) provides a standardized interface for employees and business partners to work on. The information displayed on this interface is user and customer specific.

4. **Intercompany processes with business partners**
   SAP Exchange Infrastructure (XI) is the integration component of SAP NetWeaver. The interfaces brought together here based on open standards of all internal and external systems make intercompany processes possible. They must be introduced at this point in order to make it possible to integrate and use SAP Business Information Warehouse.

6.5.1 Developing a Modern Infrastructure

The requirement that no additional IT staff be appointed at United Gas can only be met via an efficient infrastructure based on standards. In particular, administrative activities must be minimized and it must be possible for these activities to be carried out centrally.

SAP Web AS   SAP Web Application Server (Web AS) is available for meeting this requirement. As an application server, it forms the basis for the installation and is introduced first. The administrative tasks, which used to be performed via several systems and databases, are now handled centrally, and alerts and notifications are shown via an interface. Web AS is scalable and can be distributed across several entities. It also offers safety mechanisms that meet all requirements relating to data integrity, data protection, and confidentiality.

All SAP NetWeaver components have a common release cycle. Documentation, consulting, training, and customer support are geared towards supporting the SAP NetWeaver platform as a whole. This leads, then, not only to synergies in the administration of SAP NetWeaver, but also in relation to changes of release.

SAP Web AS makes it possible to use a single, common database for all applications. The various, costly database updates can be avoided. There is also no more costly user management across all systems. Centralized management means that authentication is possible via Single Sign-On.

SAP Web AS also serves as an integration platform in a Web service architecture and facilitates standard-based development using key technologies such as J2EE. This provides two possibilities for United Gas.

Java Web Services   1. Web services can be created using J2EE, which adapt the selected standard functions to the needs of the company. With the changeover from individualized to standard software, it cannot be relied upon that all desired functionalities are already provided and that no customer-specific adjustments are necessary. In this respect, Web services offer all kinds of advantages. Their mode of operation and the principles underlying this are illustrated in detail in Chapter 8.

Integration Platform   2. The application server also performs the function of an integration platform. This provides a second advantage for United Gas. This advantage lies in the connection of the content management system to the Web AS via the J2EE Engine. Because additional systems can be connected via this standard, the flexibility and future potential of this NetWeaver infrastructure component are also increased. The fact that the content management system can be used rapidly and that a tried and tested interface is used are additional reasons for introducing it as the first component.

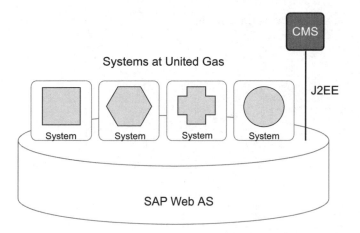

Figure 6.3 Connecting the Content Management System to SAP Web AS

6.5.2 Key Figure Models

The requirement for current, comprehensive analyses and key figures that can be used for making sound company decisions is met by SAP Business Information Warehouse (BW). SAP BW, as part of SAP Business Intelligence (BI), provides comprehensive reporting, analysis, and planning tools. With 7,500 installations, SAP BW is the most mature SAP NetWeaver component. Since SAP BW can rapidly deliver the analyses United Gas requires and is well tried and tested, it is introduced as the second component.

SAP BW

The database for analyses and reports used to be generated individually from each system of United Gas. If this was not possible, the data was compiled manually by the department in question. This is no longer necessary with the introduction of BW.

SAP BW is an independent system that is connected to other applications via the SAP Exchange Infrastructure. It therefore has direct access to all data used. Up-to-date information can therefore be accessed without any delay.

There are various predefined evaluations provided that can be used either out-of-the-box or adapted to individual requirements. Within these evaluations, non-relevant data can be hidden or aggregated by specifying important key fields.

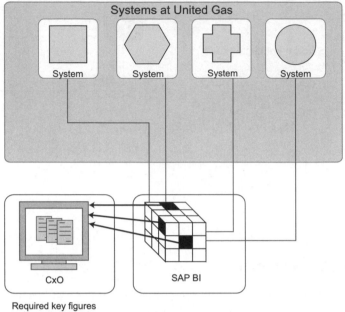

Figure 6.4 Key Figure Models with SAP BW

As you can see from Figure 6.4, to create an evaluation from all available, related data, the user selects particular information areas. This results in an evaluation for which the display can be changed using the procedure illustrated above.

In particular, the key figure models required by United Gas should provide as much compressed data as possible. With SAP BW, standard evaluations can easily be used as a basis for creating new ones.

To accommodate the special requirements of United Gas, analyses of gas consumption can be created with BW using existing data. Gas consumption can be tracked in time and broken down into customers or customer segments (industrial customers, regional and municipal gas providers).

This provides a basis for making forecasts. If forecast levels are not met, then the reasons for this can be evaluated, for example, in terms of each customer segment. These customer analyses support the manager in choosing the right measures to be taken in respect of the customer in question (additional services, recommendation for tariff change, consultancy services on gas supply, etc.).

Gas procurement can be planned in terms of quantity using these forecasts. Analyses and evaluations by BW relating to suppliers (delivery reliability, price, quality) also support qualitative procurement and assist in selecting suppliers.

United Gas revenue can then be allocated directly to each customer segment or customer. Profit accounting in relation to subsidiaries and departments is also possible. Targeted company management using meaningful, homogeneous analyses and key figures provides a picture of the company's operational situation. SAP Enterprise Portal, to be discussed in the next section, can be used to provide a defined group of employees with access to findings of analyses.

6.5.3 Optimizing Customer Relationships

SAP Enterprise Portal (EP) addresses the need for common execution of processes and automated data exchange by employees and customers via a standardized interface.

SAP EP

SAP Enterprise Portal ensures integration of all kinds of company data and applications. It also ensures control over heterogeneous IT landscapes via a standardized interface.

SAP Enterprise Portal is a widely used solution, with 2,500 installations. For companies such as United Gas that are planning to implement SAP applications for providing information and analysis functions, it becomes particularly attractive when combined with BW.

Since BW has now been fully introduced, analyses and reports can be retrieved via the portal. Thus operation is much easier. Moreover, access can be managed by means of user profiles.

The existing content management system of United Gas can also be integrated into the SAP Enterprise Portal. SAP EP supports this with uncomplicated management of business contents in a central repository, from which content is directly published.

The standardized login on the portal interface is user-friendly and eliminates costly, separate user management of all systems used via the portal. Each user is presented with individualized information according to his assigned role. The user can adapt the display to his needs. The role profile also governs entitlement to use of certain services and applications. The fact that the various user groups are addressed individually also increases user acceptance.

All mySAP ERP functions can be called up via the portal, along with other applications as required. Via common access, business transactions can be processed by United Gas process owners, some of whom are based at different company locations.

6.5.4 Intercompany Processes with Customers

SAP XI The SAP Exchange Infrastructure (XI), with its framework of adapters, provides an effective range of adapters. This ensures data exchange with file systems, message queue systems, legacy applications and database systems.

One problem for United Gas was the costly management of the interface landscape, not least due to the various self-developed solutions in this area. The SAP Exchange Infrastructure makes it possible to eliminate the existing n:n interfaces. Each connection is generally run via XI and the relevant adapter. This n:1 principle greatly enhances maintainability and monitoring.

Moreover, the open standards supported by the customer systems can then be operated. Integration of external systems can be achieved without the need for adaptations, using the mappings also supplied, and missing mappings can be extended easily using the templates. The XML expertise built up by the IT department of United Gas can be used and systematically broadened. If external expertise still has to be bought in, the results are rapidly transferable for the IT department, even without transfer of expertise and can be utilized elsewhere.

Extension of Processes Using SAP Exchange Infrastructure is a good way of extending processes beyond company limits. This can be done gradually. This advantage puts United Gas in the position of being able first to gather experience before going on to connect the most important business partners.

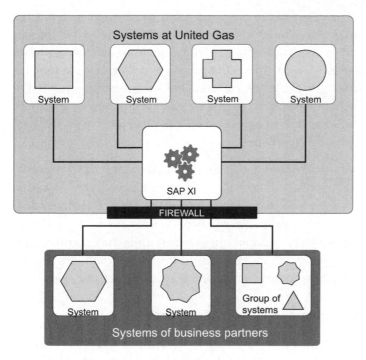

Figure 6.5 Intercompany Processes with SAP XI

6.6 United Gas—Value Consideration

United Gas is a regional gas supply company operating solely in the US market. Due to changes in regulations and the lucrative nature of the gas market, the company now finds itself up against strong competition. This increases the importance of active management of customer relationships with a competitive product portfolio. Information technology plays a strategic role for United Gas in maintaining its existing market share and expanding it further. The company wants to execute its internal processes better by introducing standard software. However, the requirement for stronger integration of customers and partners in business processes should be met by an integrated IT infrastructure. In terms of its IT strategy, United Gas is thus concentrating on the following activities:

Core IT Activities of United Gas

▶ Developing a modern IT infrastructure

▶ Developing a meaningful key figure model

▶ Optimizing customer relationships via an integrated process interface

▶ Intercompany processes with business partners

The current IT structure of the supply company is characterized by a large proportion of self-developed software. As already explained, United Gas wants to improve internal execution of processes using standard software such as mySAP ERP. Furthermore, the process of setting up a platform for knowledge management in the company has already begun, due to the fact that a content management system has already been introduced. These initiatives are now to be placed on a flexible, innovative architectural basis, with SAP NetWeaver.

To show the potential of this in objective terms, the current and target situations of the identified activities are evaluated below according to the criteria of *flexibility*, *innovation* and *cost reduction*. The value determination approach from Chapter 3 is used here. In this connection, it should be noted that flexibility and innovation are of foremost importance for United Gas. The potentials for cost reduction are important, but are not of the highest priority for the company due to its market situation.

6.6.1 Developing the IT Infrastructure

United Gas wants to modernize its IT infrastructure in order to reduce the financial costs of maintaining and managing various system platforms. The disadvantages of an old infrastructure have already been outlined in Section 6.2. The evaluation of the current IT situation as shown in Figure 6.6 confirms these disadvantages. Considerable potentials can be ascertained in terms of flexibility. In real terms, this means that: System and process flexibility are significantly impaired by a rigid basis that is hard to adapt.

These disadvantages should now be eliminated in respect of the mySAP ERP implementation via a new SAP Web Application Server (Web AS). The key advantages of this basis application lie in the areas of application development, administration, and system monitoring. For example, programming of application components is supported by using predefined templates or program modules. Thus the entire program creation process can be greatly simplified and accelerated. These advantages are also reflected in the evaluation in Figure 6.6 for a target landscape with Web AS, where flexibility and thus the speed of development show greatly improved values. Another issue, from the viewpoint of IT staff, is the endeavor to concentrate on forward-looking technologies. With its two programming layers, ABAP and J2EE, Web AS makes it possible to consolidate the individual application servers. The orientation of the IT structure towards new programming models with J2EE also results in an improved evaluation in the area of innovation in Figure 6.6.

In terms of costs, the following key potentials can be exploited with a Web AS installation:

▶ Programming using modules or templates shortens the entire development process.

Potential for Cost Reductions

▶ License costs can be reduced by system consolidations.

▶ The standardized transport system of the SAP Web Application Server considerably reduces expenditure of resources on administration.

▶ An external system such as a content management system can be integrated much more easily and rapidly with the J2EE application server.

▶ IT system monitoring is centralized and can thus be carried out more cost-effectively.

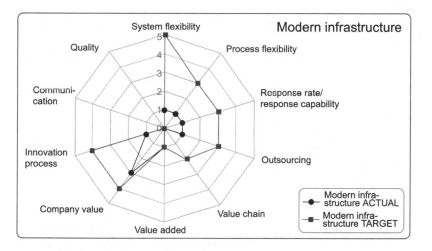

Figure 6.6 Evaluation of Infrastructure

6.6.2 Developing Key Figure Models

United Gas wants to improve its limited reporting possibilities. The current situation is characterized by distributed data sources that are either minimally integrated or not integrated at all. Thus analyses using this database are costly and sometimes inconsistent. Figure 6.7 confirms this, showing low values for response rate and quality. The controlling department can only access data that is questionable or no longer current, which, in turn, makes management of the company more difficult.

Limited Reporting Possibilities

With SAP Business Intelligence (BI), SAP offers a software solution that enables the development of an integrated key figure system. The SAP Exchange Infrastructure (XI), which was discussed above, is used to connect these distributed data sources. With SAP BI, United Gas can create and use comprehensive analyses and key figures in real time. Figure 6.7 shows clearly the advantages of an integrated and valid data platform, such as improved data currency and quality, with a higher rating for flexibility overall. Analyses and key figures result in greater cost transparency. This makes it possible to control cost distribution on the process, department, and product levels.

In terms of costs, the following savings potentials can be realized with BI:

▶ Rapid adaptation and extension of existing documents for reporting

▶ No more manual operations in terms of controlling

▶ Use of existing, predefined SAP reporting models

▶ Low expenditure of resources on analysis ("push-button reporting")

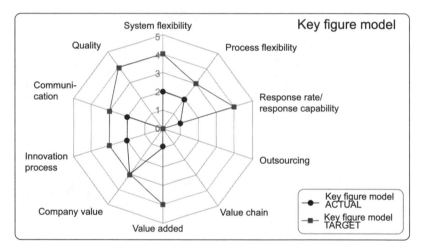

Figure 6.7 Evaluation of Key Figure Model

6.6.3 Integrated Process Interfaces

Improving customer relationships is of strategic importance for the supply company. The customer should be offered information and services via a standardized interface. In addition, it is important for United Gas to integrate the necessary application systems into one interface and display them here to employees. However, with the current Internet and Intranet applications, this requirement can either be met only inadequately or not at all. If we also compare the disadvantages of the current situation, as already mentioned, with the evaluations in Figure 6.8, then these affect rather non-distinctive criteria in the area of flexibility. Here, then, reference should once again be made to the descriptions relating to value consideration in Chapter 3.

The management of United Gas is striving for value enhancement through integrated information display and system operation via a company portal. The objective it has set for itself is to establish collaborative business with partners, suppliers, and customers. Not only should information be made available to the customer, but business applications should also be made available and this should occur via the portal. To also optimize the processes in the company, the SAP Portal with the business packages[2] offers the option of providing SAP contents particularly for target groups, that is, specifically according to roles (compare the evaluation in Figure 6.8).

Company Portal at United Gas

United Gas wants to use a portal to reduce the costs of integrated execution of processes. In this respect, the SAP Enterprise Portal offers the following potentials:

Potentials for Cost Reduction

▶ Implementation costs for changing business processes are reduced by using SAP templates.

▶ Business packages reduce processing times and thus the process costs due to predefined contents.

▶ The Single Sign-On function reduces the cost of support services for user password problems.

▶ A portal offers all information according to a user role at a glance. This has a positive influence on employee productivity and reduces process costs.

▶ Collaborative business enables delineated user groups to work and exchange information in specially defined "virtual team rooms." This reduces communication costs.

---

2 A business package contains information and applications that are preconfigured for particular user groups. For example, there are business packages for Manager Self Services or Employee Self Services with functions and data on the tasks of a manager or an employee.

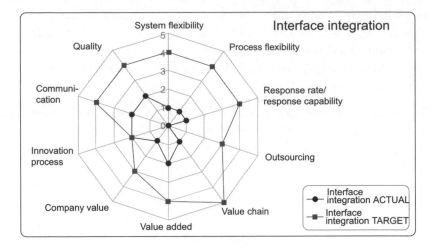

Figure 6.8 Evaluation of Interface Integration

6.6.4 Process Integration with Business Partners

Current Situation When Integrating Business Partners

Improved integration of business partners is of particular concern to United Gas. In the future, new products and services relating to gas provision will be offered. The applications developed in the past can in fact be used to execute processes, but changes can only be implemented at great cost. Another area of concern is the interfaces, which impede any flexible establishment of intercompany business processes due to the fixed nature of their programming. Figure 6.9 confirms this picture, showing weak values for current flexibility and innovation.

Process Integration with SAP XI

United Gas plans to introduce an Enterprise Application Integration (EAI) component with the installation of an SAP Exchange Infrastructure (XI). This will make it possible to connect the existing internal and external application systems to a central communication platform. Data exchange between the systems can thus take place via the standardized XML format. A great advantage of XI is the graphical modeling function for business processes. On the basis of SAP templates and models, expenditure of resources on development is reduced considerably compared with manual mapping by programming.

Potential for Cost Reductions with XI

XI also has the following cost-saving potentials:

▶ Cost savings in the development, maintenance, and monitoring of the system interfaces

▶ Fewer resources spent on operating the integration software XI

- ▶ Shorter implementation period for cross-application business processes due to graphical process modeling and when restructuring interfaces due to release changes
- ▶ Low implementation costs for connecting business partners who have IT systems that use the XML standard
- ▶ Generally low projects costs since there is no need for expensive consultants for implementing standard connections

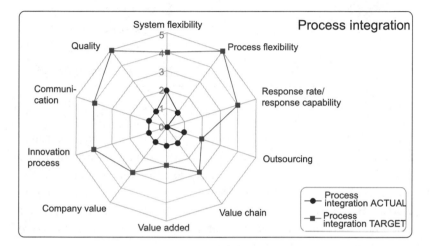

Figure 6.9 Evaluation of Process Integration

6.6.5 Evaluation and Recommendation

For United Gas, becoming a modern provider of various gas-related services is of strategic importance. To remain competitive in the future, the IT landscape must be modernized. In terms of the current situation, the company is strategically well-placed. The IT architecture meets the requirements of the specialist departments, as you can see from the ratings for the innovation criteria (see Figure 6.10, Innovation criteria scale). For the sake of simplification, the processes are summarized in the form of a diagram.

Portfolio Matrix

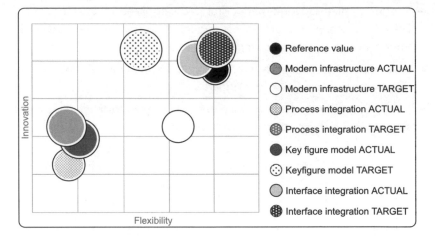

Figure 6.10 Portfolio Matrix

United Gas wants to change its processes to make them more flexible, however. In this respect, it sees SAP NetWeaver as a possible architecture platform for implementing necessary changes more rapidly as part of the IT strategy. This goal is supported by the potentials already illustrated in the areas of flexibility, innovation, and cost reduction for the scenarios considered. With SAP NetWeaver, United Gas can change its architecture to be optimally placed in the future.

7 Roadmap to SAP NetWeaver at ABC Bank

*Like many of its competitors, the German ABC Bank has sig-
nificant structural problems and needs to make lasting
improvements to its processes. Its aim is to concentrate on
core competencies. SAP NetWeaver offers a range of capabilities for supporting and expediting this modification.*

German banks, in general, are experiencing significant structural problems. During the past decade, they have hardly changed, and they have
persisted in using their old structures. Practically every bank still assumes
responsibility for each process in the value chain itself, leaving great optimization potential unrealized. Changes have constantly taken place in
other sectors of the industry over the last decade, and now these banks
have only a short time period to adapt themselves to new market requirements. Ulrich Cartellieri, former executive and member of the board of
directors at Deutsche Bank, described the circumstances of the financial
services industry by saying, "The banks will be the steel industry of the
1990s."

Pressure to Change

ABC Bank, which plays a significant role in the German banking market,
faces problems that are typical in the industry. It's under intense pressure
to make changes, and this directly affects the demands made on its IT
department. Although banks generally have high IT budgets at their disposal, in no way do they have the best possible IT systems. With their
long-standing and versatile use of computer systems, they have faced
high costs, originating from the heterogeneity of their IT landscapes. At
the same time, their complex IT structures impede fast compliance with
market requirements. ABC Bank is faced with the challenge of making
lasting improvements to the cost/revenue ratio and at the same time
optimizing its processes, particularly where outsourcing segments of the
value chain comes into play.

7.1 Scenario Description

Reunification in the beginning of the 1990s and the phenomenal market
boom at the end of the 1990s enabled German banks to achieve excellent results. However, the market boom's continuously rising returns
have led to a dangerous development. The banks' structural problems

were concealed for a long time and were then clearly manifested at the end of the market boom. In the last 5 to 7 years, banks in Europe weren't interested in the classic banking business with private customers because IPOs (Initial Public Offerings) and investment banking were far more profitable. However, the economic decline of the last 2 to 3 years (in which many IPOs were floated and investment banking had to enforce massive cuts) has prompted a change in the behavior of financial institutions. Banks are suddenly in the red because their core business has been neglected for years, and therefore has hardly grown.

Greater Competitive Pressure The crisis has been intensified by other problems in the industry, which, for example, suffers from bad loans and has to compete for customers. Although there is already a very high density of banks in Germany, new vendors are pushing into the market alongside existing competitors. The banks of automobile companies (subsidiary companies of OEMs) have achieved a respectable share of the market, for example, in the area of car financing.

The boom not only covered up the fact that business with both private and business customers had been neglected, but also that costs had risen sharply. It was necessary to lower expenditures, which resulted in layoffs throughout the entire industry. In addition, many branch offices were forced to close, because they were only profitable if they looked after several thousand customers. Although a considerable number of branch offices have closed during the past few years, there are still too few customers per branch.

Decade-Long Use of IT Banks recognized the great potential of IT early on, and have been using computer systems on a broad basis for decades. In the 1970s and 1980s, it became customary for banks to develop and install their own software in-house, and the use of standard industry software was uncommon. This use of homegrown solutions based on legacy technologies such as COBOL and mainframes has led to higher maintenance and repair costs.

When considering the typical banking IT scenario, we distinguish between the following three areas: *administration* (which includes purchasing and HR), *sales*, and *core banking* (which includes processing transactions and bookings). Standard software is used only in the area of administration. SAP has developed a core banking solution in cooperation with Germany's largest retail bank (Deutsche Postbank AG) called SAP for Banking. It has aroused much interest, but has not yet been distributed.

Even in small organizations, there may be more than a hundred different systems in use in the three different areas, leading to an extremely heterogeneous system landscape (with many legacy and mainframe systems). Some larger banks may even have more than a thousand different systems in use. The high-security standards in the banking industry, which demand certification for every type of software, have made banks wary of changing their IT systems. The relatively high number of banks with SAP R/2 installations is proof of this steadfast reluctance.

In the banking industry, infrastructure software is typically developed in-house. Although the banking industry recognized the need for infrastructure software earlier than other industries, due to the inherent use of many different systems, further developments in this area are necessary. The integration of many systems, with their numerous interfaces, leads to high absolute costs, and therefore, the costs per transaction are also very high.

Infrastructure Software

In response, banks have started a fervent attempt to reduce costs, with the primary goal of consolidating the IT landscape. Also, investments in innovation go primarily toward the migration of existing systems, or into hardware and software updates. Completely new implementations of software are planned only to a small extent. A further decline is also forecast for the area of expenditures for IT services. In spite of these savings, the banks have failed to significantly reduce their IT costs overall, as enormous costs for maintenance and care of the existing systems are still accruing due to the high system complexity.

Cost Reduction

In banks, the organization of the IT department naturally reflects the organization of the IT systems. Almost every product in operation has its own sub-department, which is made up of people who are familiar with the highly specialized software in use. Although this structure enables the creation and development of the required know-how, at the same time it also means that the respective departments are apt to adhere to "their" system, as their jobs are connected with it. Thus, there is a strong self-interest on a personal level not to remove legacy systems.

Organization of the IT Department

Banks have a fundamental structural problem that they must solve as quickly as possible: In contrast to the manufacturing industry or to high-tech enterprises, for example, a bank is in charge of its entire value chain, from the design and purchasing phases to production, and culminating in sales and services. Employing a data-processing center to manage the posting of transactions is economically sensible only for banks of a certain size. As a result, the majority of banks cover the entire process chain themselves, and high costs accrue, because of the comparatively small number of customers.

Therefore, banks have to change, just as OEMs have changed. They will only look after part of the process chain themselves, operate unprofitable areas jointly with other banks, or simply outsource. While the change by OEMs was gradual, dragging on for more than 30 years, the change in the banking sector must happen faster. International institutes identified the need for change early on and reacted accordingly, so they are now evaluated higher on the capital market than are German banks. Therefore, it is easy for them to take over German banks.

Analysis of the Banking Landscape in Germany
When comparing the banking market in Germany with the rest of Europe, the heterogeneity of the German market particularly stands out. The five largest Spanish banks share about 50% of the local credit volume among themselves. In Germany, the five largest banks collectively deal with only about 20% of credits directly. The quota for the five largest banks in Belgium and the Netherlands rests at over 75% and over 80%,[1] respectively. A comparison of the market shares of the five largest European banks is shown in Figure 7.1. The German market's problems will lead to a structural change in the medium term. Through partnerships, outsourcing, or merging, larger bank units will emerge and have a size in which, for example, transactional banking will become profitable. This "National Champions" strategy has been pursued in France, for example, where several banking enterprises have merged to form one large bank, which can assert itself well in the global market.

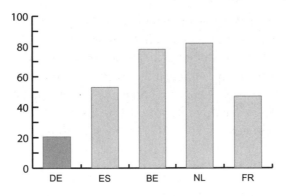

Figure 7.1 Market Share Comparison for the Five Largest Banks in Europe (Data in Percentages)

Specialization As a Result of Structural Change
Along with the trend of consolidating several small banks into fewer larger banks, there are, of course, other possibilities that meet pending structural changes. Small to medium-sized institutions can consider spe-

1 European Central Bank: *Structural Analysis of the EU Banking Sector*, 2002.

cializing in certain areas. For example, some financial service providers specialize in certain products (for example, the Norisbank specializes in consumer loans) or processes (for example, MPL specializes in sales). Other enterprises, such as Allianz, which took over Dresdner Bank, seek their fortune through offering insurance services.

The industrialization of the financial services sector is imminent. Banks must undergo fundamental change, because their operation has become too expensive. They have to concentrate on their core business areas as soon as possible, and enter into close partnerships, where they do parts of their business together (within as well as outside the industry). German banks have to explicitly cut back on their vertical integration, as controlling everything themselves is no longer expedient. In the IT area, the particular challenge exists in supporting this rapid modification.

Industrialization of the Banking Sector

ABC Bank's situation is typical for a German bank. Among the existing systems, there are many solutions that have been developed in-house, which, for the most part, are based on comparatively old technologies. Many programs were developed in COBOL and were poorly documented. A whole range of applications are not implemented in the client/server architecture, but they run in a mainframe environment.

Over the years, the number of systems in use at ABC Bank has increased to more than a thousand. Due to the acquisition of a smaller institute a few years ago, heterogeneity has increased further, as only small progress in the unification of both IT landscapes has been achieved. Overall, a significantly heterogeneous system landscape has developed, in which the IT trends of the past 30 years have left their mark.

Heterogeneous IT Landscape

The diversity in the IT landscape is also reflected in the way the IT department is organized. Almost every large system has its own corresponding specialized department. The members of these sub-units have great expertise in the use of specific applications, but they resist against system unification, afraid that the system they work on may be affected. The IT organization has been outsourced in the form of three subsidiaries.

For the most part, the integration of many different systems takes place through manually developed interfaces, which are very difficult to maintain, as proprietary technology has been applied. There are efforts to install a modern integration system based on J2EE, but this must be put on hold as the manufacturer of this software has gone out of business. Therefore, many interfaces still exist, which are predicated on the simple exchange of information on a data level, which only takes place every 24 hours.

Proprietary Interfaces

New systems comply with the J2EE standard, although relatively few software applications have been purchased. In other words, most J2EE software is homegrown. Also, first steps have been taken in the area of customer relationship management, with the use of self-developed J2EE software.

7.2 Challenges

The basic structural changes banks are currently facing are inevitable, and there are several resulting challenges that must be met. Because the main goal is to reduce cost, all projects have to focus on fast ROI and measurable results. Excessive operating costs act like a catalyst for the modification process, and intensify the effort to achieve fast and effective results.

In addition to pressure from competition and structural problems, another external factor affects the banks, emphasizing the need for change: Legislature has responded to past stock exchange scandals and has increased standards, especially with regard to transparency in lending. New regulatory standards such as Basel II,[2] tighter tax laws, and the Sarbanes-Oxley Act[3] reinforce the pressure on banks to change their processes and also the IT systems on which the processes are mapped.

To prevent a common misunderstanding (i.e., introducing new software will solve problems based on poor process design) from being perpetuated, internal processes must be managed. Practically every bank has big problems in managing its processes, and finding a permanent solution to these problems is necessary. This task can be supported by suitable software, but will never be solved by IT alone. Therefore banks must reengineer their IT organizations and processes, and then map these changes to the company's software.

In an effort toward improvement, banks will need to do the following:

▶ Consolidate the IT system, with the objective of minimizing complexity and reducing costs

▶ Disintegrate the value chain, with the objective of concentrating on real core competencies in-house and outsourcing other areas

---

2 Regulations regarding the capital and surplus of banks.
3 A law that stipulates strict accounting standards for companies listed on US stock exchanges.

- Increase focus on the customer, with the objective of selling more products to individual customers and achieving greater sales revenue per customer

- Analyze the value added (profit) by individual products, processes, and customers by value management with the objective of deducing and planning measures

- Based on this analysis, ABC Bank will be able to formulate strategies to generate more profit out of the products, customers, and so forth. This approach is contrary to what happens today—banks don't know whether or not they're earning money with a customer or product.

Under these conditions, some considerable changes in the IT area can be expected. In particular, implementing a standard platform, on which they can reorganize and optimize using standardized building blocks of software introduces a real challenge for ABC Bank, with its large variety of systems. This reorganization should simplify the system landscape considerably. The process of disintegrating the value chain will result in the need for ABC Bank to let several systems become obsolete, as the sub-processes mapped therein should be taken over by partner companies in the future. Parallel to this effort, the bank must work on successfully collecting more specific information about customers and products, and making this information available to its staff. Both of these main objectives are explained in more detail below.

Deduced Measures

7.2.1 Optimizing the Customer and Product Portfolio

Although ABC Bank uses more than a thousand different IT systems and has spent large amounts of money for its operation, it still doesn't know enough about its customers. Data is available in single systems, but not on a condensed level. Due to the huge diversity of systems, the importance of a customer is often overlooked, that is, it is not possible to get a reliable overview of a single customer. ABC Bank has systems for virtually any product so it is forced to look in each and every system to determine whether the customer is affiliated with that system (meaning that he has that product). Only some systems have reporting capabilities, which apply to individual data sources, delivering an inexact, even a partially contradictory picture.

However, it is not only the information about customers itself that is inadequate. Similarly, no comparison of the incurred costs with the sales revenue or the returns per customer is available. In fact, the bank doesn't know whether or not it makes money on a customer. Because this type of

Costs and Returns per Customer

information doesn't exist even on a customer level, it is of course also not available on the product level (for instance, for determining what a customer has purchased or would like to buy).

It is not possible for ABC Bank to get precise information at the touch of a button, for example, about a customer's profitability. Therefore, support is by no means tailored to meet the needs of a particular customer. Rather, ABC Bank distinguishes between the market segments (retail, private banking, etc.), but within these segments the individual employee cannot discern the importance of a customer. The staff must attempt to do an initial evaluation using a customer's account balance. However, this is only an improvised procedure, which does not solve the problem.

Integration of External Information

The bank must collect precise information in order to be able to serve customers better and sell more products. Less profitable customers could be handed over to special subsidiary companies or to bank units that can generate profits with this type of customer segment due to strong standardization or automation of services. Deutsche Bank, for example, pursued this idea with the creation of an Internet subsidiary bank called Bank24.[4]

Product Costs and Revenues

It is not just on the customer side that ABC Bank has insufficient information at its disposal, but also on the product side. The correlation between returns and costs of a product is based more on the use of estimates rather than on exact and comprehensible data. Because there are many systems with no direct linkage to a product or customer, the cost that it incurs cannot be deduced. The existing costs (particularly by the required IT) can be determined only for very standardized financial products, like a current account.

Even if all the information regarding individual customers and the respective products were available, it would still be difficult for users to access it. Information is largely disseminated across the company via the heterogeneity and diversity of the systems used. In actuality, this means that the staff can see only a section of the real situation, and therefore cannot always respond properly. Consequently, one of ABC Bank's important tasks is to increase the *quality* of existing information, and to simplify *access* to this information.

---

4 Meanwhile, Bank24 has been re-integrated into the parent company again due to a change of strategy.

7.2.2 Simplification of the Value Chain and IT Landscape

The second largest challenge facing ABC Bank is the transition to lean production. Just as car manufacturers are now handling only a small portion of the production chain themselves, the bank must manage to explicitly reduce their vertical integration. This entails examining practically all processes with regard to whether or not they could be implemented better or more cheaply by an outsourcing partner. If, for example, a specialized company can handle consumer loans more cheaply and successfully offers this service to other banks, then there is no reason for ABC Bank to keep offering this service. If there are no strategic arguments against or other opposition toward outsourcing, the bank can save the costs associated with handling loans, and thereby simplify its processes and the required systems.

"Lean Production" in Banks

The complexity of the IT landscape, with many in-house systems and point-to-point connections that need to be maintained, and without a manufacturer's support, along with the costs resulting from all this, practically begs for simplification. This leads to a make-or-buy decision: Should the bank continue developing its own software, or is it willing to place its bet on standardized software (that is, buy a solution and customize it)?

In most industries, including the banking industry, standard software has asserted itself. The support of a software manufacturer through updates and new releases should not be underestimated, even if regulatory changes such as Basel II require a wide range of IT customizations. As the financial industry is subject to very strict regulations, a manufacturer's support is particularly helpful here.

Advantages of Standard Software

Furthermore, standard software offers a better time-to-market; because the software manufacturer has more resources, it can bring new software into the market in a shorter amount of time. In addition, a bank's risks, which are already attached to every solution that is developed in-house, are dramatically reduced.

Depending on market power and the setting of market standards, the software manufacturers determine which standards will be applied and supported in their products (for example, currently J2EE versus .NET) so that their software offers advantages here too. While software that is developed in-house must comply with market standards, and therefore can *react* to only new standards, standard products already support an open IT architecture from the day of their initial release.

Support of Standards

Gradual Change Banks must realize that they need to make enormous changes. These changes will have a huge impact on the cost and resources side, so only a gradual approach to them is realistic. On this issue, Henning Kagermann, SAP's board spokesman, gives the following assessment:

> "The CIOs know they have to live with the heterogeneity for the next five years. You cannot just rip everything out and replace it, because that would be too expensive. Therefore you need a new blueprint for the next five years and a new architecture which you can develop over time. It's too expensive to do in one go. It is not a revolution, but an evolution."[5]

Interfaces As a Cost Driver The high number of systems that are required for the various individual needs brings an enormous interface problem with it. The combination of the many in-house software developments and mainframe applications usually relies on manually administered interfaces, for which there is of course no manufacturer's service or updates. Whenever an application is updated or modified, all interfaces involved are to be checked, tested, and, if necessary, customized. Obviously this process involves every system that is linked to the application to be customized.

As the funds for maintenance, which constitute 70% to 80% of the total IT budget, are allocated to the individual processes during a process cost inspection, the high number of interfaces inevitably means very high process costs.

System Integration Software Because the integration of existing systems in a company by manually created interfaces is very complex, maintenance-intensive, and therefore expensive, special software for integration has been used for a few years instead. The automation of electronic communication is linked with the objective of connecting all applications throughout the company. At the same time, this will avoid a disruption in media (i.e., changing the media from using an IT system to using paper for example). System integration helps to minimize the possible sources of error, and the quality of data increases incrementally with the pace of the business process. Ultimately, an integrated application will be created, geared toward the company's business processes. This type of software is referred to as *Enterprise Application Integration* (EAI) software.

Integration Types Aside from the pure integration of applications—the so-called application-to-application integration (A2A)—the integration of different organi-

---

5 *Banking Technology Magazine: In Profile.* March 2004. *www.bankingtech.com.*

zational units is especially of interest. Such an integration across company limits is known as business-to-business integration (B2B).

To be able to divide the value chain and outsource unprofitable areas, banks urgently need software for intercompany process integration. The outsourcing of processes, or "business process outsourcing," means the transfer of company responsibilities to other companies. For this you need software that can integrate processes across company boundaries and firewalls smoothly.

Intercompany Cooperation

Using software for process integration has advantages that should not be underestimated in the complex system landscape. The interfaces are configured in a central location; information on the existence of an interface is stored there, documented in a certain way, and thus made transparent. Knowledge about a manually created interface, on the other hand, can easily get irretrievably lost when an employee moves to another company.

Interfaces

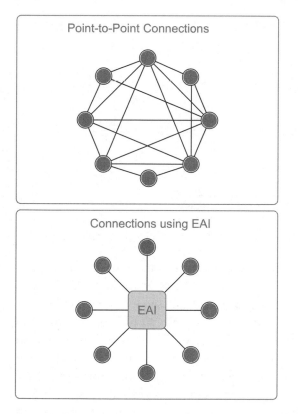

Figure 7.2 Comparison of Point-to-Point and EAI Hub Connections

While the manually generated integration of systems creates point-to-point connections via interfaces, EAI software typically creates a hub architecture. As illustrated in Figure 7.2, the number of interfaces is thereby significantly reduced, as every system has to be connected to the integration platform only once. When there's a specific number of applications to be integrated, EAI software offers large cost advantages. In Figure 7.3, the costs of the two integration types are contrasted.

Integration on the Application Level

The first form of integration software, called middleware, was primarily intended for the exchange of data. In contrast, EAI focuses on integration, particularly on a business process level, but also on an application and data level. ABC Bank invested a lot in middleware from a vendor that specialized in banking, a company that unfortunately didn't survive the commotion of the Internet market boom. The subsequent removal of this software, for which maintenance no longer exists, therefore, should be dealt with first.

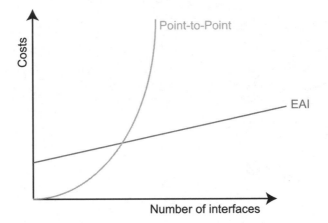

Figure 7.3 Comparison of Integration Costs (Point-to-Point and EAI Hub)

Consolidation on the Integration Market

There is a clear trend toward consolidation in the integration software market at the moment. The specialist vendors who did position themselves in the heyday of the best-of-breed architectures are in an increasingly difficult situation. Because best-of-breed causes a lot of integration cost, today's companies are looking for more cost-effective integrated solutions. That's why specialist vendors are facing a lot of competition in which they can hardly win because no one wants best-of-breed. They seem to be more exposed to competition from generalists, such as SAP and IBM, that offer comparable solutions and automatic integration with a company's applications out of the box. This is strengthened by the fact that the application server and the integration server are frequently becoming one in the same, and therefore the application vendors (with underlying application servers) find themselves in a very comfortable situation.

As a result of these developments, ABC Bank must take the following measures:

1. *Use standard software* instead of homegrown solutions
2. *Develop an integration infrastructure* to enable the outsourcing of business processes

An IT landscape that is set up with standard software—and has modern integration possibilities for the integration of external processes—has the advantages of being cost-effective and having a superior quality, because it controls the IT value chain via an effective supplier and service management.

7.3   Starting Points

In light of the developments that were discussed in the previous section, ABC Bank must do the following if it is to become a viable competitor in today's market:

1. Use standard software to reduce costs and implement process advantages
2. Increase the availability and quality of information to be able to make decisions in consideration of all relevant factors
3. Promote integration on the business process level to improve the value chain and therefore reduce interface costs

We will examine these three areas more closely in the following three sections.

7.3.1   Gradual Change to Standard Software

With its growing IT landscape that is mainly based on homegrown software, ABC Bank faces the problem that it will need to invest large sums of money into further software development. The field of software development is certainly not part of a bank's core competencies, and management must decide whether or not tying up capital in this area is a viable option. Software manufacturers invest 10% to 15% of their turnover into the development of new products, but this investment is worth it for

Software Development As a Core Competency

them, because they can sell new products to many customers, so the development costs are ultimately borne by many companies. A bank's in-house software development is self-financed only by the bank; maintenance and additional development have to be self-financed and self-managed also.

As banks are subject to strict regulatory requirements, external influences often necessitate software customization. In response to Basel II, banks must carry out far-reaching changes, and this demands further consideration as to whether a move toward standard software would be appropriate.

Integration of Standard Software At the same time, from a financial standpoint, the advantages of using standard software instead of developing software in-house are not immediately clear; at first glance, in-house development tends to look better, because it has most likely already been amortized. However, if we consider the maintenance, customization, and integration costs associated with developing software in-house, standard software comes out on top. Therefore, the choice of integration software should be considered as to which extent the integration between the technical platform and the favored application is preconfigured, as well as what costs and expenses are accrued. A big advantage of SAP is that all SAP applications that span over many different process areas are very well integrated with each other (for example, mySAP CRM and SAP R/3, for checking product availability), and the NetWeaver integration platform is very well integrated with the applications.

SAP NetWeaver's application server, SAP Web AS, enables good integration in the Java world, because not only can it work with ABAP, but with Java as well. Thus, it can be easily connected with IBM's WebSphere Java platform, for instance, which is widely distributed.

Standardization of Processes The decision in favor of standard software for mapping business processes also enables a stronger unification of the processes themselves, which can increase efficiency and consequently reduce costs. A template design is frequently chosen for it, that is, create a basic customizing and roll it out to all organizational units. Further customization can take place in the separate organizational units, but the processes are substantially the same throughout the group. Similarly, the correct balance between unification and necessary individual features is found on a client's design. (A system can be divided into technical clients with each having different customizing settings.)

Due to the unification of processes, systems can often be eliminated, reducing costs. At the same time, by standardizing its processes, the company creates the basis to enable further optimization in which certain processes in special departments, shared service centers, or other companies (in terms of BPO) are relocated. A first success can now be seen in the creation of service departments: easy telephone queries about account balances or wire transfers were outsourced to an external call center service provider. The comparatively expensive bank employee will only be required for more complex queries. Therefore, efforts toward the standardization of business processes and the systems and formats used will be intensified.

Along with the standardization of processes and the systems used to manage those processes, the standardization of desktops should also be endorsed in order to promote potential cost savings in this area as well.

All in all, the use of standard software provides a great opportunity to shift the IT landscape's build/run ratio in favor of innovation. If the bank uses ready-made software, it can concentrate more on its core business because fewer investments will be going toward maintenance of complex homegrown solutions. The make-or-buy decision has to be examined against the background of a banks' high vertical integration.

Software: Make or Buy?

The German bank HypoVereinsbank has come up with an interesting answer as to whether or not to use standard software. The company recognized the advantages of standard software, and it tried to install it in areas where it is generally not used yet. Under the motto of "Make and Sell," the bank created a banking software in cooperation with SAP for its own use, but also to be sold to other companies.

The discussion of the advantages and disadvantages of converting to standard software will not be explored further, as SAP NetWeaver is the focus of this book. In this context, it should be mentioned that NetWeaver is delivered with the new applications (i.e., almost all applications delivered in 2004 and later from SAP). The respective license is contained in the respective software package.

NetWeaver As Standard Software

7.3.2 Quantity and Quality of Available Information

The poor availability and quality of relevant information is ABC Bank's major problem. It is laborious for staff to access relevant content, as information on customers and products is distributed over several systems. A portal can help the bank eliminate this problem.

Problems do not only exist in the direct retrieval of data on individual customers. Compiling and condensing information for use in evaluations and reports is also difficult. Reporting delivers imprecise and partially contradictory information, which on top of all this is not available in the required granularity. A modern business intelligence system offers the possibility of receiving fast reliable information in this area. Only with consolidated and structured files can we evaluate the contribution of individual customers or products to the overall financial performance of the company.

Portal and Knowledge Management

ABC Bank's staff uses two words to describe the company's information situation: *intransparency* and *redundancy*. The system landscape is substantially shaped by the following:

▶ The large number of interfaces, which distribute information in an insufficient manner

▶ The use of different sources of information, which make use of individual user interfaces and require different types of operation

▶ Highly individualized programming in the individual systems

▶ Distribution of applied logic across the entire IT landscape so that employees are forced to access all systems to find the information they need

The solution would be a portal that acts as a central access point for all information. It is possible to integrate the bank's heterogeneous system landscape in the front end using the portal. This means a system layer will be implemented that conceals the complexity from the user. The availability of relevant information will be improved significantly, as the user will no longer see the confusing complexity of the system. As a bonus, training expenses will be reduced, as training will no longer have to be carried out for every individual system. The administration expenses associated with login problems and forgotten passwords will also fall dramatically.

The introduction of a portal offers the chance to implement a Knowledge Management system (KM) at the same time. All unstructured documents that are required for work can be stored there. Its primary purpose is to make current product information available. Background information on products and the bank's sales strategies are also stored here. Regulatory changes and their effects on the business process can be documented in electronic form in the KM system so that expensive paper circular mails can be dropped. Training can even be eliminated in some areas.

Easy routine queries (for example, account balance queries or wire transfers) can also be processed by lower-level personnel, who have access to all required information at the click of a mouse.

Figure 7.4 illustrates the possible front-end integration of ABC Bank's systems.

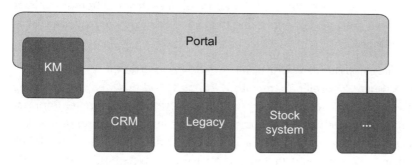

Figure 7.4 Portal and KM at ABC Bank

The simplification achieved by improved access to information and the structural arrangement of information eventually serves one large objective: to make the bank's entire knowledge about customers and suitable products available to the employees by collecting all relevant information.

You can introduce the portal step by step. While one user group is already using it and therefore gets integrated information, the other user groups can still access the systems individually (for example, a KM system) without the portal. While some user groups will immediately start using the portal, others will be not impacted right away by its implementation. Little by little, use of the portal can be expanded to more user groups, and the integrated contents can be refined. For example, the area of *private banking* could serve very well as a pilot for implementation. As a relatively small group of staff is affected, the volume of the project size for improving their work environment is limited. Because very wealthy customers are looked after in this area, a realized success can have a positive impact on the overall result. If you manage to improve the customer satisfaction in this rather small segment, it can have a remarkable impact on your overall financial result because there is a lot of money involved. **Procedure: Step by step**

Another objective that should be achieved by the optimization of available information is the improvement of customer care. In the past, ABC **Improve Customer Care**

Bank has undertaken its first steps in this direction by developing CRM software. This software allows you to retrieve detailed customer data and uses data from other source systems for that reason. Certain additional information about customers can be stored, so that, for example, information is available about a customer's interest in certain products. The management team will now try to align this information with categorized product information, so that products can be suggested automatically. The system is based on the J2EE architecture; however, it is not enhanced, because the consolidation of files from different sources requires a great deal of effort, and the expected degree of success has not materialized.

Necessity of CRM The first steps toward CRM were made in an attempt to increase the bank's low cross-selling rate with IT support, and this idea was taken up again using SAP NetWeaver. Accessing the distributed customer information will become significantly easier with the implementation of the portal, and with the possibility of accessing the different data sources via the unifier technology. Fortunately, the legacy CRM system is based on J2EE, so a large part of it can be used again. The algorithms in particular, which align customer and product information, don't need to be changed. Additionally, the capabilities of the KM system can help here as well. Based on recommendations, detailed product information is supplied at the touch of a button, which informs the bank staff of current conditions or of legal changes, for example.

Stronger Customer Focus ABC Bank is also counting on this solution to help it provide more customer-focused products. In terms of *mass customization*, financial services should be offered that are relatively easy to develop, and at the same time correspond to the customers' specific requirements. The difficulty here is in finding the right balance between standardization and customization.

In the medium term, a stronger focus is applied to one-to-one marketing, which is supported by sales activities in the area of e-business. In a similar time period, financial services in the form of mobile business is expected to serve customers better, and at the same time gather more information about them.

Profitability and Risk Evaluation of the Customer Business

Access to necessary information is drastically improved by the portal, and working with this information becomes more efficient, however the quality of the underlying data remains unchanged. Therefore the next logical step for ABC Bank is to implement a data warehouse that can extract and process all necessary information from the many source systems. Not only should the current data be available, but it should also include target figures and estimates.

The objective is to make progress, particularly in the area of cost and profit accounting. This accounting method is used to analyze the cost-effectiveness of individual products or customers, and can be used to compare different time periods or organizational units with each other. Measures for controlling the company are devised from this analysis, for example, it might identify the need to improve certain areas. By comparing two profit centers, for instance, it is soon clear where the strengths and weaknesses of a bank can be found.

Methods to Ensure Success

Furthermore, the data warehouse can process important information from the administrative systems. Knowledge on the number of employees on sick leave in a department, for example, or the quality of the staff's time recording facilitates conclusions about efficiency in these areas.

With the introduction of a central reporting and analysis platform, one of the bank's basic problems is being addressed. As a result of the highly heterogeneous system landscape, the information situation is characterized by a high degree of redundancy. Information is available in various locations in a different context, whereby it is not often clear how the system processes the displayed data due to a great deal of individual logic being used. In the worst cases, the information is even contradictory.

Avoiding Redundancies

Because of the large number of interfaces between systems, information must not be consolidated or gathered over many systems, but instead extracted from individual sources. This way, errors that could ensue as a result of individual programming can be avoided.

The data warehouse should serve as a central source of information that is used as a basis for decision-making processes. Due to the multitude of different systems, master data isn't always reliable (it's changed in one system but not in the next system and so on). The data warehouse will be used as the foundation for the unification of master data to increase the quality and consistency of data in the heterogeneous environment. With the approach of implementing a central system instead of procuring information from a multiplicity of sources as before, a cost-effective central administration of the system will also become possible.

One Central System

The main objective of the implementation of the data warehouse system is to make exact value and risk analyses available. On the basis of this information, it is possible to determine a customer's profitability and provide that customer with service accordingly. To do this, the accumulated economic result, which is deduced by totalling all products sold to the customer, is taken into consideration.

Contacting the Customer

Knowledge of the profitability of a customer (or under marketing factors, possible profitability) is used as a foundation for better customer care. The financial institution has accumulated a huge amount of data during its support relationship, which is not used in the optimization of the business. For example, thanks to account movement, it has information about which leasing contracts a company handles. Due to the pattern in the expense behavior (for example, if, in the past, the leasing amount changed every three years because a new machine was acquired), customers could be individually addressed, and a suitable offer could proactively be submitted to them.

The specific customer sales approach should be viewed with the understanding that the capital market conditions for an individual institution are predetermined. That means the margin between what the bank may charge for a loan and what it has to spend for the loan cannot be changed. The financial market sets this margin. Therefore, the primary way the company can distinguish itself is by providing offers that are tailored to the customer's individual situation.

Consideration of Actual and Planned Data

ABC Bank's objective is to better serve the customer. From a financial controlling standpoint, it is therefore now important to focus on the customer's possible revenue potential, and not—as in the past—on the cost factors generated by a customer. Thus it is essential to maintain planned values along with the actual values, and to always align both with each other. The considered data should incorporate the following points:

▶ Customers

▶ Products

▶ Market

▶ Competing vendors and their products

Integration of External Data Sources

If a sufficient amount of this type of data is not available, of if the data lacks quality or detail, it can be bought from an external company. This practice already plays a large role in the context of benchmarking. The integration of (purchased) data from market research must therefore be considered in the conceptual design of the data warehouse.

In addition to the revenue side, we also have to consider the risk side in detail. As a result of the increased standards imposed by Sarbanes-Oxley and Basel II, it is very important to have an information system that is based on key figures to enable a suitable risk. (They use the key figures to create a risk classification from which, for instance, refinancing costs can be derived.) In this context, planned figures and simulations are also very important, as stress tests analyze how solidly a bank has safeguarded its risks in the portfolio.

Product Portfolio Optimization

The bank's lack of information about its products can be viewed in the same terms as its lack of information about its customers. The initial circumstances are the same; information is decentralized and not transparent. As the accrued costs are directly allocated in only a few areas, it is hard to estimate the degree to which individual offers are profitable. ABC Bank does not know exactly what added value it attains with its individual products. For the same reason, a comparison of various organizational units is only possible to a certain extent, as the resulting conclusions don't really have a solid foundation.

With the implementation of the data warehouse, you can analyze a product's added value and, if necessary, optimize it. Depending on whether a product is self-financed by fees and provision or by an interest margin, information about current accounts, loans, and services can be processed and interpreted. By comparing actual data with planned data, you can expect more reliable information about the contribution of individual products to the company's overall success.

Analysis of the Value Added

Using this exact information, the bank can decide which business option is best for each product. Successful core products can be further developed and promoted in terms of both sales and processes. The positioning of products that are successful only within a certain target group can be adjusted (for example, they can be handed over from one of the company's organizational units to a shared service center), and less successful products can be outsourced to specialized companies.

7.3.3   Cross-Company Integration of Processes

Many bank services, such as a current account, (a bank giro account) are so highly standardized that they are basically interchangeable. Nevertheless, most banks handle such transactions and business processes themselves, without making cost-conscious decisions in this area. By no means do the accrued costs reflect the benefits. The operation of different systems is necessary for a comparatively small number of customers, and the bank has to absorb relatively high costs per customer.

Economies of Scale To achieve economies of scale and to clearly reduce the costs per customer, it is critical that larger units process the back-office operations. This can be done either by using data processing centers (in the case of savings banks and mutual savings banks), or by entering into partnerships with various financial institutions (as with Deutsche Bank and Dresdner Bank in the area of payment processing). In the medium term, we can expect to see the development of *bank factories*. These are banks that specialize in individual transaction procedures and offer these services to other banks. The German Norisbank, for example, specializes in consumer credits. Thanks to a good scoring model to classify potential and existing customers, (i.e., they assess the risk of a credit loss), the company has been very successful. Furthermore, Norisbank offers the service of transacting credits to other banks.

Outsourcing of Business Processes Needless to say, in practice the outsourcing of business processes involves more than just simply handing over a loan application form. Because the intermediary bank must have access to all information relevant to the loan, combining the systems of both companies is necessary. As a matter of fact, all processes related to the allocation and processing of loans are outsourced. For some time, outsourcing in the area of securities trading has also become standard. But in general we can say that in the area of outsourcing, German banks have a long way to go, especially compared to their European competitors.

Apart from those business processes that deal directly with banking, another area that has the potential to be outsourced is administration. Deutsche Bank, for example, made headlines with its decision to outsource its whole purchasing department.

Need for an Integration Platform However, to enable such a cross-company collaboration, there must be an integration platform in place that facilitates electronic links between the participating companies on a business process level. Such a process integration solution allows the systems to connect and operate even through the firewall boundaries. Of course, besides the simple and cost-effective operation of the platform, security must also be considered. Lastly, the transparency that exists for interfaces—as well as the ability to monitor them during operation (for possible troubleshooting)—must be ensured.

184   Roadmap to SAP NetWeaver at ABC Bank

The linking of the different systems does not take place via manually created interfaces, but through adapters that create the connection between the integration hub and the applications involved. For communication purposes, XML has now become the standard language of integration systems. While the costs for point-to-point connections with every other connected system tend to rise exponentially, the use of Enterprise Application Integration (EAI) software stabilizes costs per integrated system, due to its hub architecture.

The decision to use EAI software should not be based on operational reasons alone, despite all the cost advantages and persuasive arguments based on practical experience. Rather, the decision for an integration platform should be strategical, as it plays an integral role in affecting the foundation and the direction of the company. The decision must help to separate the bank's value chain in an economically sensible way, and to change the entire organization accordingly.

Strategic Role of Integration

In our particular example, ABC Bank has decided to outsource the processing of classic bank transactions. For these purposes, in cooperation with another bank, ABC Bank has recently founded an operating company to handle these transactions for both institutions. In the medium term, the German market expects to see consolidation in this area, and in the future probably only five vendors will remain. ABC Bank may very well outsource to Postbank, which is one of the companies that insources these exact processes.

7.4 Integrated Project Planning Procedure

In order to optimize the identified approaches, a project planning procedure is designed, consisting of the following three sub-projects:

1. Establishment of a portal with an integrated KM system

2. Implementation of an analytics platform

3. Implementation of an infrastructure for business process integration

These three sub-projects are explained in more detail in the following sections.

7.4.1 Quick Win: Introducing SAP Enterprise Portal (EP)

As already explained, the users at ABC Bank work with many different systems. They need to use all of these different systems in order to get a comprehensive picture of a customer's financial situation. By introducing a portal, ABC Bank hopes to benefit from two big advantages:

1. The (front-end) processes will be optimized and unified across all organization units
2. By automating and finally removing frequently recurring routine tasks (such as system logins or searching for customer data), the users will save a substantial amount of time

Introduction by Department

To master the comprehensive integration approach, a gradual process is recommended for portal projects. Typically, one organizational unit at a time is allowed to access the portal, so that all the required content is provided for each organizational unit. Larger organizational units can be broken down into departments. ABC Bank has decided to create business cases that specify previously defined and prioritized individual steps. The advantage is that the scope of the individual sub-projects is precisely defined, and the particularly relevant project areas are derived from the business cases.

"Think Big, Start Small"

In planning the project procedure and the definition of the sub-project, the bank will attempt to incorporate the final objective of a company-wide portal rollout, and at the same time implement the individual departments' special standards. According to the motto "Think big, start small," the individual sub-projects enable the gradual implementation of the bank's various individual business areas. Due to the short timeframes of the sub-projects, fast results can be achieved relatively quickly, constituting a success factor that should not be underestimated. These early successes are critical when it comes to motivating the persons involved.

Moreover, ABC Bank puts great emphasis on an elaborate security concept that controls the authorizations for access to different content. This means that it makes sense to create an organizational plan that spells out how different users will be grouped together at a very early stage in the project, so that both the distribution of content and the assignment of authorizations can be managed relatively easily.

Information Flow Between the Project Team and Users

The gradual approach to implementation ensures that there is a constant flow of information between the users and the project team, which continually increases quality. Problems and optimization potential can be discussed based on existing practical examples. Alternative solutions can be considered and discussed at length. The expertise in the individual departments grows because of the tight collaboration with the project team. Generally, the inclusion of all those concerned is extremely important. The experts who know the (future) portal content best can be found among various departments. Therefore, these departments must be involved in the definition of the project or sub-project scope from the very beginning.

In portal projects, contrary to conventional software projects, content is key. A portal is worthless without content. If too little content is provided, the user will not accept and use the portal. This means that the project planning team should spend much more time on contextual topics than on questions that pertain to conventional IT areas, and everybody involved in planning the project should be prepared for this shift in emphasis to content. The applied technology is not that important, as long as a certain degree of functionality is ensured. Instead, the concepts of integration and processing of content, as well as of structuring and navigation, have a much bigger impact on user-friendliness, and thus on results.

The Importance of Content

A portal is an integration platform that has points of contact in practically every organizational unit. Nearly all processes will be modified; at least the way that process steps are carried out and operated will radically change.

All companies have information structures that were not planned or developed in a logical manner, but that instead grew "organically." Although these structures are far from optimal, they are astonishingly resistant toward change. However, with the introduction of the portal, and especially the Knowledge Management component, great changes can be expected.

Information Structures

The integration of existing homegrown software for CRM-type tasks in particular is supposed to increase the quality of customer care, which should have an effect on the bank's revenues. Due to the unification technology contained in SAP Enterprise Portal, it is relatively easy to integrate the various data sources required for a comprehensive view of customer data.

7.4.2 Implementing an Analytics Platform

The second big step in the transformation of ABC Bank's IT landscape is to implement SAP Business Intelligence (BI)—SAP's data warehouse solution—with SAP Business Information Warehouse (BW). The goal is to significantly improve the quality of information that serves as a basis for decision-making. The implementation project includes providing a central information warehouse that gathers and processes data from source systems and answers the questions of all users.

Authorizations   The basis for this central information warehouse is a sophisticated authorization concept that allows users to access all necessary information, and simultaneously ensures that no unauthorized access to confidential information takes place. Access rights can be granted to employees with certain roles, or on an individual basis.

One advantage of SAP's BW system is that data is available on the Web front end, or alternatively in Microsoft Excel format. This way, it can be easily provided and processed. Above all, the possibility of navigating deep down into the data structure from data that is currently displayed enables users to navigate through the interrelations within the reporting structure.

Key User Concept   From an organizational standpoint, the portal should allow the establishment of key users in each separate department in addition to predefined user queries. Besides the predefined queries, you should try to have key users in every organizational unit who can implement additional special queries for the "normal" users. The key users in ABC Bank's different departments can develop specific expert knowledge and will then be in the position to create queries and reports themselves and customize them according to their respective department's requirements. Aside from the basic data, the derived key figures are of particular interest here.

Administration   The concept of using just one centralized system also facilitates administration. The administration of SAP BI can be done centrally in order to cut costs. The actual evaluation processes and the creation of reports can then be done by the individual departments, so that the required information will be autonomous and separate.

From a technical standpoint, the central reporting system takes a lot of load off the operative systems, which, in turn, will then be fully available for handling the actual processes. They will only be used for current evaluations (for example, to get status information such as "open orders" or "orders to be processed"). Consolidated reports will be retrieved from the BW system.

When implementing the BW system, usually data from only the most important sources will be available at first. More systems will be integrated successively until all relevant information is available in the single system. In conjunction with this gradual system growth, legacy systems will also be removed gradually.

A deeper integration into the portal is planned in a further expansion stage of the system. Although the information from the BW system will be available on the Web from the time of implementation and can be retrieved from the portal, there is still room for improvement: the combined use of both components makes it possible to work with the content on a much higher level of collaboration. In particular, the controlled information exchange within the team and the freely defined order in which the work is done (with regard to BW reports) offer great potential.

Integration into the Portal

7.4.3 Implementing an Integration Hub

Finally, the third step (implementing an integration hub) will allow ABC Bank flexibility in the design of processes, especially in processes that cross the borders of the company. The basis of this is the EAI solution from SAP. With the implementation of SAP Exchange Infrastructure (XI) as a central integration component, it will be possible to integrate systems relatively easily and to replace them if required. Given the fact that ABC Bank's vertical integration is too high, as is the case with many other banks, using XI opens up many exciting possibilities. For example, unprofitable process areas can be grouped together and outsourced with the help of XI. There is also the opportunity to use business process outsourcing (BPO) offerings to unload processes that aren't part of the company's core competencies.

Not only does XI offer advantages in the modification of the process landscape, it also enables you to reduce the complexity of the existing system landscape, particularly with regard to the multiplicity of existing interfaces. Instead of having many separate connections between the systems, every system connects to XI, which, in turn, handles the distribution of process information.

Disintegration of the Interface Chaos

When you have SAP XI, it is less costly and takes less time to make changes to the IT landscape, such as installing a new system, because you only have to ensure that it integrates with XI, not a variety of systems.

Similarly, changes that are carried out solely in the process area can be implemented faster and with much more ease, because only the affected systems have to be customized, not the interfaces. Thanks to the modular structure of the integration landscape, the required time decreases while flexibility increases when developing new processes or customizing existing processes.

To implement all these advantages, you must consider all the relevant factors when creating the plan that precedes the technical implementation of XI. Aside from general technical considerations such as the types of protocols available, organizational questions must also be addressed. Of course, the design of the platform is particularly important. And it would be "fatal" if the system's integration were to be put on hold because the used hardware did not meet the requirements. Therefore, sufficient contingencies—and upgrade possibilities—have to be planned for in order to prepare for both peak loads and company growth.

The top-down approach has proven itself to be the best approach in the design of the EAI architecture. Based on an analysis of the system and processes, and considering the company's strategy, the large EAI structure and architecture is first defined and validated. The sequence in which the individual systems will be implemented is already being planned at this stage. Only after this step is completed will planning of the activities associated with the technical implementation begin. The objective is a smooth transition from the existing to the new architecture, which includes the gradual removal of the legacy interfaces.

The imminent modification of the IT landscape is also felt in other areas. ABC Bank has already started its first projects testing the use of Web services. Banks are typically early adopters of Web services; from a technical standpoint, it obviously makes sense that Web services would be used to solve integration problems that are evident within the banking industry.

7.5   ABC Bank—Value Consideration

ABC Bank has seen decreasing profits during the past years, which acted as a strong impetus for change. Compared to its European competitors, ABC Bank does not have enough revenue, and it's spending too much money per bank customer. Last but not least, the CIO is under increasing pressure to take action to reduce the high costs of the computer systems. It is imperative for those responsible at ABC Bank to cut the costs of the IT landscape. At the same time, the bank's new innovative products need to be supported by corresponding IT systems and processes. Therefore, the focus is not only cost reduction but also the implementation of a modern IT landscape as a basis for flexibility. Management has decided to modernize the information systems and would like to start in this direction with the following processes:

- Creation of a standardized user interface for application integration
- Improvement of analysis possibilities due to data integration
- Development of a flexible architecture for IT system integration

Take a look at the current IT situation at ABC Bank: it is characterized by a high amount of in-house software development as well as a heterogeneous system landscape. The potential of an IT architecture based on SAP NetWeaver is shown in the following paragraphs.

Current Situation at ABC Bank

As already noted, the question of whether to *develop software in-house or use standard software* is particularly important to the bank. Due to the high costs of homegrown software, the managers of the IT department must insist on the transition to standard software. In our evaluation, we will now focus on the advantages of using SAP NetWeaver.

7.5.1 Standard User Interface

The success of a bank is considerably influenced by whether employees have fast and easy access to reliable information. Because ABC Bank currently has a heterogeneous system landscape, information about customers and products is disseminated throughout the IT landscape. The company has taken the first steps toward improved customer care by implementing a CRM system. Figure 7.5 shows an interesting picture. The ratings in the areas of flexibility and innovation, which deal with the company's added value, are hardly distinctive (the two areas got low ratings) (compare value chain, value added, and company value). Implementing a company portal is considered the optimal solution for improving this situation. SAP Enterprise Portal (EP) provides users with a unified view of the different IT systems and supports them in their daily work. Thus, a bank employee can concentrate on providing the best possible customer care instead of on the process of searching for information.

Portal for User Integration

Knowledge Management (KM) is another important requirement in the development of an information platform. All product information that is available in the form of unstructured documents, such as PowerPoint, Adobe PDF, or MS Word files, can easily be made available to every portal user. If we look at the evaluation of the target concept (i.e., the blueprint with SAP NetWeaver in the diagram), we can see that there is still room for significant improvement in the areas of communication and quality.

Provision of Information with KM

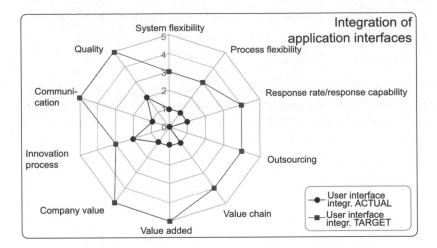

Figure 7.5 Evaluation of Portal Integration

At this point, we would like to mention the evaluation of outsourcing. Recently, banks have been outsourcing their non-core-competency processes to external companies. With a portal solution, this process can be supported by an integrated application interface across system boundaries.

Potential for Cost Reductions In terms of costs, the following points stand out:

► A portal solution cuts the processing time of business processes considerably via the use of a role-based approach to granting access to necessary information.

► Saving potentials in the area of knowledge management are mainly found in centralized information access and in the consolidation of existing application systems.

7.5.2 Data Integration

Insufficient Data Quality Even the best portal installation is useless if the data displayed is not of good quality. For this reason, it is of strategic importance for ABC Bank to consolidate heterogeneous data sources into one single system. Figure 7.6 clearly shows the present low ratings for innovation and flexibility. According to the illustration, the bank is hardly in the position to use its operative data for significant analyses. This is particularly emphasized by the rating of quality.

SAP Business Intelligence (BI) With SAP Business Information Warehouse (BW), SAP Business Intelligence (BI) provides a platform for integrating the various data sources. As a result, improved data is available regarding the risks and profitability associated with the bank's customers This is indicated in the evaluations in Figure 7.6, which show higher values for the forecasted situation in the areas of added value and flexibility and the now possible increase in the company value. In terms of costs, BI provides the following advantages:

Here are the potentials for cost reduction:

Potential for Cost
Reduction

▶ Fast customization and enhancement of existing reports

▶ Removal of manual tasks in the context of financial controlling

▶ Use of predefined SAP reporting models for the implementation of modified reporting requirements

▶ Decreased analysis efforts ("reporting at the touch of a button")

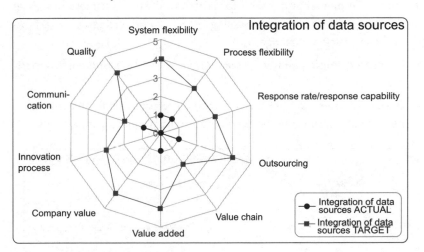

Figure 7.6 Evaluating Data Integration

7.5.3 Process Integration

Two considerable tasks are the main focus during process integration at ABC Bank. One is the outsourcing of business processes that are not profitable or are not part of the bank's core competencies, such as software development. The other is the simplification of the complex process infrastructure, which is the responsibility of the managers of the IT department. The actual situation is determined by little flexibility and innovation possibilities. In the AS-IS situation (regarding process integration) we have little flexibility and it is difficult to implement innovative new solutions. As shown in Figure 7.7, the current IT architecture is not prepared for these requirements.

Today's IT Process
Integration

SAP Exchange Infrastructure (XI) provides the tools to tackle this problem. With the help of this software, ABC Bank can organize its processes
more flexibly, which is enabled by unifying the interface architecture. In
this way, the integration of third-party systems in the context of business
process outsourcing (BPO) is made easier and considerably cheaper. Figure 7.7 shows the potential that could be realized in all areas by implementing XI.

Other potentials in the area of cost savings are:

▶ Savings in development, maintenance, and monitoring of the system
  interfaces

▶ Reduced effort in the operation of the XI integration software

▶ Shorter implementation time for cross-application business processes
  due to graphical process modeling or when converting the interfaces
  because of release changes

▶ Decreased implementation costs when integrating outsourcing partners

▶ Generally lower project costs, as no expensive external consultants
  need to be hired for the implementation of standard connections

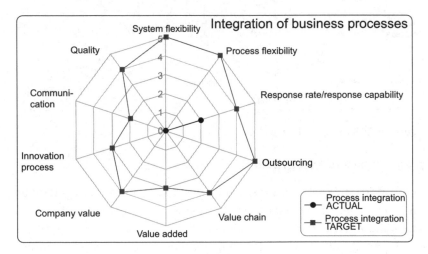

Figure 7.7 Evaluation of Business Process Integration

7.5.4 Evaluation and Recommendation

It is vital that ABC Bank modernize its entire IT system architecture. This
does not mean replacing individual systems with new ones, but rather
that fundamental changes like the implementation of standard software

or of an integrated infrastructure solution have to be carried out. To illustrate the considered processes, we will now draw a comparison to the reference value. (The reference value is based on the IT strategy of a company. To determine what the contribution of a single project will be, the projects can be compared with that reference value.) The reference value represents a subjective evaluation of the criteria of *flexibility*, *innovation*, and *cost reduction*. Figure 7.8 illustrates this comparison.

It is apparent that the greatest potential lies in the area of process integration. In the portfolio matrix, the evaluations for the actual process and the target architecture are at opposite ends of the spectrum.

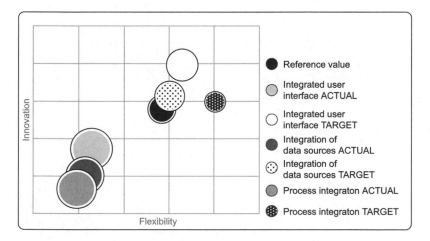

Figure 7.8 Portfolio Matrix

An interesting picture ensues in the area of the forecasted processes enabled by the SAP NetWeaver components. Costs can be reduced through *data integration* and *process integration*. The cost-saving potential for a standard user interface is lower in comparison. This phenomenon is explained by the fact that a company portal can realize only indirect cost advantages (for example, through the consolidation of several legacy applications). In a nutshell, ABC Bank should be aware of the great IT challenges it will face in the coming years, and implement planned investments promptly.

8 ESA—Enterprise Services Architecture

In this chapter you'll learn what is meant by a service-oriented architecture (SOA) and why this type of architecture is currently the most popular IT trend. You'll also discover the reasons behind SAP's vision of an Enterprise Services Architecture (ESA) based on a service-oriented architecture. Lastly, you'll find out about the advantages of an SOA.

The previous discussion and, in particular, the roadmaps in Chapters 4 to 7 have already established that flexibility, innovative ability, and cost transparency and controlling are the essential requirements of modern IT systems. However, in order to achieve new potential in relation to these criteria, new concepts are needed, not only in IT strategy, but also in the area of technology.

Both this chapter and the next will deal with these technological concepts. We'll examine the platform architecture first (in this chapter). Then we'll look at the individual technical components of SAP NetWeaver in more detail (in Chapter 9).

8.1 The Gentle Revolution

Before examining SOA and ESA more closely, we'll study the history behind current IT landscapes, which will explain why SOA became important in the first place.

8.1.1 IT Developments of Recent Years

In recent decades, many businesses have invested heavily in the development of their IT architecture. In the early '70s, mainframe systems like those from IBM were the main focus, because they were best suited for the centralized structure of businesses, and they delivered information that could be used to process business operations. However, this centralized way of doing business meant that business processes were more or less "written in stone," and it was only possible to change the process structure or add new processes when undertaking larger projects.

Mainframe Era

In the mid-1980s, external market requirements forced a huge change in IT architecture. Suddenly, decentralized systems that allowed greater flex-

Decentralized Systems

ibility to react to market changes were required. Consequently, companies developed their own software or used applications from many different manufacturers. This resulted in expensive, initially non-integrated standalone solutions that were interlinked with each other via equally complex interfaces. These less than optimal conditions prompted businesses to look for alternatives.

Client/Server Architecture Client/server architecture became popular in the early 1990s. Software systems such as SAP R/3 were designed to meet the market demands for decentralized and scalable systems. They also included a feature recognizable from the mainframe era—integration. Once again, companies could react flexibly to external market changes and also manage their business processes in an integrated manner.

Business Processes via the Internet Then, in the late 1990s, the Internet laid the foundation for managing business processes across company borders. The idea was to use the software systems to set up business-to-business (B2B) scenarios, which would be used to simplify or accelerate the processes between market participants (for example, customer, company, and supplier). Companies chose the most optimal solutions from those offered by the software providers. This was the beginning of the Best-of-Breed[1] era, which brought with it not only new problems, but unresolved old problems as well.

Best-of-Breed Businesses today have built up heterogeneous and very complex system landscapes using the best-of-breed strategy. These businesses are opportune because their individual components offer maximum functionality, however, integration requires a great deal of investment. What we mean by integration in terms of business processes is application integration and cross-company integration.

Integration at All Levels In the future, IT will be required to use more of its available budget on innovation and less of it on maintenance and the servicing of existing interfaces. This could be achieved by integrating the processes and the data. Furthermore, applications and ultimately the user interface should be integrated (see Section 9.1).

Which Is the Right Platform? Service-oriented architectures almost achieve such comprehensive integration. Once an SOA has been designed, however, a suitable platform must be chosen for its implementation. In order to choose a suitable platform, many questions must be answered, such as: How widely-used is the platform? What are the system requirements necessary to connect

---

1 Best-of-breed: Selection of software for a specific process from the best provider, for example, for purchasing or sales over the Internet.

agents? What is the service versioning concept? What is the authentication and authorization concept?

What is considered most important when it comes to the protection of investment is the use of recognized standards and the degree of expandability.

The distribution of the platform gives important information on the degree of maturity of the product and on the quality of the service structure.

8.1.2 Another Paradigm Shift

In the IT industry, alarm bells ring for many IT professionals when they hear talk of a paradigm shift. The new buzzwords of consultants are often equated with trends started solely to increase consultation turnover. This mistrust is probably due to past negative experiences. And who could blame the CIOs? In recent years, they have had to accept that creating value in an IT system is an imperative company goal.

Mistrust As a Reflex

When we speak of a gentle revolution in subsequent sections, we are referring to the challenge of realizing the demand for radical changes in the IT landscape, while ensuring that previous investments were not made in vain (investment protection).

Gentle Revolution?

The service-oriented architecture approach appears to answer this challenge. Just one indication of this is that the big manufacturers (IBM, Microsoft, and others) are adopting SOAs for their own products.

What Are Service-Oriented Architectures?

SOAs are not ends in themselves—they focus on the business processes of the company. At first glance, this does not appear to be anything new, because the concept of business process modeling has existed since the Business Process Reengineering (BPR) boom.

However, if we consider that because of the best-of-breed philosophy, "functional silos" in the form of ERP, CRM, SCM, and SRM systems still exist side by side in many companies and are often ill-equipped at exchanging information, it becomes apparent that business processes running across functional silos cannot be executed efficiently.

Focus on the Business Process

Integrating services into a comprehensive service-oriented architecture should solve this operational and information logistics problem. As already indicated, SOA is an IT concept in which emphasis is placed on

SOA—Componentizing Applications

the business processes, and the technology with which they are implemented is of minor importance. In other words, the old monoliths are "broken down" into manageable services, which are really new applications based on component and service-oriented programming. These services can now be interlinked in order to execute business processes. This interconnection is quite loose, and the services can be incorporated into multiple different processes.

It is also comparably easy to create new business processes using existing services, or to add to or change existing business processes—a feature which, given the business world's high fluctuation of assets, can greatly accelerate integration or spin-off with correspondingly favorable financial effects.

What Is an Enterprise Services Architecture?

ESA = SOA with Added Value

If we develop the SOA approach further, we arrive at an Enterprise Services Architecture (ESA), which in addition to the technical possibilties of SOA, also provides a business focus. In other words, business-process oriented structures are predefined, which enables companies to quickly develop reusable components. These components are so flexible that they offer a real competitive advantage.

It is therefore assumed that business processes will no longer be developed using traditional programming, but will instead be defined with the help and correct design of these services. Needless to say, this requires a new platform with new functions. This platform can be termed an ESA platform, and in order for it to work not only across applications but also across companies, it uses recognized, open standards.

8.2   Reasons for Service-Oriented Architectures

"The industry desperately wants vendors to move away from proprietary systems that lock firms into technology."[2]

Why is it that SOA is on the tip of everybody's tongue at the moment and all big system integrators have taken up its cause? The following section will describe the specific developments that have occurred in companies, the economy, and society to lead to this trend.

---

2   Bob Hallstone, Director of Software Infrastructure, IDC.

8.2.1 The Burden on Businesses

Rapidness is an important quality for businesses that want to assert themselves in the market and generate growth. Rapidness refers to the ability of management to recognize market requirements and to promptly implement respective products in specific processes. Of course, the price at which the product can be made available plays an important role in this regard.

Rapidness

If products and processes are adjusted in reaction to market or customer requirements, the success of the adjustment and the efficiency of the processes must be measured. This monitoring must happen in real time, which is why we speak of a "realtime enterprise" in this context.

Although successful efforts have been made in recent years toward implementing business intelligence concepts, in many businesses there is still a large gap between the information required and the information actually made available. Bridging this gap is critical to successful corporate management.

Failings

8.2.2 Squaring the Circle

Being aware of this burden and actually taking specific steps to alleviate it are two different matters.

The "fat" years of corporate IT are in the past. IT budgets are being reduced everywhere. Every project planned must first be subjected to a detailed ROI analysis. If management suspects that a project is being suggested only because it would be "nice to have" rather than contribute to process automation and thereby reduce costs, it has little hope of being implemented.

IT Doesn't Matter?

Although this may be an understandable reaction, it brings with it the risk of blocking innovation. Under these conditions, too much emphasis is put on the benefit of short-term cost optimization, and the company may soon find itself at a dangerous competitive disadvantage.

Nevertheless, IT departments are still being asked to initiate innovation, and some even say that the abbreviation "CIO" should be changed to stand for "Chief Innovation Officer" instead of "Chief Information Officer."

Chief Innovation Officer

It would therefore appear that the CIO is charged with a "mission impossible." He or she is supposed to increase the portion of the budget spent on innovative ideas and projects, while the overall available budget is actually shrinking. And, of course, the expense of maintaining the current IT landscape is fixed or is even going up.

8.2.3 Developed IT Landscapes

After the mainframe era, many companies concentrated on implementing modern client/server systems, and some built up powerful ERP systems, which automate the financial and general administration processes.

It wasn't long before other departments also wanted to automate their processes. Therefore, every department head was given his or her own application. These were identified by three-letter acronyms such as CRM, SCM, PLM, or SRM.[3]

Isolated Silos It also didn't take long to realize that many important processes began in CRM, moved to ERP, and finished in SCM. However, not many applications could communicate with each other or even execute a cross-application process. Thus many companies were forced to tackle this limitation by implementing human interfaces (so-called "brain interfaces") or by developing and maintaining very expensive technical interfaces.

Nevertheless, investments that had already been made were to be protected. It was not possible to demand a complete transformation in IT. This is why integration has been one of the top five topics on the agenda of CIOs for many years now.

8.3 Web Services

The term "Web services" has been mentioned several times, and its potential for solving existing integration problems in IT has been discussed. We will now look at Web services in a little more detail.

Although the buzzword SOA is mentioned again and again in relation to Web services, SOA is an architecture paradigm that is independent of Web services. An analogy with the automotive industry is often used to explain the SOA approach.[4]

Monoliths In the past, a car was considered to be a large collection of various parts. A model was a self-contained monolith consisting of parts produced specifically for it. Parts from other monoliths were of little or no use.

---

3 Woods, Dan: *Realtime: A Tribute to Hasso Plattner*. John Wiley & Sons Australia, 2004. p. 237.
4 Woods, Dan: *Enterprise Services Architecture*. Sebastopol 2003. p. 4.

The implications of this type of production process are well known. This approach had a negative effect on construction costs as well as production and servicing costs. As a result, modular systems were established. Modular systems are standardized and can be used by different manufacturers. The different components fit together like a plug and a socket.

Components

Of course, the use of components does not reduce the complexity of a product, but it does make the production cheaper. This concept, known as "lean manufacturing," has become popular in many industries.

8.3.1 Increasing Standardization in IT

But why do we need new standards, when we already have standards available that offer this type of componentization (for example, CORBA and DCOM)? The usual answer given to this justified question is that "the summation of the features of Web services" would already be considered to be better, as they are easy to understand and easy for humans to read—therefore instantly appearing "nicer."

"Nicer Services"

A significant argument in favor of Web services is the fact that several hundred software companies, including Microsoft, Sun, SAP and IBM, support them or have promised to support them in the future.

Wide Support

The adoption of the lean manufacturing concept (see above) in the IT industry leads to the SOA approach. Applications are modularized, and the resulting components communicate with each other via defined Web service interfaces. They work in a type of service relationship, in which one program module requests a service from another, such as checking a credit rating, calculating a delivery date, or documenting an invoice.

Service Relationship

Some of these services reside in different applications, different systems, or even different companies. In order to make them generically available, they must be designed in such a way so that they can be easily identified, so the service they fulfill can be easily recognized, and so they can be easily and transparently invoked using a standardized protocol.

For this to work smoothly, various manufacturer-independent standards have been defined in recent years with the cooperation of the big IT integrators. Some of the standards defined to work with Web services in this way are XML, SOAP, UDDI, and WSDL. Here's a brief description of these terms:

Manufacturer-Independent Standards

▶ **XML (Extensible Markup Language)**
   XML is a data content description language. It defines data as well as the metadata belonging to it (data type, quantity, and restrictions). The

revolutionary characteristic of XML is that it is a data format that is capable of describing itself.

▶ **SOAP (Simple Object Access Protocol)**
SOAP is the "command language" of the Internet. It is used to call methods and functions contained in applications on remote systems. To do this, SOAP uses XML as a base language.

▶ **UDDI (Universal Description, Discovery, and Integration Services)**
UDDI is like the yellow pages of the Internet. It is used to find functionality provided in the form of Web services.

▶ **WSDL (Web Services Description Language)**
WSDL is an XML-based language for describing Web Services and how to access them.

▶ **BPEL/BPEL4WS (Business Process Execution Language/for Web Services)**
This is a description language that specifies the order and conditions under which services created work together in order to generate a (sub-)business process. This is called "choreography."

As a result of this technology, Web services can be used across firewalls, are supported by many programming languages, and are flexible with regard to synchronous or asynchronous processing.

Web services are characterized by the three-part *Web service stack*. It consists of:

1. SOAP, the protocol used to access Web services

2. WSDL, the language used to describe Web service interfaces

3. UDDI, the directory structure for publishing Web services

8.3.2 Communication Between Web Services

In order to execute a business process using Web services, the respective requirements must first be met. This is the topic we will cover in this section.

Generating and Publishing

In order to create a Web service and make it available, the service provider must carry out the following steps:[5]

---

5 Färber, Günther; Kirchner, Julia: *mySAP Technology Roadmap. When, where and how to incorporate mySAP Technology in your IT landscape.* SAP PRESS 2002.

1. The service provider creates a service (a function) based on the service requestor's preferred programming language, infrastructure, and platform.

2. The service must then be described along with the transfer parameters and background information. This is done using the language provided for this purpose—WSDL.

3. The service can now be registered in the UDDI registries (service broker) along with the URL where it can be reached and the WDSL description. These global "yellow pages" are usually managed by big IT companies.

4. The service provider makes it possible for the service requestor to access and use the services using SOAP.

Figure 8.1 shows the entire process.

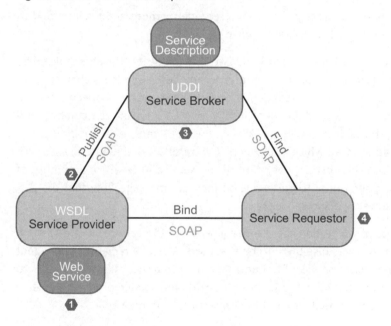

Figure 8.1 Using Web Services

Digression: Explanation of Further Terminology

The following section explains concepts and relationships you should be familiar with in order to understand service-oriented architecture. It includes the terminology of the *service-oriented model* (SOM), a component of the Web Services Architecture (WSA), which is currently being developed by the W3C. This is a framework for further development of future Web services-related standards.

Action and Agent An *action* is an activity carried out by an *agent* as a result of receiving a message, or in order to send a message. An agent is a program acting on behalf of a person, organization, or process. It can provide and invoke services.

Choreography A *choreography* defines the sequence and conditions under which multiple cooperating independent (Web) services act in order to perform specific functions. *Choreography Description Language* is used to describe a choreography in a machine-processable format. It specifies the interactions allowed between a large number of services and can specify the lifecycle of a call as well as the conversations possible between service requestor and service provider.

Task A *task* has a specific goal and involves one or more actions intended to achieve this goal. Tasks are assigned to services.

Service A *service* is a collection of tasks related to each other. They are realized by one or more agents acting as a service provider. A service is characterized by an unambiguous identifier, a service interface, and specific service semantics. It should be dynamically publishable and detectable, and allow remote access using a *service end point*. A service end point is a network address at which the *service interface* is implemented. A service interface is an abstract definition of the service in terms of a number of service operations. The interface defines the message flow that the service can receive and send.

Service Provider and Service Requestor A *service provider* is an agent that can execute the actions of one or more services or can cause them to be executed. A *service requestor* is an agent that requests a service. The term "service semantics" is used to refer to the contract between the service requestor and service provider concerning the requirements for and the impact of using the service.

8.3.3 The Benefits of Web Services[6]

So how can Web services help a company meet business requirements? The following section summarizes the most important points:

▶ Cross-applications
  Web services make it considerably easier and more cost-effective for

---

6 cf. Woods: *Realtime...* pp. 238 f.

existing (old) SAP or non-SAP applications to contribute to cross-application and cross-company processes.

▶ **New functionality**
Web services make it much easier for IT manufacturers and users to add new functionality to existing applications.

▶ **Versioning**
Web services make it much simpler to develop, roll out, and maintain various versions of sector-specific solutions.

▶ **New applications**
Web services make innovation possible by allowing the creation and integration of new applications that extend the process automation capabilities of existing applications.

▶ **Reusability**
Web services are reusable, which means that redundant developments, common in the past, are avoided.[7]

▶ **Investment protection**
The move to a service-oriented architecture can be carried out very cautiously. Whole system architectures therefore don't need to be replaced as a result of the move, which used to happen, for example, when a host in a client/server architecture was replaced.

And in particular, existing applications can be integrated via encapsulation. The point-to-point connections are broken down one by one.

8.4   ESA—SAP's Blueprint for SOA

A brief definition of an ESA has already been given in Section 8.1.3. The following section will look at the topic in more detail, and how it relates to SAP.

SAP has declared that ESA is its framework or philosophy for SOA implementation, based on Web services standards.

ESA is a collection of fundamental principles and handling instructions, with which it is possible to construct a flexible IT landscape offering the greatest number of business uses at the lowest cost.[8]

---

7   cf. Woods: *Realtime...* pp. 238 f.
8   cf. Woods: *Realtime...* p. 231.

In order to achieve a better understanding of ESA, it is necessary to break down this marketing-oriented description into its individual components. We will now attempt to describe ESA more simply, while also considering the SOA details.

Extension of the Web Services Concept

ESA extends the concept of Web services to that of an architecture for business applications (enterprise services). While Web services is primarily a purely technical concept, ESA is the blueprint for all-inclusive and service-based business applications. In this regard, ESA supports everyone involved in a business process, whether they are internal or external to the company itself. It also includes all information that is relevant for a business process.

Comprehensive Integration

Furthermore, ESA integrates all systems relevant to the process, whether they are internal or external, SAP or non-SAP systems. ESA allows the design of a complete business process solution into which existing systems and applications can be incorporated.

However, despite this detailed description, ESA remains what it is—a philosophy. This doesn't mean that SAP is stuck at the visionary level. The philosophy can be implemented using a number of specific tools that are collected together and integrated into a toolbox. This toolbox is SAP NetWeaver, and its technical components are described in more detail in Chapter 9.

The following more detailed description of ESA will be limited to detailing the ESA topics related to SAP, since the history, need for, and advantages of the service-oriented architecture have already been discussed in Sections 8.1 to 8.3.

8.4.1 From ERP to the Cross-Application Business Process

SAP views the road to ESA as at least as important as, if not more important than the road to a three-layer client/server architecture in the early 1990s.[9] Figure 8.2 shows the reasons why it may be even more important. It is sometimes necessary to replace the complete infrastructure of a client/server architecture due to a change in the host world. The transition to ESA therefore stands out in that existing applications do not need to be replaced, protecting earlier investments.

---

9 cf. Woods: *Realtime...* p. 248 f.

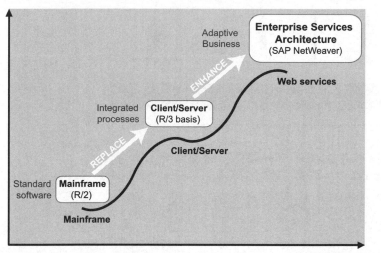

Technological progress

Figure 8.2 The Road to an SOA

Of course, it is not possible to do it all for free. The necessary skills will change, no doubt resulting in training costs. The ERP systems that were previously the focal point of the operational universe have decreased in importance. Their role has now been assumed by a consistent company strategy and the business processes resulting from it. Of course, these business processes are usually cross-application business processes.

We now come to the point at which it is necessary to discuss the structure and individual components or building blocks of the architecture.

8.4.2 The ESA Structure

All optimization efforts up to now have concentrated on the business processes taking place in the ERP systems. In conjunction with the shift of focus mentioned earlier, business process definition and control now also move to a new level outside of the applications. This is the "hub" or "integration broker." Figure 8.3 shows the architecture and the main components.

Integration Broker

The hub is responsible for connecting a number of different applications. In other words, all these connections between applications guarantee integration.

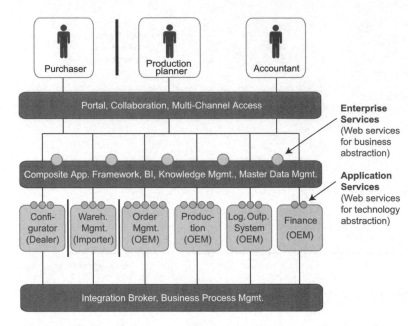

Figure 8.3 The ESA Structure

Let's use a car for comparison again: Besides the engine, there is other technical equipment under the hood that acts to ensure smooth cooperation between all components involved, for example, the cylinders, the crankshaft, the gears, etc. Since the detailed processes do not concern the driver and he only needs control information (Am I going too fast? Do I have enough gas? What is the engine temperature? What is the oil pressure? etc.), he is interested only in specific information or the final result of processes, and this is displayed on his dashboard.

It is the same for people responsible for business processes. For them too, the result is what is important, and not the detailed techncial implementation. They also have a "dashboard." This dashboard is displayed using a special layer that enables employees to retrieve information, take action, and collaborate, and it can also be personalized. This dashboard is implemented by a portal.

Figure 8.4 illustrates the main concepts related to ESA.

An *application service* is a Web service that makes the services of a business application available. One example would be canceling an order in a CRM system. Application services are located at such a deep technical level that it is not necessary to display them on the dashboard.

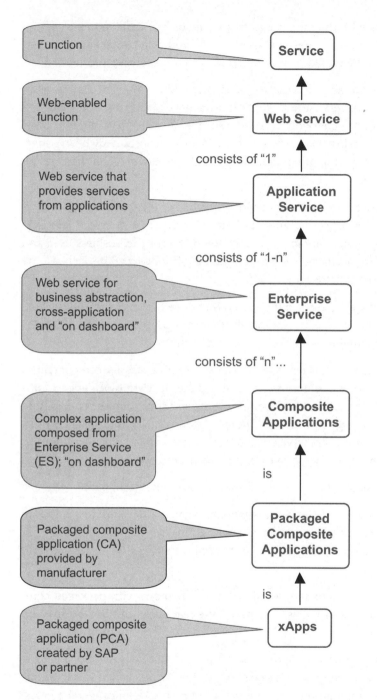

Figure 8.4 Terminology Overview

Continuing with the car analogy, this would be comparable to making the function of every spark plug visible. This would not interest the driver, and if anything would overburden him with unnecessary information.

Enterprise Services

An example of an *enterprise service* (ES) would be the cancellation of an order that triggers various application services, such as cancelling the order in CRM, checking SCM to see if any parts have already been ordered, checking finance to see if any invoices have already been generated, and triggering other applications that were involved in the creation of the order.

An enterprise service therefore works at a higher level than an application service and can use multiple application services to carry out its work. Enterprise services are important for the driver, or the business user, and are therefore displayed on the "dashboard," from where they can also be switched on or activated.

The advantage for users in this case is that once they press the cancel button, they do not need to give any further thought to the complex process and its dependencies. The ES takes care of this.

Composite Applications

Figure 8.4 shows a layer called *Composite Applications*, which contains a number of tools. Composite applications are building block applications created using Web services. Composite applications can use services from multiple existing applications. The hub groups different application services into enterprise services, and composite applications can then use these enterprise services to carry out the necessary work.

Composite applications can also be set up using the dashboard.

Packaged Composite Applications

The term *packaged composite applications* generally refers to composite applications packaged and developed by software manufacturers or specific companies. Packaged composite applications can be created individually.

xApps

The term *xApps* (cross-applications) is synonymous with packaged composite applications (PCAs). xApps are the realization of PCAs by SAP and SAP partners.

One of the first usable xApps to be completed and delivered by SAP is the Resource and Program Management (RPM) xApp, which collaborating companies and corporate groups can use for cross-application and cross-company resource and project management.

8.4.3 Sample Scenario

The nature of Web services has already been discussed in Section 8.3, and some important terms have been introduced. Since we have also discussed the ESA-specific components and respective terminology, we will now use a business scenario to show how Web services or enterprise services can be used to execute a business process in an ESA structure.

Product
Development
Scenario

As a sample scenario, we will consider a process initiated by product development of a production company. This area is of particular interest for many companies, as it generates huge costs. But in contrast to these high costs, there is a weak success rate of 15% on average in the Consumer Products division.

A common reason for low success rates and high costs is that responsibility for the process has not been integrated, and therefore none of the departments involved really promote the process.

No Respons-
ibilities

The goal must be to reduce as many non-value-adding (sub-)processes in the company as possible. This can be achieved by extensive automation. For car suppliers in particular, this pressure is continually growing (see Chapter 5). Car manufacturers, which are continually reducing their vertical integration (see Figure 5.2 in Chapter 5), sometimes also demand active participation from their suppliers in innovation and research activities, which is the same as outsourcing parts of the research departments.

In an optimized process, there is increased collaboration between the departments involved and the (potential) suppliers, whereas for many companies today tedious paperwork is still associated with carrying out such a process.

We will now look at how such an important process can be implemented using Web services or enterprise services in an ESA structure. As already stated, this scenario is fictitious. SAP does not (yet) deliver the enterprise services mentioned below.

To begin, let's look at the people involved, the process, the problems that exist, and their possible solutions using enterprise services.

The process starts with an operations director who needs new raw material for the piloting of a new product. The problem is that the material required is very new and is therefore not in stock, and has also never been used before. No material master record is available, and there are no known suppliers. The director will check the availability of the material,

New Components

and in the case of non-availability will initiate the procurement process. To do this, he uses the "Availability check" and "Create BANF" services.

Because no supplier of the required material has been identified, the employee from the purchasing department who is responsible for choosing suppliers must find a suitable supplier for the material and obtain an offer for it. In doing this, he uses the "Discover Supplier," "Evaluate Supplier," and "Accept Offer" enterprise services.

Including Suppliers Typically, the supplier will want to submit its offer as quickly as possible. Therfore, the supplier secures access to the portal of the requesting company, and enters the offer there.

When the purchasing department accepts the offer (see above), it is then time for the employee who is responsible for issuing orders to take action. She obtains the necessary information from a colleague, and issues and dispatches the order using the "Create Order" service.

The supplier either confirms or rejects the order using the "Confirm Order" service.

Finally, the accounts payable department activates the "Payment Process" service.

Figure 8.5 shows a use-case scenario to more clearly illustrate the people involved and the processes they carry out.

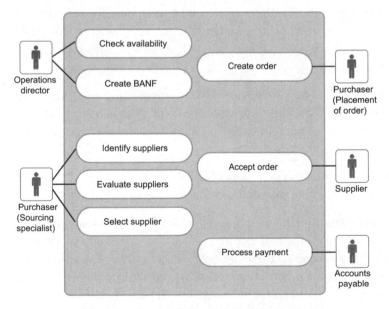

Figure 8.5 "Product Development" Use-Case Scenario

A simplified version of the business process is shown in Figure 8.6.

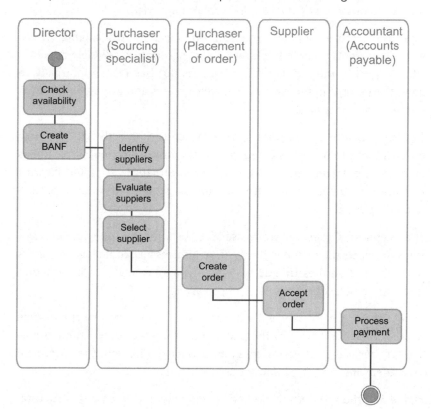

Figure 8.6 Simplified "Product Development" Business Process Model

The added value of an enterprise service in comparison to a simple Web service is now easy to explain based on the scenario and the enterprise services that have been discussed. Even in the context of product development, an increasing number of checks (for example, supplier evaluation, informing participants, etc.) are necessary between the individual process steps. These additional services are each part of an enterprise service.

Enterprise Service Added Value

For example, the "Create BANF" enterprise service automatically provides information on the requestors and the product, and checks the material numbers offered. The "Discover Supplier" service looks for known suppliers in the internal system, as well as for new suppliers in the Web directories, and searches for additional marketplaces.

The "Evaluate Supplier" service accesses internal and external ranking lists in order to obtain information on the potential supplier's quality, delivery reliability, and other key qualifying data. More checks on specific formalities to be observed by the supplier are also included.

Next the "Choose Supplier" service determines the most suitable suppliers, and presents them in the form of a list or automatically selects a specific supplier. If the supplier it chooses has not been listed internally to date, the enterprise service automatically creates and dispatches an RFQ (request for quotation).

The "Create Order" enterprise service, which is then activated, not only ensures that the order is created in all relevant systems, but also obtains all necessary documents (plans, contract information, etc.) and informs the internal purchasing department (sourcing specialist) and all participating suppliers.

The "Reply to Order" enterprise service, initiated by the supplier, confirms or rejects the manufacturer's offer, informs all people involved of its decision, and ensures that all systems involved receive the information necessary to execute the order if necessary.

Finally, the "Payment Process" enterprise service ensures that the invoice data is correct and handles the payment. If there has been no confirmation of the receipt of goods when an invoice is received, the enterprise service ensures that this information is obtained.

Figure 8.7 shows how this process is implemented in an ESA structure. The enterprise services assigned to the different process phases are also shown, as well as the systems and applications involved. The users can concentrate on doing their actual jobs, as they don't need to be involved in the continuous maintenance of the system or manually instigating administrative processes.

ESA = Flexibility An enterprise services approach takes the emphasis off of users and thus opens up the possibility of great flexibility. Process participants can be replaced, process steps can be reused, and new steps can even be added, all without reprogramming in the traditional sense.

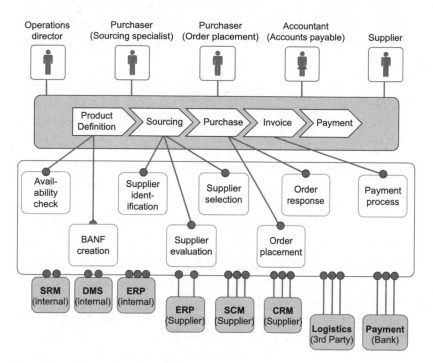

Figure 8.7 Enterprise Services Optimize Business Processes

8.4.4 SAP's Road to ESA

As already mentioned, SAP has specific work to do in order to implement the ESA vision. Paradigm shifts are rarely implemented without some cost.

For one thing, all applications must be altered so they can be available as Web services and so they can use Web services. The development process must also be adjusted so that new products can take advantage of what Web services has to offer.

Furthermore, SAP must preconfigure the integration within and between different applications and tools, so that as much integration as possible can be made available to customers more or less "out of the box."

In order for the hub to become the pivotal point of integration in the future, it must be made available at the beginning of the process. It promises to be responsible for the cross-application processes and the "very very many" connections. It performs these services with the support of Web services.

All these things will make it possible to reduce operational costs and the costs of adjusting applications to new business strategies and business processes.

8.4.5 The Road to ESA As a Process

The process of introducing an ESA into a business generally consists of four phases:[10]

1. **Analysis of the core business processes**
   The contribution of every system should be examined very carefully in the analysis phase. The basic components available to improve the architecture are taken into account. The architect identifies the basic data objects, services, and processes of the company, and provides an outline of how the existing systems automate the most important processes.

2. **Forecast (componentizing)**
   The forecast phase specifies the areas in which ESA can be used. Particular consideration is given to the business areas that need the most change and must be flexible. Areas outside IT (such as the customer base, the market, and the economic situation) are also analyzed in this regard.

3. **Design of the services**
   In the design phase, which is perhaps the most challenging phase, objects, services, and components are added to the architecture on the existing system to meet the demand for flexibility and process optimization. On the basis of the prognosis, a decision must be made concerning which parts of an application can be converted into components.

4. **Implementation**
   The implementation phase improves the architecture in a series of small steps.

8.5 Conclusion

Focus on the Process

The ESA concept provided by SAP is an integration platform. SAP is therefore supported by the big software providers. In terms of placing the focus on business processes and protecting previous investments, SAP fully meets today's software development requirements. The service-ori-

---

10 See Woods: *Enterprise Services Architecture.* pp. 80 f.

ented approach is a model that seems to answer the challenge of meeting the demand for innovation in companies that have reduced IT budgets.

This is supported by the fact that it is possible to cautiously (incrementally) install an ESA. Customers' and users' trust must not be affected by complicated and expensive release and maintenance politics. There should be no "big bang."

No Big Bang

However, some questions still remain unanswered. While "SAP NetWeaver" explains how SAP plans to realize these objectives (see Chapter 9 for more information), there are still some reasonable questions, which must be answered so that there can be cooperation based on mutual trust.

The Solution: SAP NetWeaver

Some of these questions involve the areas of security, test environments for cross-business processes, and rollback. Efficient management to administer the large number of Web services and to ensure quality must also be built up. Many of these Web services were permitted to have redundant functionality.

Open Questions

When these issues have been resolved, ESA could become a real success story, because with it SAP is providing a roadmap and a comprehensive concept that will promote the introduction of many successfully implemented products.

9 Technology

Integrating software applications lets you escape the problems of heterogeneous IT landscapes. SAP's NetWeaver technology platform addresses the challenges created by increasingly complex system architectures. SAP NetWeaver enables the integration of users, information, processes, and applications.

9.1 SAP NetWeaver Integration Platform

Integration has its roots in Latin, and roughly translates to "creating a unit" or "inclusion in a larger whole." For enterprises, the integration of software systems is more important now than ever before. Why? During the course of the past several years, many companies installed software systems to deal with a wide range of business challenges. Whether these were systems for handling internal processes or systems for integrating customers and vendors, they were all intended to automate process flows. Today nearly every enterprise has software that is capable of managing its core processes. Accordingly, IT departments are no longer faced with the challenge of implementing requirements from different user departments, but instead with the challenge of reducing growing system heterogeneity. This is especially true in four areas:

Heterogeneous IT Architecture

▶ Typically, each application has its own user interface, and users often operate with them in parallel. Many users find it complex and cumbersome to deal with these different user interfaces.

Requirements of the IT

▶ Coherent information is of crucial importance for enterprise decision-making processes. It is pretty much impossible to achieve reasonable data aggregation in a heterogeneous system landscape.

▶ The enterprise business processes are usually not limited to a single system, but instead distributed across multiple applications. For them to work across systems and enterprises, communication is required. Therefore, connecting the individual IT systems through defined interfaces is a major task.

▶ From the IT department's perspective, different application systems always mean different basic technologies as well. To keep the complexity to a manageable level, you should consider switching to a uniform platform as soon as possible.

How can an enterprise deal with the challenges of a heterogeneous system landscape? The ideal solution would be implementing a technology that reduces the number of interfaces on the user side, while also integrating the back-end systems: a system architecture with an integrated structure that reduces the complexity of IT landscapes.

Transitioning to a service-oriented IT architecture is a promising approach here. The development of Web services and their corresponding standards are major steps toward the integration objective.

9.2   The Integration Layers of SAP NetWeaver

Of course, none of these statements are new. There are already software solutions on the market for integrating interfaces both user side and technical architecture that enterprises are using to try to simplify their heterogeneous system landscapes. But these software systems differ in a critical area: They don't have an integrated overall architecture, but instead consist of individual products, each of which represents a standalone solution for all the discussed requirements above.

With the SAP NetWeaver integration platform, enterprises overcome the challenges of heterogeneity. SAP NetWeaver offers integration at the following layers: *people*, *information*, *process*, and *application*. Figure 9.1 shows the structure of SAP NetWeaver.

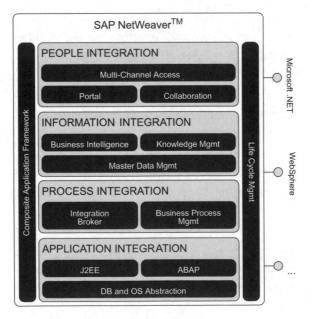

Figure 9.1 Overview of SAP NetWeaver

9.2.1 People Integration

People Integration is the top integration layer of SAP NetWeaver. It brings the functions of a software product to the users, who expect a single navigation platform despite the many different systems. Regardless of whether employees, customers, or suppliers are involved, each of them has role-specific access to the enterprise systems. A portal lets you integrate the functions from several software systems in a single user interface. It provides a single point of access for all sources of information and represents the front-end component for SAP NetWeaver. It is a uniform user interface that provides access to the applications involved in a business process. With its role-based content and its personalization function, the portal helps users concentrate on the data that is relevant for their day-to-day decisions.

SAP Enterprise Portal

The *collaboration* component of SAP NetWeaver supports intense collaboration between different partners. It consists of services that simplify communication and information exchange within business processes. Collaboration brings team members together regardless of time zone or geographical distances.

Collaboration

People integration works only when all participants have unrestricted access to the media, which requires *multi-channel access* to the IT systems. Access to the enterprise applications is thus possible regardless of the medium—either through an Internet portal or with a mobile device such as a cell phone.

Multi-Channel Access

The People Integration layer features all these alternatives for reducing complexity at the user layer.

9.2.2 Information Integration

The objective of *Information Integration* is to merge enterprise information for specific business processes from distributed, heterogeneous sources and supply it in a targeted manner, to supply business processes with the relevant data and increase their efficiency. The NetWeaver components at this integration layer provide integrated, targeted access to information. They represent an important step toward an integrated, enterprise-wide business process. One benefit of this is that business processes become more efficient because information delivery is optimized. Another is the potential of information integration for automating electronic business processes and making them more flexible.

SAP Business Information Warehouse

We differentiate between access to structured and unstructured information. The integration of structured information is best managed with a data warehouse. These systems are capable of accessing content from a wide range of databases, to consolidate and analyze it. They are the foundation for reliable reporting, and therefore for successful enterprise management. *SAP Business Information Warehouse* (SAP BW) is SAP NetWeaver's integrated data warehouse component.

Master Data Management

In this context, it becomes clear how important it is for enterprises to avoid problems with the inconsistency of structured data. When datasets are distributed among heterogeneous system environments, synchronization or consolidation of the most important data is required. To meet this requirement, you need centralized master data management for customers, products, business partners, and so on. In SAP NetWeaver, this function is handled by *SAP Master Data Management* (SAP MDM).

Knowledge Management

Another frequently required function is the integration of unstructured data, such as, for example, Word, PowerPoint, Adobe PDF, or Web pages documents. It is this very information that you often need for your day-to-day work, and whose retrieval requires a large amount of time. The *Knowledge Management* (KM) functions of SAP NetWeaver help users structure information and supply it to the right target audiences.

9.2.3 Process Integration

Process Integration

Process Integration makes it possible to implement cross-system business processes, which you can define, control, and monitor. It involves primarily managing the interfaces that exchange data between the involved systems via XML-based communication. A wide range of services support the definition of scenarios, interfaces, and mapping rules.

Business Process Management

If you need to integrate processes across enterprise and application boundaries, you can use NetWeaver's *Business Process Management* (BPM) functions. It lets you graphically model, implement, and monitor complex process flows in an IT landscape, which generally involve processes between different business partners that are loosely coupled through a messaging scenario.

By integrating business processes with the NetWeaver components, you can significantly reduce the effort required for system modifications or architecture enhancements, therefore lowering your costs.

9.2.4 Application Integration

Most enterprises do not purchase all of their application software from a single vendor. This results in a wide range of IT technologies, whose combination results in a heterogeneous system landscape. The ideal solution would be to have one application server for all systems. The structure of the NetWeaver *Application Platform* lets you execute SAP programs written in ABAP or Java. As a result, enterprises can continue using their existing SAP applications, while at the same time program new applications in an open, standards-based development environment like J2EE.

Application Platform

SAP Web Application Server (Web AS) is the foundation for SAP NetWeaver and the software components that build on it. More importantly, the process applications from *mySAP Business Suite*, such as mySAP CRM, are based on this technology. Consequently, SAP Web AS represents the technological foundation for all SAP products.

SAP Web Application Server (Web AS)

The *Composite Application Framework* (CAF) in Web AS represents a development environment for a completely new generation of applications, xApps (cross-applications). The CAF provides the tools for creating this type of application, based on enterprise services.

Composite Application Framework

Solution Life Cycle Management (SLCM) is a key part of SAP NetWeaver. It provides the technology required for the entire life cycle of the solution, from implementation and operation to ongoing changes and upgrades.

Solution Life Cycle Management

9.2.5 Summary and Outlook

Enterprises have to promote the integration of software systems in order to regain control of complexity, costs, and innovation. The SAP NetWeaver integration platform fulfills these requirements by integrating the following areas:

► People (users), through a uniform user interface

► Information, through a data platform

► Processes, through an integration layer

► Applications, through a shared system base

The integration platform makes entirely new business processes possible. The composite applications were developed specifically to handle the requirements from operative business processes quickly, flexibly, innovatively, and cost-effectively.

In the following sections, the integration layers with their components are described and SAP software solutions are introduced.

9.3 People Integration

9.3.1 Market and Solution Requirements

Lack of Integration

Presently, the handling of business processes at an enterprise is characterized largely by the use of several computer systems for each process. This is surely the result of companies' long-lasting ambitions to install best-of-breed solutions in different areas such as customer or vendor management. Such systems are wonderful for covering single tasks. However, when cross-system business processes are needed, which is frequently the case today, the disadvantages of this strategy come to the fore. Users are forced to design their own integrated processes in the various systems. Therefore, this type of integration is also described as involving "human integrators" (see Figure 9.2).

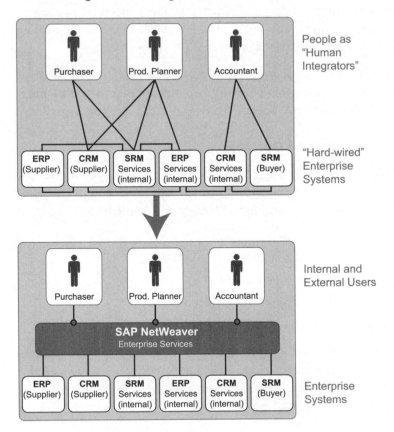

Figure 9.2 "Human Integrators"

Using human integrators contradicts our goal of simplified, and therefore faster, handling of business processes. Examining the technology required for this scenario, it becomes apparent that one central point is required for the integration: a layer that integrates the systems on the front end and supports people doing their jobs; an architecture that integrates people—*People Integration*. The SAP NetWeaver integration platform features the following products for people integration:

▶ *SAP Enterprise Portal* (EP) provides uniform, personalized, role-based access to heterogeneous IT environments.

▶ *Collaboration* with NetWeaver empowers communication between teams and communities, and contains virtual rooms and tools for real-time collaboration.

▶ The *SAP Mobile Infrastructure* (MI) makes it possible to connect to the back-end systems through speech, cellular, and radio technology.

The following section describes process handling with the People Integration layer, followed by an introduction to the individual components and their features.

9.3.2 SAP Enterprise Portal

Requirements from the User Perspective

The demand for technology that makes complex systems easier for people to use is well known. Consider the example of a car dashboard.[1] If you compare the displays with the complexity of a modern engine, it is clear that the dashboard "portal" represents a simplification. If you analyze the typical work patterns of office staff,[2] their required information sources can be divided into the following categories:

▶ *Application systems* such as SAP R/3 and their databases. The databases are also called *back-end systems*.

▶ *Unstructured documents* such as email, Internet or intranet documents, regardless of their storage location (for example, local hard drive or a central file server)

▶ *Analysis data* such as reports and KPIs, for example, from a data warehouse system

---

1 Compare to description in Woods, Dan: *Realtime: A Tribute to Hasso Plattner*. John Wlley & Sons Australia, 2004. pp. 233 ff.
2 Delphi Group, Nathaniel Palmer: *What functions should be included in a Portal software*. 2003. p. 34.

Depending on the interest group, the information requirements can be split up by customers, employees, suppliers, and partners. At this point, it becomes apparent that a portal has to meet the demands of several different user groups, and can therefore become the central access point for an enterprise's or organization's systems. Figure 9.3 illustrates the major requirements from a user perspective.

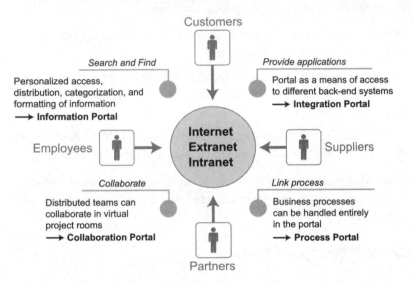

Figure 9.3 Portals—Requirements from the User Perspective

Requirements of the Technology

The appropriate technology is needed to meet the users' requirements. When comparing customer expectations with the manufacturer information, the components for a portal product can be summarized as the following:

▶ **Presentation**
Including display of Web-capable content on mobile devices

▶ **Navigation**
Portal user interface with different hierarchy levels

▶ **Personalization**
Assignment of role-specific content and portal settings

▶ **Integration**
Technology for integrating products from different vendors and connectors

- ► **Security**
  Authentication and single sign-on

- ► **Administration**
  Management of users, roles, and content

These are the most important components of a portal.

Presentation

The presentation of portal pages always depends on the presentation device used to access the portal. Depending on whether the display is on a PC or a mobile device, the portal server composes the pages and displays them in accordance with the user profile.

The content is displayed in the SAP Enterprise Portal using *iViews*. iViews are small Java or .NET applications that integrate information from a wide variety of sources—including ERP applications, databases, and HTML pages from the Internet—and display them as text, numbers, tables, and charts. Therefore, an iView represents the smallest unit of information in the portal. You can use containers to group several iViews together. A portal page can contain several containers with the corresponding iViews.

<aside>iViews</aside>

When defining iViews, it is essential to determine which ones support the user's process. In this context, SAP offers a variety of preconfigured iViews that you can adapt to your customer processes.

Navigation

In the future, the portal will be the interface for all users' applications. SAP Enterprise Portal renders this desktop according to ergonomic aspects such as usability and user-friendliness. Many user interface design experts were involved in the development of SAP Enterprise Portal. Both the appearance and navigation of the interface have been designed according to the latest findings in ergonomics research.

<aside>Ergonomics</aside>

From the user perspective, portal navigation is very important. To simplify navigation in a portal, it has to be modeled at different levels of a logical structure. Starting from the top-level navigation (see Figure 9.4), the user sees the higher-level content areas such as purchasing, sales, or marketing. Second-level navigation then represents the specific content for the levels (for example, the display of product information or customer information for sales). The detail navigation can be used to display content for product groups, for example, in the product information area.

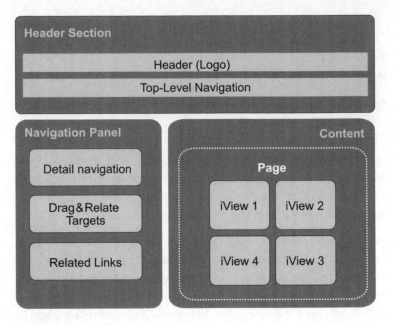

Figure 9.4 Portal Desktop

Personalization

Personalization
of the
Portal Interface

The process of configuring the portal interface is called "personalization." Each user defines what content he or she wants to see in the portal (subject to the respective authorizations) and how to display it. We differentiate between three layers in SAP EP:

1. Assignment of preconfigured content based on the user role. The assignment can be based on user analyses, or job profiles can be used to model the portal content.

2. Users can customize the appearance of the portal interface, such as page layout and font size. They can also display and hide entire subscreens.

3. SAP Enterprise Portal uses iViews to display the information, which can also be personalized by displaying or hiding information.

Integration

A portal installation aims to integrate systems, applications, and information for handling business processes. SAP EP supports several technologies for promoting integration.

SAP's unification technology is one method for combining data from different source systems. Unification in the portal context means homogenizing the content from different applications (such as Oracle, PeopleSoft, or Siebel), rendering them useable for an integrated process. The portal's Drag&Relate function enables portal navigation based on unification. The required data is taken from the databases of the application systems and displayed in an iView. Users navigate in the portal without knowing the source of the data, enabling them to concentrate on the content. The portal simplifies navigation and gives users the impression they are working in a single system, as emphasized in the following example:

Unification

A customer needs information about her order. A clerk retrieves the customer's data from the CRM system and displays her orders. The clerk clicks and drags the requested order number from one iView to another, which displays the data from a logistics service provider. The delivery status information appears instantly. Another application case involves displaying customer data with the Drag&Relate function. During the course of his work, a salesperson is asked to provide the number of customers in each region. In this case, you can use the Drag&Relate function to determine the region-customer link (see Figure 9.4).

Drag&Relate Example

Another integration option is *eventing*, which involves communication between individual iViews at the portal layer—that is, the iViews exchange data with one another. In one example, clicking a customer data record in one iView triggers the display of additional information for that customer in another iView.

Eventing

Security

Because portals are operated as customer, employee, supplier, or partner portals, depending on their instantiation, the access for different user groups has to be separated in a secure manner. You can configure an authorization concept to protect sensitive data against unauthorized access. The security mechanisms in SAP Enterprise Portal are described below.

To ensure secure communication between the user and the portal, as well as between the portal and the applications, encryption mechanisms are needed (cryptography). SAP EP supports common methods such as Secure Sockets Layer (SSL) and Secure Network Connection (SNC).

Secure Communication

Authentication mechanisms verify the authenticity, or genuineness, of persons and systems. Authentication is required to protect portal content

Authentication

against unauthorized access. Conventional procedures are based on a privacy principle, which means users log on to the portal with a user name and password.[3] Modern authentication methods utilize digital certificates based on the X.509 standard or external systems that support biometric processes.

Authorization   Authorization follows authentication and ensures that each user can access only the authorized portal resources. The user is assigned a role, which defines the content the user is authorized to see in the portal and which authorizations he or she has. It also defines the appearance of the portal view and which functions are displayed in the navigation bars. In this context, we can also speak of a role-based authorization concept.

Single Sign-On   Single Sign-On (SSO) simplifies interaction with the application systems that are accessible through the portal. As soon as a user has been authenticated and assigned an authorization profile, information can be accessed from all the necessary systems. Please note, however, that the local authorizations in the individual applications cannot be overridden by the portal authorizations. In other words, even when logged on to the portal, users see only the information that they are authorized to see in the back-end systems.

The portal offers two procedures for SSO: it can log on to the individual systems using the SAP logon ticket, or it can log on to the systems automatically with a user name and password, a method that is also called *user mapping*. Both variants let you avoid repeat logons to the information systems once the user is authenticated in the portal.

Administration

The administration component in portals consists of central functions such as user management and role management.

User Management   User management refers to the tasks associated with creating, changing, and deleting user accounts. It does not always make sense to establish separate user management in the portal, however; instead, it is more effective to utilize existing data. The *Lightweight Directory Access Protocol* (LDAP) has established itself as the standard for user management. SAP Enterprise Portal supports this standard, enabling access to the central user data. One advantage of central user data storage is that it helps you avoid redundancy. This procedure also increases the security of portal systems enormously.

---

3   Basic authentication via HTTP.

In addition to portal users, the user role is another organizational instrument. Roles represent a collection of logically related content that is required for day-to-day work. The "Salesperson" role, for example, contains content for customers and products. We differentiate between the following elements to set up roles in the SAP Enterprise Portal:

▶ **Service**
A complex task. Several tasks can be grouped together to form worksets, for example, to display customer information.

▶ **Workset**
A collection of related services from one or more work areas, for example, for account management.

▶ **Role**
A package of one or more worksets that model a work area, such as the Sales Manager role.

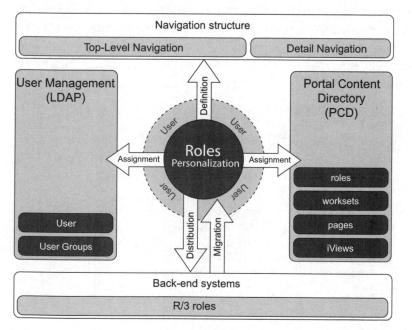

Figure 9.5 Role Management in SAP Enterprise Portal

The portal roles are saved in a hierarchical structure in the *Portal Content Directory* (PCD). All information regarding roles, worksets, services, iViews, and users can be managed with the PCD. The roles and their content are then assigned to the employees within user management in the portal (see Figure 9.5).

Business packages represent predefined, role-based portal content. A business package contains information and applications that are preconfigured for specific groups of users. For example, business packages are available for:

▶ **Manager Self-Service (MSS)**
Beginning with the tasks of a manager, the content—cost center accounting or employee management, for example—is put together.

▶ **Employee Self-Service (ESS)**
All of a user's administrative activities—such as leave notices, illnesses, and time recording—are provided in one central location.

9.3.3 SAP NetWeaver Collaboration Services

The communication between the individuals involved in a project or process is a critical, and can influence whether a deal succeeds or fails. Because the users of the application systems are often separated—organizationally and geographically—a shared collaboration platform is a huge benefit. The collaboration toolset developed by SAP is available everywhere in the portal through the *Collaboration Launch Pad* (CLP). These services can also be offered to members of a *Collaboration Room* (see Figure 9.6).

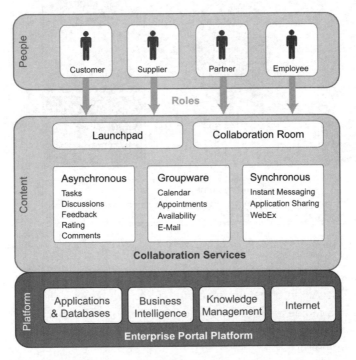

Figure 9.6 Portal with Collaboration Services

Collaboration Rooms

A Collaboration Room is a virtual room that a project team, for instance, can use as a work platform. Each user sees the rooms available for their specific authorizations. In this context, we differentiate between three types of Collaboration Rooms:

A *public room* is a room that is available to every portal user. It is generally used as an information and communication platform.

Public Room

It is also possible to configure a room with access restrictions. Although these rooms appear in the room overview, only authorized individuals are allowed to enter them. The room owner can invite users and manage authorizations in the *self-service mode*. This room category also permits differentiation between public and closed areas. Rooms can be used by project teams, for example, who only want to publish selected information (milestone documentation, and so on), while the actual work takes place in a closed area, which can be displayed in the room overview.

Self-Service Mode

The third concept involves the *private room*. A private room does not appear in the overview of available rooms. This means no information is published for non-members. The room owner must invite new members directly. You can use private rooms, for example, to edit confidential documents within projects.

Private Room

Collaboration Launch Pad

SAP has developed a central starting point for collaboration—the *Collaboration Launch Pad* (CLP), which gives direct access to the provided functions such as *instant messaging* or *application sharing*. The launch pad is designed to be an intuitive tool, and also lets you check and display the online availability of specific users. At the same time, the CLP has characteristics of both a start menu and a buddy list,[4] because the user's most important tools and contact persons are directly accessible. These tools can be provided by either SAP, customers, or third-party vendors, for example, if a customer has already hired an external provider for application sharing with external project team members. In this case, its services can also be recorded in the CLP.

Collaboration Launch Pad in the Portal

---

4 A buddy list contains all partners (such as colleagues and customers) that have registered for the Collaboration Service. As soon as a user logs on, the other participants receive notification of their status.

Third-Party Integration

SAP NetWeaver Collaboration is useful to customers who want to set up a communication and collaboration platform. It also lets you use existing products from third-party vendors. The following two components are available for integrating third-party products:

▶ Integration with groupware solutions such as Microsoft Exchange and Lotus Domino

▶ Integration of real-time service providers such as WebEx. This service permits portal users to exchange information with non-portal users.

9.3.4 SAP NetWeaver Multi-Channel Access

Mobile
Computing

The rapid technical developments in mobile computing are providing entirely new possibilities for business applications. SAP NetWeaver offers additional ways of accessing the systems, in addition to the familiar methods such as the Web browser and SAP GUI (SAP Graphical User Interface). Two major areas to watch for in the future are access via speech-controlled systems (voice access)[5] and *radio frequency identification* (RFID) technology. To enable mobile access, and thus *mobile business*, SAP NetWeaver is equipped with a *mobile infrastructure* (MI).

The Mobile Business Scenarios

Mobile business scenarios have to deliver specific benefits, not just flashy features. To guarantee this, it is important to analyze the enterprise processes and only then equip the most promising ones with mobile access. The following diagram shows four areas where mobile access can be useful (see Figure 9.7).

Collaboration
Scenario

Enterprises can use mobile technology to develop and supply new products and collaboration services for customers, partners, and suppliers. Potential lies in a shared mobile learning platform or mobile administration of editorial processes at a publishing house, for example.

Customer
Scenario

Solutions that focus on direct customer contact are very important in mobile scenarios. Direct (or indirect) access to customer data makes for faster, more efficient, higher-quality sales and consulting processes. Examples include *mobile sales* and *mobile services*.

Supply Chain
Scenario

The speed at which inquiries are processed is very important in a wide range of industries. Mobile scenarios can be used in production and logis-

---

5 Speech-controlled access is possible with third-party products.

tics. Current purchasing data, stock levels, and delivery quantities support the tasks along the enterprise supply chain. In another possible application case, mobile devices can be used to accelerate maintenance of machinery and process-critical assets such as logistics conveyor systems.

Employee Scenario

Mobile applications give employees entirely new ways to access IT systems. An enterprise consultant can enter a trip report and release it for further processing, for example, or an account manager can run a report of current customer sales.

As shown, mobile scenarios can be used in various ways to handle business processes more effectively. For a mobile application to communicate seamlessly with the back-end systems, it requires a corresponding technical infrastructure, which is described in more detail below.

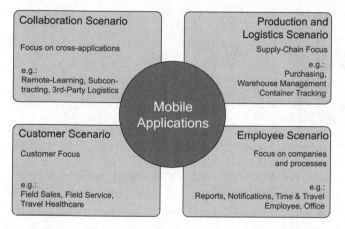

Figure 9.7 Mobile Business Scenarios

SAP Mobile Infrastructure

Mobile Infrastructure (MI)

SAP Mobile Infrastructure (SAP MI) is the foundation for mobile scenarios and an extension to SAP Web Application Server (Web AS). We differentiate between two connection types for mobile devices: *connected* and *disconnected* mobile architecture.

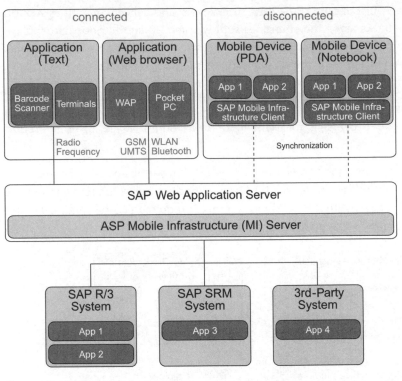

Figure 9.8 SAP Mobile Infrastructure

Connected Infrastructure

A *connected* architecture is one that links the mobile device directly with SAP Web AS through a browser, and is not dependent on the mobile infrastructure. The data in the back-end systems is accessed in real time. In this mode, WAP- (Wireless Application Protocol) capable cell phones and pocket PCs can communicate with one another via a WLAN/Bluetooth connection or a cellular network such as GSM/UMTS. In the connected infrastructure, the mobile device does not require synchronization, because it is connected to the server continuously. This is the fastest, easiest way to access information.

Disconnected Infrastructure

SAP Mobile Infrastructure features a platform-independent framework for disconnected communication with mobile applications. Mobile devices such as handheld computers or personal digital assistants (PDAs) have a client-specific installation of SAP Mobile Infrastructure. It is capable of executing transactions without a network or wireless connection. As soon as the client is reconnected with the SAP MI server, the data is synchronized and any changes to the datasets are updated. The greatest challenges in a disconnected scenario are data synchronization and the limited memory available on mobile devices.

If mobile applications cannot display a graphical interface, SAP MI supports a conversion to the respective text language. In this context, we typically speak of radio-frequency (RF) devices such as bar code scanners and mobile, text-based terminals.

The MI Client Component

The mobile infrastructure for the mobile devices features a platform-independent, Java-based environment, which makes it possible to run Java applications. The most important features of the infrastructure are:

SAP MI Client

▶ It enables secure, packed data transfer between client and server based on HTTPS with a 128-bit RDS method and zip algorithm.

▶ Data synchronization occurs between client and server. Synchronization guarantees the latest data and freedom from redundancies on the client and back-end systems.

▶ A local database on the mobile device enables access to the business data without requiring a server connection.

The MI Server Component

The server component of the mobile infrastructure is an extension of the SAP Web Application Server. The two primary tasks it performs are:

SAP MI Server

▶ **Client deployment and administration**
Mobile applications are transferred to the presentation devices automatically during synchronization. This process is controlled and administered centrally by a function in the deployment integration layer. System administrators can configure various settings.

▶ **Synchronization**
During the synchronization process, the mobile device communicates with the synchronization integration layer of the SAP Mobile Infrastructure Server. A variety of tools are available for administrators to monitor the data exchange.

Developing Mobile Infrastructure Applications

The mobile business scenarios introduced in this section are applications that have been implemented using standard software. The following options are available to adapt these processes to specific enterprise requirements:

MDK

- ▶ **Customizing**
  Modification of system parameters

- ▶ **Personalization**
  Adjust the user interface based on the mobile device

- ▶ **Modification**
  Adapt the SAP program objects to the process requirements

- ▶ **Enhancements**
  Customer developments as an add on to the standard processes

- ▶ **Customer development**
  Proprietary customer development based on the mobile infrastructure

The platform for developing mobile scenarios is the *SAP Mobile Development Kit* (MDK), which features a large set of tools and comprehensive documentation. It is also possible to use *SAP NetWeaver Developer Studio* (NWDS) to develop mobile scenarios. The tool also features a graphical programming interface to support the software development process.

9.4 Information Integration

Information is one of the most important factors of production for an enterprise. It represents the foundation for optimized control of the production process, and thus plays a decisive role in achieving defined enterprise goals. The following sections describe today's management information system (MIS) requirements and explain how the functions of SAP NetWeaver meet these requirements.

9.4.1 Market and Solution Requirements

In the past, several IT approaches failed to meet the high demands of an MIS completely, or even at all. Simply put, an MIS is a system for supplying the information that management decisions are based on.

Information Glut and Information Deficit

Today, many decision-makers spend the majority of their time collecting, preparing, and disseminating information, yet they still feel insufficiently informed. While they're faced with a glut of data and information, there is a deficit of truly useful information. There is apparently a shortage of suitable information systems that filter the ever-growing inundation of information and provide it in the exact method and format that managers need to support their decision-making processes.

The first MIS approaches failed miserably in the late 1970s, and it was a long time before the first truly usable variants of the MIS concept were established. The past failure was due mainly to the fully integrated systems of the time, which were highly inflexible and could only be modified with great difficulty. Performance left much to be desired, and a suitable graphical user interface for uniform navigation was lacking. At the time, MIS projects were heavy on the IT, but neglected the necessary business modeling. Ultimately, a great deal of data was collected in databases, but could not be used to generate any consolidated information.

Decision-makers rely on information systems that support decisions, and are therefore strategically important. Enterprise managers must be given access to systems that can provide intelligent, targeted consolidation and analysis. These systems should be easy to use and provide for optimal presentation of the gathered information. In addition, this collected, decision-relevant knowledge has to be channeled, structured, and intermixed. After all, only formatted information is tangible and usable for an enterprise.

Information Systems Have Strategic Character

The main problem today is the variety of enterprise systems that contain this decision-relevant information. The main challenge in merging this decision-relevant information is achieving the vertical and horizontal integration of these information systems. Figure 9.9 illustrates this problem.

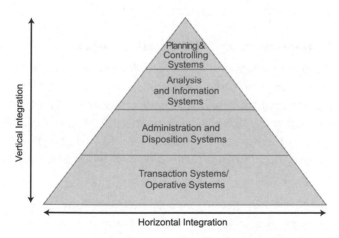

Figure 9.9 Vertical and Horizontal Integration of Information Systems

Managers need information from various levels of the enterprise hierarchy, and have to process it to get specific results. If no integrated information system is available, they will have to retrieve the information from the various systems themselves. They (or more accurately, their assistants) log on to the different operative systems, such as an accounting system to

Local Data Collection versus Integrated Information Systems

retrieve a P&L report. They also require planning data, but it is saved in a separate planning system. This information has to be formatted in Excel and then saved somewhere where it can be accessed in future.

This process is complex and time-intensive, and offers many opportunities for mistakes: manual report preparation can result in transposed digits, while locally created reports cannot be adjusted automatically to the current dataset. Instead, the data has to be entered in the reports again manually. In most cases, combining and accessing data from different operational areas requires a large technical effort. The IT department has to render assistance in such cases, because the users do not have the required skills, nor can they be expected to as decision-makers. Ideally, they will be able to retrieve the information quickly and independently, and spend their time interpreting this information, to make the right decisions to achieve the defined enterprise goals.

OLTP versus OLAP In the operative systems, the data is usually stored in relational database management systems (RBDMS), which are primarily suited for running transaction-based enterprise processes with large data volumes. They are sometimes also called *online transaction processing* (OLTP) systems. In most cases, you must write a specific program to analyze this data. From an analytical perspective, the data has to be stored multidimensionally to enable access.

Management Requirements of an Information System

Data Warehouse As Analysis Tool An MIS requires a separate data warehouse, where the relevant data from the entire enterprise value chain can be extracted, using ETL (extraction, transformation, and loading) tools, and stored as analysis-capable information. Multidimensional database management systems are usually involved. This type of data storage is generally used for the analytical, report-based processing of information with *online analytical processing* (OLAP) systems.

The process is complicated by heterogeneous, non-compliant systems that require master data cleansing to obtain a uniform enterprise data basis (a uniform master data management).

Flexible Integration of External Data Sources In addition to this internal data environment, which largely models the individual enterprise areas, managers also need data from a wide range of external sources (such as the Internet) for additional analysis and comparison. It can involve both structured and unstructured information (documents, for example).

Managers have to design transparent business processes and analyze the enterprise results for specific targets. To do so, they needs suitable instruments (analytical applications) to analyze the collected information independently of outside help. This makes it possible to optimize and improve the business processes through actions derived from the analysis process.

Simple Data Analysis Tools

Aside from the world of current data, managers also need planning instruments that they can use to plan the individual business processes in the individual business areas, based on the collected data. They also need analysis instruments that can provide standard reporting functions, as well as specific analysis without undue effort.

Integrated Planning

Specialized data mining tools let managers investigate their data for unexpected dependencies, for example, creating ABC classes or determining frequency distributions. Benchmarking lists (such as competitor analyses) can be created from internal and external information. Direct comparison of internal KPIs with those of your competitors can help illuminate potential within your own value chain.

Data Mining and Benchmarking

It is becoming increasingly important for companies to make targeted use of enterprise knowledge to steer their business activities. Prepared information must be made available transparently and in usable form.

Knowledge Management

Once the relevant information has been prepared, managers need the suitable media for presenting it (spreadsheet programs, Web browser, portal, and so on). To present the relevant information, you must ensure that all the decision-makers involved in the value-adding process have access to all the relevant information, in order to optimize and improve the actions.

Portal As Uniform User Interface

In the past several years, several MIS systems have established themselves on the market, each with its own specific strengths, particularly simple graphical user interfaces and graphical analysis options. One major problem here, however, is the integration of the variety of different upstream systems (interface problems), especially the legacy systems.

As a result, many enterprises have developed a best-of-breed approach: Individual areas and departments have gone it alone and implemented a multitude of systems. The result is a collection of different information systems that aren't necessarily integrated in the enterprise landscape.

Best-of-Breed Approach

9.4.2 The SAP Solution

How can SAP NetWeaver satisfy the demands for a powerful MIS? What options does SAP NetWeaver give managers for finding the decision-relevant information easily and publishing it as needed, to make the generated knowledge available within the enterprise?

Information Integration The solution in SAP NetWeaver can be described as having the following components:

▶ Data integration and transformation

▶ Data analysis and planning

▶ Reporting and analyses

▶ Data cleansing

▶ Knowledge Management

People Integration The first integration layer, *People Integration*, also plays a decisive role in accessing the specifically formatted information. Within this integration layer, central access is provided through a uniformly designed, easy-to-use interface within *SAP Enterprise Portal* (SAP EP).

In addition to integration and data transformation, *SAP Business Information Warehouse* (SAP BW) also supports data analysis with various tools. The integrated planning functions in SAP BW are represented by *SAP BW-Business Planning and Simulation* (SAP BW-BPS). SAP BW and SAP BW-BPS are referred to as *Business Intelligence*.

The data cleansing that is required for optimum data quality is performed using *SAP Master Data Management* (SAP MDM). *SAP Knowledge Management* (SAP KM) is a solution that lets you access structured and unstructured information centrally through SAP Enterprise Portal. As a result, managers can access all the enterprise information within the uniform user interface through a single point of access.

In the following sections, the individual products are described in more detail, along with their interaction within the layers of SAP NetWeaver.

9.4.3 SAP Business Intelligence

Business Intelligence with SAP BW SAP's data warehouse solution provides the internal and external data that managers need to make the right decisions. This is supplemented by the integrated planning (BW-BPS) within SAP BW. Figure 9.10 shows the most important areas within SAP BW and their functions.

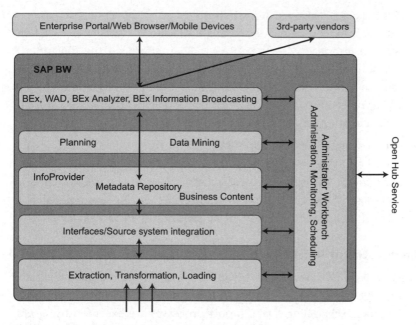

Figure 9.10 The Main Components of SAP BW

Extraction, Transformation, and Loading Processes

Extraction, transformation, and loading (ETL) tools let you import data into SAP BW from a wide variety of data sources through various interfaces, and transform, enrich, consolidate, and cleanse it in many different ways. Aside from the familiar BAPIs (Business Application Programming Interfaces) and functions for importing simple text files to BW, the following options are available:

ETL Process

▶ **DB Connect**

The DB Connect interface gives you direct access to relational databases. You can address Oracle tables directly, for example, and import their content into BW.

▶ **Universal Data Integration (UDI)**

The UDI, which is based on open standards, is another potential technique for enhancing the data import process. Its integration in SAP Web AS, through the J2EE platform, makes it possible to access a wide variety of source systems through a group of four Java-capable connectors (JDBC, XMLA, ODBO, and SAP Query connectors). Examples include almost all relational and multidimensional data sources. Therefore, access to third-party products such as *Hyperion* or *SAS* is also possible.

▶ **JDBC (Java Database Connectivity)**
SAP Web AS communicates through a Java UDC (universal data connection) interface with the ABAP-UDC interface on the BW side. A data source wizard is available for generating a data source with UDC. You can use this generated UDC data source to import the data into appropriate InfoProviders. More than 200 JDBC connectors are currently available for importing data to SAP BW.

▶ **SAP Exchange Infrastructure (SAP XI)**
SAP XI and Web services let you integrate additional data in SAP BW using the SOAP (simple object access protocol) service, which is an XML-based protocol for information exchange. An example of how data can be loaded through SAP XI is illustrated in Section 9.5.2.

Administrator Workbench

The *Administrator Workbench* (AWB) is the main tool for managing and controlling the SAP BW. You use it to monitor all the import processes and manage scheduling. Data import processes are executed using *process chains*. Large interdependent import processes are controlled using higher-level process chains (meta chains). Follow-on actions can be activated dependent on which events occur. Process chains can be scheduled and activated either by time-dependent events or triggered by events.

Multidimensional Data Analysis (OLAP) The AWB is used to define and structure all the data models that decision-makers can access with the various analysis tools. The decision-relevant data is loaded into *InfoProviders*. To facilitate the analysis process, this data is saved in multidimensional data models, to enable simple, flexible access. After all, the decision-makers who need this information should be capable of retrieving it themselves through the corresponding analyses.

The OLAP (online analytical processing) functions enable a multidimensional, conceptual perspective of the provided dataset. The *drill-down* functions enable users to "see through" decision-relevant data and examine it in a variety of ways. A user can navigate from an aggregated view to the detail levels until he or she has found an explanation for the problem or inconsistencies in the dataset.

The *metadata repository* can be considered the information system for SAP BW: it describes and explains all the objects within SAP BW centrally and demonstrates their interdependencies. It is important for BW users to know which objects are used in which InfoProviders, and how these objects are defined. Several thousand objects can be managed in the metadata repository, depending on its complexity.

One major advantage of SAP BW is its integrated *Business Content* (BC). SAP offers predefined models (both role-specific and task-specific) and components, based on consistent metadata, to support the entire data warehouse process from data extraction to analysis. BC is a predefined component of SAP BW that can be activated as needed and used immediately. BC supports the "rapid warehousing" approach, which lets you achieve initial results extremely quickly within a data warehouse project.

Business Content

In the BC context, SAP provides specific, preconfigured extractors (plug-ins) that you can install as add-ons to SAP systems. You can use these extractors to import both master data and transaction data to BW. Within BW, complete, preconfigured business models can be activated, including a wide range of reports that build on this model. Over time, more and more models have been developed in projects, together with customers, and are now available within BW as *Business Content*. These models can be used and adapted according to specific customer requirements.

Individual user access to the data in SAP BW is controlled through a detailed, role-based authorization concept. Existing authorizations can be transferred automatically from upstream R/3 systems, saving you from having to define them again in SAP BW. The authorizations within a cost center hierarchy, which are saved in detail in Cost Center Accounting in R/3, are an example of this. Special extractors are used to import this authorization information into the specific InfoProvider for this purpose. You can use this information to generate authorizations automatically in SAP BW. Authorizations in SAP BW are much different than the authorization concepts in the operative R/3 systems, however: While authorizations in these R/3 systems are transaction-based, the authorizations in SAP BW are defined more by analytical aspects.

Role-Based Authorization Concept

The *open hub service* makes it possible to integrate third-party products in SAP BW. You can trigger a process chain externally from a third-party product, which in turn imports the generated data extract into an Info-Provider on the BW side. An API (Application Programming Interface) can be used to access metadata and generated data.

Open Hub Service

Integrated Planning

The integrated planning component, SAP BW-BPS (SAP BW Business Planning and Simulation), gives decision-makers complex planning func-

SAP BW-BPS

tions that permit them to set up planning applications and scenarios without requiring SAP SEM (SAP Strategic Enterprise Management) to be installed.

A brief example will now illustrate the functions and possible procedure for integrated enterprise planning. You define a special planning InfoProvider in SAP BW with reference to the InfoProvider where the actual data is stored. The special feature of this planning InfoProvider is that you can write data back to it. Put simply, you can copy the actual data to the planning InfoProvider. Based on this actual data, the planning data can be moved to specific planning levels in the planning InfoProvider in Excel and saved. The new planning data is then available for reporting immediately. To enter the planning data, you can use the Web Interface Builder to generate a browser input template that can be integrated immediately in SAP Enterprise Portal, as an alternative to Excel. Users then log on to the portal and can use the input template to assemble the planning data for their enterprise areas, based on the actual data.

Controlling the Planning Process A status and tracking system is used to control the planning process. When combined with SAP Workflow, communication with all participants can be controlled through the planning status. Even complex planning scenarios, in which the planning data is first generated automatically using planning functions, are possible.

So far, we have discussed the alternatives for data import into SAP BW, and options for integrating the data in the data warehouse. But what possibilities do managers have for finding and reacting to undiscovered connections in their data?

Data Mining

SAP's data mining solution is the Analysis Process Designer (APD). It helps you explore and detect connections in existing data. You define an analysis process in a graphical user interface. In the process, one or more data sources are merged in individual steps, transformed using mathematical and statistical calculations, and prepared for further examination. You can then save this new data in the appropriate InfoProvider and analyze it. The determination of frequency distributions is just one example of a data mining application.

SAP Business Explorer

Reporting One of the most important functions in a data warehouse solution is the simple analysis of the integrated data and setup of a reporting framework.

The reporting framework supplies the decision-makers with information. The delivery medium needs to be flexible. In addition to conventional spreadsheet programs, such as Excel, the information should also be available through Web browsers or an enterprise portal. Different groups of recipients need different media to work with the information efficiently. Employees in the controlling area work mainly in Excel, and find the functions to format their information there. In contrast, a top manager who only occasionally uses information systems needs a central point of access, where he or she can log on once and then access all information centrally in the familiar user interface.

SAP Business Explorer (SAP BEx) is the umbrella term in SAP BW that stands for a variety of analysis tools that meet these requirements. The *BEx Analyzer*, *BEx Web Application Designer*, and *BEx Information Broadcasting* let you publish information via Excel, Web browsers, enterprise portals, and various mobile devices (PDAs).

BEx Analyzer

The BEx Analyzer is the conventional Excel application, supplemented with add-ins for the BW functions. You use it to call existing reports and present them in Excel. You can also use the *BEx Query Designer* to create new queries and reports, even if you don't have any programming skills at all: you simply access existing InfoProviders and use the Drag&Drop technique to create new reports. This function lets you create even extremely complex profitability reports, which you can also publish automatically on the Web.

The BEx Analyzer is also integrated in SAP Enterprise Portal. Any report created with the BEx Analyzer can be integrated in the portal instantly, making it available to a specific group of users.

BEx Web Analyzer

Simple, intuitive access to BW reports is also available with the BEx Web Analyzer. You can use a browser interface to log on via single sign-on (SSO), giving you access to the necessary reports. Special functions make the reports especially easy to use; you can save the data in a report with different charts, for example, which you can select from a dropdown box. Predefined functions in the user interface let you display additional information for the reports.

BEx Web Application Designer

The *BEx Web Application Designer* (BEx WAD) lets you develop demanding Web applications that you can integrate in SAP Enterprise Portal. Web items (radio buttons, dropdown boxes, graphics, tables, and so on) are linked with the appropriate elements from the reports, which were created with the *BEx Query Designer*. To format them, you can use a *cascad-*

ing style sheet (CSS) that corresponds to your corporate identity. The *BEx Web Application Chart Designer* lets you create demanding charts and graphics within a Web application and start them from within the BEx Web Application Designer. The design of the business graphics is wizard-based—you are prompted step by step through the definition process. As soon as the last step is complete, the chart is generated automatically.

Please note the following regarding graphics: Previously, the *Internet Graphics Server* (IGS), which only ran on Windows systems, was required to deliver the graphics on the Web. This function was integrated in SAP Web AS in SAP BW 3.5, which means you can forgo the IGS completely. Beforehand, however, all the graphics that were developed using the IGS have to be migrated to the new platform before you can shut down the IGS permanently and simplify your system landscape.

BEx Information Broadcasting

Until now, information from SAP BW was called by BW users through reporting. A completely new function for forwarding and distributing information outside an enterprise is BEx Information Broadcasting. This function requires SAP Enterprise Portal with Knowledge Management (KM), which was described in Section 9.3.2. BEx Information Broadcasting transforms existing Web reports and reports from the BEx Query Designer, and distributes them in a variety of ways. KM functions can also be used. The preliminary reports can be saved as KM documents or provided as KM links for online reporting. In the process, the reports are scheduled and updated to recalculate the data. The reports are published in the portal as KM documents, where they can be queried and used by properly authorized BW users.

Another option is a subscription service that lets you subscribe to specific reports for a specific period of time. When interregional teamwork is required, the reports can also be placed in Collaboration Rooms, where the authorized users have access to the reports and can discuss their content together.

The *BEx Broadcaster* can be called from the various SAP BEx analysis tools, to publish the reports in the various dialog views. You can also send the reports by e-mail.

When we consider the SAP BW functions listed above, we could come to the conclusion that SAP BW represents a data warehouse within SAP NetWeaver that more than fulfills the requirements of an MIS. Comprehensive data formatting and delivery tools can access all the data that is important for the decision-making process. The integrated planning functions let you implement a wide range of planning scenarios. In addition, users are given a powerful analysis tool for generating a wide variety of reports and sending them to the addresses through various media.

9.4.4 SAP Master Data Management

The most important functions of SAP BW were described in Section 9.4.3. To make the right decisions, however, you need to have the correct data quality within the controlling system. A simple example illustrates the problem:

Enterprise growth—resulting from acquisitions or joint ventures—creates a homogenous IT infrastructure consisting of a number of different systems. After an enterprise-wide controlling system is implemented, you discover that the definition of the *vendor* business object is not consistent between sites. However, a globally standardized view of vendors is essential to streamlining and optimizing the purchasing process. If the individual subsidiaries of an enterprise group negotiate separately with the same vendor, the results will be far from optimal, but a central negotiation view is not possible due to the differing master data of the *vendor* business object. Because the business object is not integrated uniformly in the enterprise's business processes, wrong decisions can be made.

Inconsistent Data Between Systems

SAP Master Data Management (SAP MDM) is used for consolidating, harmonizing, and/or centrally integrating the master data at the enterprise in the above example. These three functions are performed on the master data server. Figure 9.11 shows the master data server and other main components of SAP Master Data Management.

The MDM Concept

The main components of SAP MDM are:

▶ Master data server
▶ SAP Content Integrator
▶ SAP XI
▶ SAP MDM adapters

The *master data server* (MDS) is the target system for data transfer and consolidation. The master data is defined and maintained here. The MDS also distributes the cleansed master data to the upstream systems or SAP BW.

Master Data Server

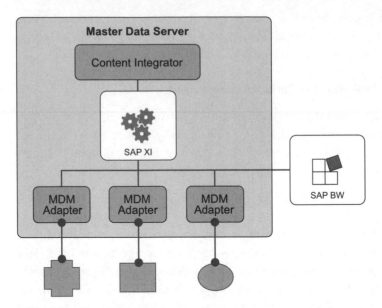

Figure 9.11 Primary Components of SAP Master Data Management

SAP Content
Integrator

The *SAP Content Integrator* (CI) performs consistency checks of the master data on the MDS. It also manages ID mappings. If the CI detects identical master data with different attributes, a *CI group ID* is generated and appended to the master data as an attribute, guaranteeing complete data access.

SAP XI

SAP XI is responsible for ensuring communication between all the involved systems.

SAP MDM
Adapters

SAP MDM adapters link all the systems from which master data is imported to SAP MDM for data cleansing, or *master data clients* (MDC). They are also used to distribute the cleansed master data to the MDCs.

The scenarios below introduce the three options for master data cleansing that are available in SAP MDM. The interaction between the major components of SAP MDM is also described in detail. The individual scenarios in SAP MDM are built on one another and illustrate the possibilities for enterprise-wide master data management, which is essential for enterprise-critical controlling. After all, consistent data is required to achieve a uniform view of the entire enterprise.

Master Data Consolidation

Consolidation of the master data from the different upstream systems detects identical master data records in a first step and may cleanse them instantly. The various upstream systems are connected to SAP MDM through the SAP MDM adapters. The master data is uploaded to SAP MDM from the upstream systems. The *content integrator* (CI) automatically starts consistency checks to detect identical or duplicate objects. When identical master data records are found, the CI creates a standard CI group ID. In the consolidation scenario, no master data is saved physically on the MDS; the *CI group ID* information is available, and can be imported into SAP BW through various data sources using one of two processes:

In the *pull process*, the data upload from SAP BW is triggered by the data sources. The data is uploaded to the *delta queue* in SAP BW and then processed with the master data.

Pull Process

If you want the data to be placed in the delta queue automatically, you use the *push process*, in which SAP XI takes care of automatic distribution to the delta queue. The appropriate processes for processing the data further are defined and scheduled on the BW side.

Push Process

By implementing enterprise-wide object type attributes as CI group IDs, you create a standardized view with SAP MDM without changing the master data in the upstream systems. Distributing the object type attributes to SAP BW lays the foundation for uniform, standardized reporting.

Master Data Harmonization

Consolidation of enterprise master data in SAP MDM and forwarding it to SAP BW are not always sufficient for enterprise-wide data cleansing. In addition to SAP BW, the subsidies of an enterprise group also need the cleansed master data on-site. For this reason, the cleansed master data has to be transferred back to the upstream systems. The procedure is similar to that of consolidation, with the exception that globally defined master data is saved on the MDS in addition to the CI group ID information. This global master data is generally valid in all subsidiaries. The harmonized global master data is distributed to SAP BW analogously to the consolidation process.

In addition, the harmonized global master data is also distributed to the upstream systems, using the distribution queuing and format conversion functions in SAP XI. Moreover, the subsidiaries can assign regional or industry-specific attributes to the globally valid master data in their respective systems. As a result, in addition to SAP BW, all the upstream systems that are connected to SAP MDM are supplied with harmonized master data.

Central Master Data Management

The last SAP MDM scenario describes the centralized solution for master data management in SAP MDM. Whereas the globally defined master data is loaded from the connected upstream systems to SAP MDM in the harmonization process, in this last scenario all the enterprise master data is maintained centrally in SAP MDM. The centrally maintained master data is then distributed to the upstream systems, like in the harmonization process. There is hardly any regional maintenance of the master data at all.

In the previous sections, we described how structured data can be supplied to the decision-makers at an enterprise with a certain level of quality in a certain way. The proportion of structured data is relatively low compared to the overall data volume required. The remaining data is available in unstructured form: documents, e-mails, and Web content. But how can this critical unstructured data be integrated in an MIS so decision-makers can access and process it without problems?

SAP's solution to this problem is SAP Knowledge Management (SAP KM).

9.4.5 SAP Knowledge Management

As mentioned previously, making targeted use of enterprise knowledge plays an important role in enterprise decision-making processes. The knowledge that employees acquire over time has to be rendered transparent, yet usable at the same time.

What possibilities does SAP KM offer? How can you integrate the various knowledge resources in enterprise workflows?

You access SAP KM through *SAP Enterprise Portal* (SAP EP). The central point of access in the portal provides role-based access to all the unstructured information saved in SAP KM. A generic framework lets you integrate unstructured information that employees have collected from a wide variety of sources for access in SAP KM. Various functions within SAP KM let you retrieve, edit, and distribute this information.

The most important functions in SAP KM are described below, showing:

▶ How data can be integrated (data integration)
▶ How data can be processed (data processing)
▶ How data is accessed (data access)

A specific example will then illustrate how SAP KM works.

Data Integration

Frequently, the most relevant information is spread around the various file systems at an enterprise. This information is integrated and accessed in KM using *repository managers*. The *repository framework* is responsible for physical storage of the information, for example, documents can be saved in virtual hierarchies.

The integrated documents can be classified in different ways, for example, by content or organizational aspects. This is done using TREX (*Text Retrieval and Information Extraction*), the integrated search and classification engine for KM. A hierarchy structure of categories used to classify documents is called a *taxonomy*. One particularly important feature is that the documents for classification can be saved in different repositories, for example, documents involving orders from different vendors that were previously filed by month. These documents can now be saved in KM and sorted by purchasing department, creating structures that help users find their way around more effectively.

Classification

Generally, every authorized KM user can create information and integrate it in a KM folder in KM, making it available to others. A memo regarding a certain problem, which an employee writes on a local PC, can be integrated in KM immediately. Users can also save information in KM directly, using a Web browser and the appropriate forms. To facilitate retrieval of this information, the documents can be assigned various attributes, which can be filtered during the search process.

To prevent every user from publishing information immediately, you can configure an approval workflow in which a document is reviewed and released by a superior. Similarly, documents that have already been checked in can be downloaded to a local PC, edited, and integrated again. Lastly, you can use the BEx Broadcaster to publish preliminary reports from SAP BW or links to queries in KM.

Approval Workflow

Data Processing

The *Content Management Service* in KM contains various functions that you can use with the saved information. You can define subscriptions, for example, that are valid for a certain period of time. For example, you can place profitability reports from controlling in KM that are to be supplied to a certain group of people at regular intervals, for evaluation or for soliciting personal notes, for a specific period.

Data Access

Any employee can access any folder in the repositories through the portal interface, provided he or she has the necessary authorization. You search for information using a conventional search engine. The system searches all the repositories that the user is authorized to read. In addition to the search options, the user can also specify keywords to search in the information attributes. TREX automatically groups the classified information together into taxonomies. One of the main tasks is the integration of internal and external information through the repository manager.

Example Mr. Smith is an employee at an automotive supplier. In the coming months, he will be working on a project team responsible for developing a new locking mechanism for the door of a new car model. To perform his daily work, Mr. Smith logs on to the portal, which gives him easy access to all the functions he needs.

Mr. Smith's colleagues have prepared initial design reports that he must review, but he's forgotten the folder names. The search function is available to retrieve the documents. Although Mr. Smith is a terrible typist, a fuzzy search helps him find the right ones. Now that he has reviewed the design, he can write his report. To do so, he needs supporting material from cost accounting, so he searches for cost reports from controlling. He needs this information for various cost efficiency analyses.

Once he has written his report, Mr. Smith has his superior approve it and place it in the project KM directory. Here, Mr. Smith's colleagues can add their personal notes to the report. Accordingly, the portal can be used to exchange unstructured information, and even allows employees from other subsidiaries to participate online.

9.4.6 Outlook

The integration of information from the *business intelligence* area will continue to increase in importance. If an enterprise does not have access to the decision-relevant information, whether structured or unstructured, it cannot be managed optimally. In the coming years, it will become increasingly important to be able to retrieve all the relevant information quickly through a uniform user interface. The integration of unstructured information, to make employee knowledge available to the enterprise, is increasingly critical.

Knowledge Is Power
: The *knowledge society* has been the subject of much attention in the past. The eminent claim "*Knowledge is power*" is still valid today. Modern IT

systems such as SAP NetWeaver provide the technical foundation for successful knowledge integration and distribution. It is the organizations that use these systems that have to adapt their structures to the new situation. As soon as the possibilities and advantages of these new technologies are recognized, the NetWeaver concept can begin to bear fruit.

9.5 Process Integration

In the NetWeaver concept, process integration encompasses everything that assists the data flow between the individual systems. The main application is SAP Exchange Infrastructure (XI). While the SAP XI component is the functional successor to IDocs (Intermediate Documents, the standard format for exchanging data between R/3 systems) and the SAP Business Connector (a relatively new, XML-based tool for exchanging data between R/3 and non-R/3 systems) in SAP R/3 to a certain extent, it goes far beyond these solutions at the technical level. IDocs and the Business Connector were pure EDI (Electronic Data Interchange) solutions that exchanged data containers between systems. Therefore, we will examine the SAP XI components in more detail below.

SAP XI As Successor to the SAP Business Connector?

9.5.1 Market and Solution Requirements of an Exchange Infrastructure

To understand the market and solution requirements of enterprise application integration, you first have to consider the changed business environment. Whereas business processes were formerly modeled in parallel to the internal organizational structure, the focus now is more on customer processes. These processes no longer run in a single system, but instead are distributed across many different systems. A customer sales process is an excellent example of this new type of process. To execute it without any integration gaps, all the necessary information has to be available at the time of the sale, including:

▶ Stock levels of the desired products

▶ Pricing for the customer

▶ History of the customer

▶ Production planning data

▶ Credit standing check for the customer

To check all these items and execute the customer order, you need an IS (information system) architecture that enables direct access to the data in the respective subsystems involved in the sales process. SAP XI is just such an architecture.

Figure 9.12 illustrates how SAP Exchange Infrastructure establishes the connections between the individual systems.

One Defined Access Point for All Systems
As the diagram clearly shows, each involved company has one defined access point to the other systems (instead of building separate access points for each system), and it is always an XI system. The advantage of this solution becomes even more clear when we compare the previous approach (without XI) and the technology that is now available (with XI) in Table 9.1.

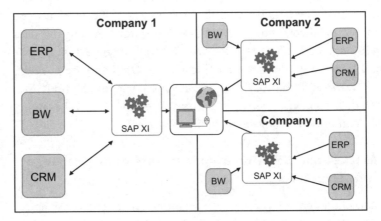

Figure 9.12 The Position of SAP XI in an Open Systems Group

Without XI	With XI
Most XI tools stem from third-party vendors.	The tools now come from the software vendors.
EDI was the previous standard.	XML, an open standard, is now used.
The tools were ERP-dependent.	XI is an independent, scalable application.
Mapping between the systems was static.	All systems at an enterprise are linked with each other through one platform.
The data format was tailored to the application.	Multiple adapters are available.
Most of the mapped relationships were n:m.	Through system reduction (1:n), connections have better performance, synopsis, and security.
Data transfer was usually asynchronous (batch).	Synchronous (online) data transfer is now possible.

Table 9.1 Comparison of System Connections with and without XI

During the transformation from an EDI environment to XI, enterprises face the following challenges:

▶ Integrating the internal applications in XI
▶ Querying from external applications in XI

Integration of Internal Applications

Enterprises want to link all their applications with one another in a central system quickly and cost-effectively, to exchange data and information online. This development is called *internal process integration*. To implement it, you need a coordinated procedure that precisely determines which system within a process is integrated with which other systems.

Fast, Cost-Effective Integration

Accordingly, the requirement of an IT solution is to provide as many *connectors* as possible, to link the systems together. A connector is a piece of software that establishes connections between two systems, without requiring any major programming modifications, based on general interface descriptions.

The advantages of connecting systems include:

▶ The use of a hub architecture reduces the number of interfaces and point-to-point connections
▶ The use of mapping rules in a central instance reduces data inconsistencies
▶ Synchronous processing and control through a single platform increases process speeds

Integration of External Applications

Another relevant feature is that *business process management* (BPM) can also integrate data about the process itself and its logic. This was possible in the EDIFACT standard, but only at the technical (field) level. It is required to execute business processes quickly, completely, and seamlessly in real time.

Business Process Management

Accordingly, the requirement of the IT solution is: A minimum number of simple, non-application-specific interfaces from the EAI (enterprise application integration) has to suffice to connect all the data from third-party systems flexibly and securely.

The advantages of this type of connection:

▶ By connecting the data directly through the business process, you can access other companies' data directly

▶ The business process runs in all involved systems without any interruptions

▶ An EAI component represents a single, defined point of access to the enterprise, eliminating the maintenance of n different access points.

Connect New Systems Without Changing the IS Architecture In the past, whenever you integrated a new system, you had to adapt the interfaces in n other systems. The attraction of an XI solution: to connect new systems, you no longer have to review or modify the IS architecture at your company. Instead, all communication takes place through SAP XI.

9.5.2 SAP Exchange Infrastructure in Detail

SAP Exchange Infrastructure (XI) consists of two main components (also see Figure 9.13):

▶ Shared collaboration knowledge

▶ Execute collaborative business processes

Both components are needed to configure, maintain, and operate an XI landscape.

We will first examine the configuration of the XI system.

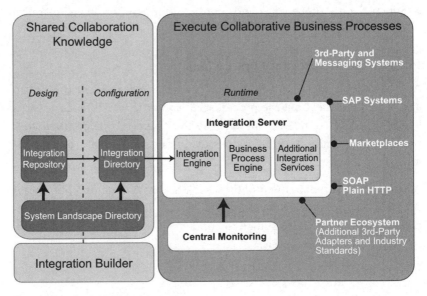

Figure 9.13 The SAP XI Architecture

260   Technology

Shared Collaboration Knowledge

The *shared collaboration knowledge* area serves to configure SAP XI. It contains the following components:

▶ System Landscape Directory

▶ Integration Repository

▶ Integration Directory

All these components are managed with one central tool, the *Integration Builder*. The Integration Builder is a Web-based tool that runs in the Enterprise Portal (and does not use a conventional SAP GUI interface). You use it to successively perform all the necessary configuration steps, which are described for each individual component below.

The *System Landscape Directory* describes all the systems (SAP, non-SAP, Web services, and so on) within an enterprise, as well as the systems (SAP, non-SAP, Web services, and EAI systems) at partner enterprises. It defines what kind of system is involved, which message types and exchange parameters exist, and how the communication works.

System Landscape Directory

As a result, each system only has to be defined once in the system landscape and can then be used in all XI-based integration scenarios.

The *Integration Repository* is the central repository within an XI landscape. It contains the knowledge for all existing business objects (such as business partners, for example), and knows the source system of each object. SAP provides a wide range of Business Content in this area—predefined business objects from SAP applications that can be used "out of the box." As such, there are predefined objects for each SAP system that can be addressed via IDoc, RFC (Remote Function Call), or BAPI (Business Application Programming Interface), which you can use almost immediately.

Integration Repository

Therefore, the main task in setting up an XI landscape involves the Integration Directory, to ensure that every business object is defined exactly once and that the data flow between the systems utilizes the correct business objects.

In the second step, you configure the *Integration Directory* with the connections between the systems and the objects defined in the Integration Repository, using mapping rules that you can define graphically. Mapping rules describe how objects are connected between systems. When you create them, you can define precisely how the data flow will take place and whether processing will be synchronous or asynchronous.

Integration Directory

The attraction of this centralized variant: when changes are made in the source system, you only have to change the object references in the Integration Repository; the Integration Directory is not affected.

Execute Collaborative Business Processes

The second area in SAP XI is the runtime environment. It establishes the connections to the systems specified in the *System Landscape Directory* (SLD), using the mapping rules from the Integration Directory. The Integration Server is the central element within the runtime environment. It consists of the following components:

▶ Integration Engine

▶ Proxy framework

▶ Adapter framework

▶ Runtime Workbench

▶ Business Process Engine

These components ensure that all the information required for a process is delivered where it is needed. In addition, the *Business Process Engine* provides for central integration in the *Composite Application Framework*, specifically with the xApps. For more information, see the section on the Business Process Engine later in this chapter.

Integration Engine   The *Integration Engine* is the runtime environment within the *Integration Server*. It consists of the individual components listed above and represents the centerpiece of a production XI environment. The engine is based on Web AS technology and primarily uses its standard interfaces, such as the SOAP adapter.

Proxy Framework   The *proxy framework* establishes communication between SAP XI (specifically, the Integration Engine) and SAP Web Application Server. The proxy framework is a Web AS component that is used by XI. It serves as an abstraction layer between SAP XI and the underlying technology.

A proxy framework is used here because it gives SAP XI a standard interface to SAP Web AS, regardless of whether J2EE (Java 2 Platform, Enterprise Edition) or ABAP services are executed on SAP Web AS. We should note that the proxy framework is the general component for accessing SAP systems that run on SAP Web AS. If non-Web AS systems are used (such as SAP R/3 4.6C and earlier), communication takes place using adapters, as described in the next section.

The *adapter framework* is an integrated component of the XI solution for connecting all relevant systems with one another. The following rules apply:

Adapter Framework

▶ If an SAP system based on Web AS 6.20 or later is involved, the proxy framework is used as a connection.

▶ If a connection is based on XML and the SOAP protocol, it uses the Web services framework, which is a native Web AS component.

▶ The adapter framework is used to connect all other applications.

Figure 9.14 illustrates the possible connections and indicates where the individual technologies are used.

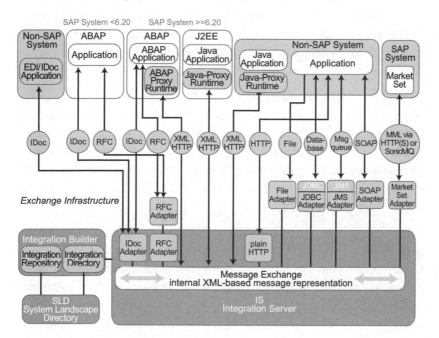

Figure 9.14 Adapter Framework of SAP XI 3.0

Adapters

There are three ways to connect systems to SAP XI, depending on which systems are involved. Each connection uses an adapter from one of the following groups:

▶ SAP-to-SAP adapter

▶ SAP-to-non-SAP adapter

▶ B2B adapter

All three connection types feature a variety of individual adapters. We will first examine the adapters that are used for SAP-to-SAP integration.

The SAP-to-SAP adapters include:

► IDoc adapter

► RFC adapter

The exchange of messages based on IDocs (Intermediate Documents) is a well-established method for exchanging information between SAP systems. The underlying technology is called ALE (Application Link Enabling), and nearly every SAP system uses this technique to exchange information with other systems. Common uses for ALE (IDoc) include connecting SAP systems to SAP BW and master data exchange between different SAP systems (cost center distribution between FI and HR, for example). You configure the IDoc adapter in the Integration Engine in SAP XI.

Exchanging data and messages using RFCs (Remote Function Calls) is another well-established method in the SAP environment. The underlying concept is that a program in one system calls a function module in another system, which processes a certain function (such as checking a delivery status) and reports this information back to the calling function module/program. Before a function module can support this, it must be made "remote-enabled."

A special application of RFC modules are BAPIs (Business Application Programming Interfaces). SAP defines a BAPI as a function that can not only be addressed from within SAP systems, but is generally available for all connected systems (such as office applications). Another difference between BAPI and RFC is that BAPIs are "guaranteed" to remain unchanged, while RFCs are subject to potential change at any time.

The RFC adapter in SAP XI is responsible for intermediating between the systems—that is, transforming inbound RFCs to XML messages and forwarding them to the Integration Engine. Similarly, it transforms XML messages from the Integration Engine into RFCs and forwards these outbound messages to the subsystems.

SAP-to-non-SAP adapters can be divided into the following categories:

► *File adapters* for reading files

► *JMS adapters* for addressing Java-based messages

► *JDBC adapters* for connecting to databases

- ▶ *HTTP adapter* for connecting to HTTP applications
- ▶ *SOAP adapter* for reading data from Web services

Many third-party systems, particularly older host systems, do not offer standardized interfaces. As a result, extracting the data in file form and connecting it individually to SAP XI is often the only possibility. A *file adapter* often represents the last possible option for integrating systems.

File Adapters

Many modern systems feature open messaging interfaces. Although such interfaces are not based on defined industry standards, their widespread use has given them a certain validity. One example is *MQSeries* from IBM. When a system that communicates using MQSeries message types is connected to SAP XI, a *JMS adapter* implements the connection. This JMS adapter converts inbound messages back to XML and is also capable of implementing Java-based mapping rules.

JMS Adapters

Using *JDBC adapters* is the best way to connect non-SAP systems with their own databases to XI. JDBC is the standard for connecting databases through Java means. The XML syntax that is used in this connection is also capable of forwarding specific database commands (such as SELECT, INSERT, and DELETE), and can therefore facilitate true process integration.

JDBC Adapters

The *HTTP adapter* is used for communicating with a Web application that does not use a database, or when database access is not possible. This adapter transforms the inbound message to XML and forwards it to the Integration Server.

HTTP Adapter

SOAP (simple object access protocol) is a pseudo-standard for exchanging XML-based data between systems. Almost all major software vendors now support it. Accordingly, the *SOAP adapter* is often the correct choice for integrating ERP systems with one another. The SOAP adapter is implemented in SAP Web AS, not in the XI system, as it has also been used by other applications (such as BW) for some time now.

SOAP Adapter

B2B adapters are those adapters required to connect SAP XI with other, EAI/EDI-based systems. It includes industry standard adapters such as *RosettaNet* (RNIF adapter) and *EDIFACT*.

B2B Adapters

The SAP environment also features the *Partner Connectivity Kit* (PCK), which lets you integrate smaller enterprises without their own XIs in an XI landscape, and is especially useful for connecting suppliers or smaller customers to existing XI systems.

Partner Connectivity Kit

Runtime Workbench

The *Runtime Workbench* within XI is an environment where you can monitor the active processes and intervene if there's an error. The Runtime Workbench is a graphical user interface that is also integrated in the *Solution Manager*. The individual steps are monitored here. It can even be integrated in the *ARIS Toolset for SAP NetWeaver*.

Business Process Engine

The *Business Process Engine* represents the main difference between the XI environment and other solutions available on the market. While conventional EAI (enterprise application integration) systems merely create a mapping between the fields in the corresponding systems, the Business Process Engine is capable of much more. It contains information regarding:

▶ Where the process is currently located

▶ Which Web (application) service is currently active

▶ Which functions a specific Web service offers

▶ Which of these functions are used at runtime

BPM As Central Control Medium for Business Processes

All this information helps to build, monitor, and optimize business processes across different platforms. Figure 9.15 shows the Business Process Engine in the XI context.

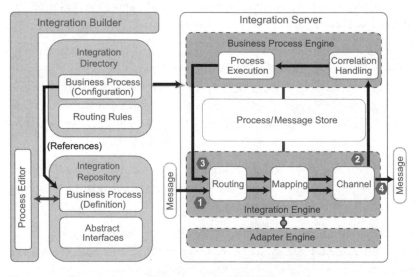

Figure 9.15 Business Process Management in SAP XI 3.0

In this diagram, the XI is divided into the *Integration Builder* (design) and *Integration Server* (runtime). However, the business processes are defined on both sides, in addition to the mapping rules.

But what does the implementation process look like? To explain, we need to review several facts from Chapter 8. This chapter described how an existing client/server architecture is changed such that each application provides its services as *application services*, which in turn are bundled to form *enterprise services*, creating new applications that combine these enterprise services within the *Composite Application Framework*. These "new" applications, which do not have any native data retention, are called *xApps* and are described in more detail in Section 9.7.

Because the xApps contain data, however, they have to use a uniform interface to access all enterprise applications and Web services within an enterprise and its associated partner companies. This interface is SAP XI.

xApps Also Use XI Technology (BPM)

The data flow shown in Figure 9.15 is divided into the following steps: SAP XI receives a message in step 1 (inbound). This message is processed by an adapter or through the proxy framework. It is distributed further using previously defined mapping rules (which were designed in the Integration Directory during the design phase) and passed on. In step 2, the data is passed on to the Business Process Engine, which maps the business logic and determines which business processes have to run. The engine knows which systems have to receive a message and what happens to it there. Because it also knows where the process is currently located, monitoring is possible.

Process Flow at System Runtime

If the engine decides that the process has to be forwarded to another system, the routing rules are passed again in step 3. Finally, in step 4, a new (outbound) message is created, and then processed again in the subsystem.

If we expand our focus somewhat, the following situation results: XI, combined with the Business Process Engine, will become the central component of an IT landscape in the long term, because all processes are designed and monitored there. This is then the responsibility of the *SAP Solution Manager* or ARIS for SAP NetWeaver.

To model a landscape like this, however, you need to have the right tools. SAP customers can decide whether they want to use the provided tools, most of which are based on the open *Eclipse* platform, or use a tool that is used widely in other areas, the ARIS Toolset for SAP NetWeaver from *IDS Scheer*. If you elect the latter, we recommend using SAP NetWeaver

ARIS and Solution Manager for Modeling the Business Processes

Developer Studio to define the mapping rules based on Eclipse first, and then modeling the business processes in ARIS in SAP Solution Manager.

Both tools enable you to define the processes, usually with one of the two approaches described below. The model is displayed in "swim lanes," in which each system is portrayed as a lane in a swimming pool. When a process is drawn in this model, the interaction and points of intersection between the systems are clear.

9.5.3 Summary and Outlook

As we learned in the previous sections, XI is more than just an EAI component. You often read in the press that XI is an integration solution, or even that XI is the same as NetWeaver.

XI Is More than EAI

As the previous section showed, however, XI can do much more than EAI. While it maps the physical data flow between all systems, it also does more—it transfers the data and additionally makes the process manageable in *Business Process Management* (BPM). The added value consists of the ease of manageability of processes. Moreover, you have to consider that XI is only part of SAP NetWeaver, as it models the process integration layer, an advantage that you should not underestimate.

Using BPM adds value to the XI solution, because it models the logical data flow between different systems in addition to the physical data flow. Combined with the graphical implementation models mentioned previously, you get an application that permits you to finally model end-to-end business processes.

Business Content As the Starting Point for an Implementation

The described solution may be too much for many customers to handle, however—not understanding the solution, mind you, but operating the XI toolkit. For this reason, SAP also provides Business Content in all SAP systems: preconfigured XI scenarios and processes based on SAP's experience and expertise. Some 40 of these integration scenarios are currently available in the system, and can be supplemented by a further ten or so that are based on industry standards (such as RosettaNet, for example).

The Future Belongs to Integration Scenarios

The future will certainly bring a variety of additional integration scenarios, further reducing the time required to implement such systems.

The decisive factor will be the availability of adapters for each application requiring integration. The adapters in the SAP and Java environment are currently excellent, however, adapters for all other systems are lacking— especially for the competing ERP systems from *Oracle*, *PeopleSoft*, and

Baan. In this area, in particular, enterprises need adapters that are fast, easy to use, and cover a large scope of functions, not only mere message exchange. But steps are being taken in the right direction here as well. New adapters are being developed and deployed all the time, and these adapters are often based on open standards. If all software vendors conform to these standards, the dream of an integrated IT world could become reality in the near future.

9.6 Application Platform

9.6.1 General Market Requirements and Solutions

In today's economy, many industries find themselves faced with increasing globalization. Companies have to collaborate with their partners. With this trend comes the demand that the deployed IT systems support these integrated, cross-enterprise business processes. The term "e-business" continues to increase in importance.

The IT infrastructures that were developed in the past were initially charged with ensuring intraenterprise system integration. Business processes were modeled in complex, heterogeneous system landscapes and adapted to changing circumstances at great expense. The Internet changed all this. Now companies demand interoperability and communication between various systems that are spread across a wide range of locations and that are connected by Internet technology. Moreover, these solutions have to demonstrate a high degree of system independence.

By using new, generally valid standards and technologies such as XML and Web services, a Web-centric model can be defined to overcome the current obstacles to communication in heterogeneous IT systems. In the past, different vendors have presented a variety of different approaches to solve this problem.

In 1996, SAP introduced the *Internet Transaction Server* (ITS), which **ITS Technology** makes it possible to access an R/3 application server from the Internet. Under this technology, external queries can be sent from a Web browser to an SAP system and are transformed such that the Web browser emulates an SAP GUI (graphical user interface). As a result, transactions and reports can be called externally, using the browser technology. True system integration, however, in which cross-enterprise functions trigger workflows and exchange the generated results with one another, is hardly possible with this approach, at least not without an unreasonable effort.

SAP Business Connector The *SAP Business Connector* was developed to exchange data in heterogeneous IT environments. A separate application server enables the bidirectional exchange of XML messages through the Internet, synchronously or asynchronously via RFC or tRFC, respectively. Like the ITS technology, the Business Connector represents a possibility for linking different systems. However, the demand for comprehensive process integration goes far beyond simply linking systems.

SAP Java Connector SAP created another method for communicating with non-SAP systems in the Java programming language with the *SAP Java Connector*. Java has proven highly successful for Internet programming and affords a high degree of platform independence. To implement system integration and communication here, Java programs access classes that encapsulate BAPIs (*Business Application Programming Interfaces*). When a Java program calls an encapsulated function module, the Java Connector executes the corresponding coding in the R/3 system and sends the result back to the Java environment.

J2EE General demands for a uniform, system-independent standard for system communication, as a technical prerequisite for e-business, continued to grow. In response, Sun Microsystems launched the *Java 2 Platform, Enterprise Edition* (J2EE) in 1999, a development architecture for Internet applications in which Web-based information systems can be developed based on a layer model and component technology.

Over time, the additional e-business solutions IBM *WebSphere* and Microsoft *.NET* also began to spread. They are described in more detail in Section 9.6.2, along with the methods available for integrating these different concepts with *SAP Web Application Server*.

9.6.2 SAP Web Application Server

Web AS—an Integrated Solution *SAP Web Application Server* (Web AS) provides the complete infrastructure for the development and operation of all SAP NetWeaver components and forms the foundation for all SAP applications. In addition, it is also the foundation for all customer developments, as well as J2EE-compliant third-party applications. Figure 9.16 illustrates the fundamental position of SAP Web AS.

SAP Web AS was developed by supplementing SAP Basis with additional functions. In addition to support for existing SAP applications, Web AS enables the development and implementation of Web applications, particularly Web services, within a shared infrastructure.

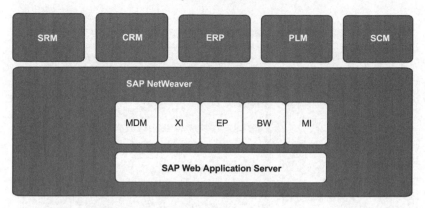

mySAP Business Suite

Figure 9.16 Central Position of SAP Web Application Server

In contrast to standalone solutions, some of which were described above, Web AS represents a uniform development environment with integrated life-cycle management based on standardized development and installation tools. Within this uniform application environment, both the familiar ABAP runtime environment and a J2EE-based development environment are available, the latter equipped with functions from the SAP world, to provide optimized support for enterprise-wide software development.

Uniform Environment

SAP Web AS enables the integration of both environments, with support for open Internet standards, meeting the most important requirements of an enterprise application server with regard to:

► Security

► Reliability

► Sturdiness

► Scalability

► Ease of maintenance

► Platform independence

Figure 9.17 shows the most important components of SAP Web AS in a multilayer architecture. You can use these components to develop and run ABAP-based and J2EE-based Web applications and Web services.

Overview of the Most Important Web AS Components

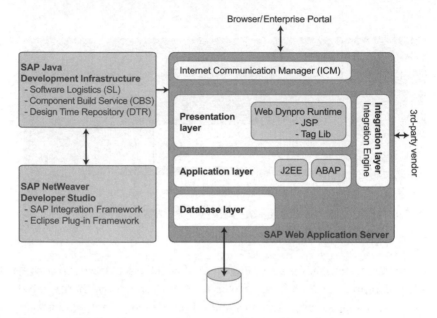

Figure 9.17 The Most Important Components of SAP Web Application Server

The Internet Communication Manager and the Integration Layer

Exchanging Data with the Outside World The *Internet Communication Manager* (ICM) is an independent process that manages data exchange with the outside world, and plays a dual role as both server and client within SAP Web AS.

For external requests, the ICM acts as a Web server, for example, to provide functions to external applications. When a request is received, the ICM sends the content to the *Integration Engine*, using XML and SOAP protocols, where it can be generated in ABAP or Java applications using the proxy framework (see Section 9.5.2). The Integration Engine connects all the applications to SAP XI. It receives and sends the messages to all connected systems in XML and SOAP protocol.

Conversely, the ICM has a client for internal requests of external Web services. To communicate with the outside world, the Web AS uses standard protocols such as HTTP (Hypertext Transfer Protocol), HTTPS (Hypertext Transfer Protocol over Secure Sockets Layer), and SMTP (Simple Mail Transport Protocol).

Caching In addition to its client/server functions, the ICM employs a caching technology that conserves server resources when building pages. As a result, frequently requested pages do not have to be created each time from scratch.

Application Layer

Figure 9.17 shows the application layer as represented by the *J2EE* and *ABAP instantiations*.

J2EE is based on a layer model and component technology as the ele- J2EE mentary principles for creating Web-based information systems. The business logic for Web applications is defined within the application layer using *Enterprise JavaBeans* (EJBs), which represent the connection between the presentation layer and the business data. The EJB components are provided in EJB containers. In turn, these containers form a runtime environment that enables the execution of the components in the first place.

In addition to the technical description within the EJB, *middleware services* utilize standardized interfaces to access the required persistence, security, and transaction services. In the declarative approach, the technical program logic within the EJB is separated from the middleware services, which are saved in a configuration file.

The J2EE architecture uses *Java servlets* and *JavaServer Pages* (JSPs) to specify Web components for server-side presentation logic. This is also the foundation for providing *Web Dynpro* as the user interface in SAP Web AS. Web Dynpro is described in more detail below.

We should also mention the vendor-independent Java interfaces (APIs), which have already proven their worth in the standard Java technology, including *Java Database Connectivity* (JDBC) for access to relational database connections and the *Java Connector Architecture* (JCA), which is used in systems integration.

The J2EE environment makes it possible to create Web-based applications and Web services based on J2EE technologies. The integration of ABAP and J2EE technologies in SAP Web AS now makes it possible to define method calls between the technologies. The *SAP Java Connector* (SAP JCo) lets you use the BAPIs (Business Application Programming Interfaces) from the ABAP environment.

In the ABAP environment, which is based on the proven applica- ABAP tion/server development and implementation environment, the business logic is provided using business objects, which are analogous to EJBs. This environment has been enhanced with simple Web technologies, such as simple XML transformations and a Web service infrastructure.

We should mention, however, that the J2EE Engine and ABAP Workbench each have separate database management, which prevents direct access at the database table level. There are no database transactions that support cross-environment library access. Currently, the only option for combining the J2EE and ABAP environments within a uniform architecture is at the application level, with SAP JCo, SAP XI or Web services. In the future, direct access from both environments should be possible, which means the current solution is a step towards this end.

The SAP Java Development Infrastructure and SAP NetWeaver Developer Studio

When it comes to enterprise-wide software development, the conventional Java IDEs (integrated development environments) are not as powerful as the ABAP Workbench. They do not support repository-based development, nor management or distribution of byte code.

SAP Java Development Infrastructure

The *SAP Java Development Infrastructure* within the SAP NetWeaver platform extends the proven ABAP development concept to the Java environment, eliminating the major deficits of the previous Java development environment. The following core functions close the gap in the existing Java development environment:

▶ Software Logistics (SL)

▶ Component Build Service (CBS)

▶ Design Time Repository (DTR)

The local coding developed by the individual developers is managed centrally by the DTR, which ensures its consistency. The CBS builds and manages the finished Java archives. SL represents the *change management service*, which is responsible for distributing the finished Java archives to the J2EE server. Existing Java applications are also maintained centrally.

SAP NetWeaver Developer Studio

The local development environment is supported by *SAP NetWeaver Developer Studio*. Every developer can write code in a local development environment based on the *Eclipse Plug-in Framework*, which is used to create tools and desktop applications. It is free of charge and provides the functions as a plug-in. The individual coding blocks are composed and managed using the functions described above.

Presentation Layer

The conventional SAP R/3 system has a three-tier architecture, with data retention, application logic, and presentation logic. The presentation logic is located completely on the client, in the SAP GUI. One of the main disadvantages of this architecture is the need to install the graphical user interface on the client. Users have to install the GUI locally again whenever changes occur, which prevents the successful dissemination of Web applications over the Internet. For this reason, demands to implement Web applications with a standard browser increased as Internet technology spread.

In the thin client concept, the presentation logic is divided into client-side and server-side components. In this model, the client side is the browser, which is responsible for user navigation and visualization, while the server side houses the presentation logic, with input validation and conversion of results into HTML or XML. In addition to thin clients, there are also more powerful browsers, or *advanced clients*, that can implement this conversion themselves. In this case, the XML transformation and JavaScript are executed on the client, which means server-side HTML generation is not needed.

Browser Technology vs. SAP GUI

A major advantage of browser technology is its independence from the underlying client technology. As a result, a large number of clients can be reached with a Web application. In the past, however, many Web applications were equipped with insufficient user interfaces, for example, lacking important functions such as user help and input validation.

This lack of support in entering data in the correct format, or in handling input errors in the user interface, greatly reduced the usability of Web applications. A tremendous effort is required to eliminate these technical deficits with conventional Web application tools.

SAP's Web Dynpro is a new user interface technology that meets the demands for high-quality interface development with a reasonable development effort. Web Dynpro is a development and runtime environment that is based on the JSP (JavaServer Pages) model and tag libraries. It supports both the thin client and advanced client concepts.

Web Dynpro

A decisive advantage of the Web Dynpro technology is its division of presentation logic and application logic in accordance with the MVC (Model View Controller) approach. As a result, a role-based development process is supported that separates the development of the user interface from the implementation of the application logic.

In *SAP NetWeaver Developer Studio*, various tools are used to develop Web dynpros. In addition to graphical implementation tools for UI design, SAP NetWeaver Developer Studio also provides tools for the

Development Tools

development life cycle. The *View Designer* supports Adobe form functions for application interfaces, while the *Data Modeler* enables the graphical definition of data flows between application units.

UI patterns can be used for fast, standard development of user interfaces. We differentiate between three different levels. *Controls* are frequently used UI elements, such as radio buttons. *Components* are reusable blocks that are used for specific purposes. Lastly, *floor plans* contain layout, interaction, and semantics for a generic application. These UI patterns make it possible to develop standardized, consistent application interfaces even for large, long-running projects.

Developing Web Dynpros with SAP NetWeaver Developer Studio ensures integration with the *SAP Development Infrastructure*. In addition, a wizard is available for effortlessly integrating Web Dynpro in the portal infrastructure. As a result, you can create demanding user interfaces with a homogenous layout within the portal.

Integration with Third-Party Software

In addition to the multilayer architecture of SAP Web AS, with the *SAP Java Development Infrastructure* and *SAP NetWeaver Developer Studio* as development tools, the possibilities for integrating non-SAP systems in a heterogeneous enterprise environment represent another important feature of SAP Web AS. The interoperability with *IBM WebSphere* and *Microsoft .NET* are described below.

WebSphere Based on J2EE

IBM's WebSphere solution is based on standard technologies such as Java, XML, and J2EE, and can be divided into three areas:

▶ Foundation and tools

▶ Business integration

▶ Reach and user experience

In the *foundation and tools* area, the centerpiece of IBM WebSphere Studio, *Web Application Server Version 5.0*, represents the complete Web service infrastructure. Support is also available for mainframe integration and application development. In addition, the *business integration* area contains functions for integrating all kinds of back-end systems.

Microsoft .NET As Proprietary Approach

Microsoft has introduced the .NET platform as a separate product and an alternative to the J2EE standard; the *.NET Framework* consists of proprietary components. The *.NET Framework Classes* contain a collection of functions to support application development. The *ADO.NET Data Sets* contain ActiveX data objects, for example, to save database content. The *.NET Remoting Protocol* enables client access to distributed servers. The technical foundation for .NET is the *Visual Studio .NET* development environment and *Windows Server 2003*.

As you can see from the structure of the Web AS application layer, the Java environment has been completely integrated in SAP Web AS, making it automatically compatible with J2EE. SAP Web AS is also based on open standards such as XML, SOAP, WSDL (Web Services Description Language), and UDDI (Universal Description, Discovery, and Integration). In addition to these standards, the *J2EE Connector Architecture* (JCA) and *Java Message Service* (JMS) offer interoperability with IBM WebSphere and Microsoft .NET.

Connecting Non-SAP Systems

SAP NetWeaver Developer Studio is based on the *Eclipse* open-source framework. It is closely related to *IBM WebSphere Studio Application Developer* (WSAD), which is based on the same foundation. The Java classes that are used to access BAPIs and RFCs are also used in WSAD. In addition, the development objects implemented in WSAD are compatible with the Web AS runtime environment.

The *SAP Java Connector* is a toolkit for bidirectional communication with J2EE application servers, and enables SAP Web AS to communicate with Java application systems. This enables calls from SAP to WebSphere objects and vice versa.

The *SAP .NET Connector* is provided for bidirectional access to Microsoft .NET applications, which lets you integrate .NET services in SAP Web AS and vice versa. The *SAP .NET Connector* supports the *Visual Studio .NET* development environment.

In closing, we can reiterate that SAP Web AS relies on J2EE to provide a platform-independent integration and application base for Web applications (Web services). It replaces the previous, ABAP-only runtime environment. As a result, integration, middleware, and security functions have been shifted to the Web AS.

J2EE or .NET

Microsoft implemented .NET as its alternative solution. In contrast to the J2EE approach, .NET is a proprietary architecture that is tailored to Windows and consists of vendor-specific components, which means native SAP support is not possible.

Summary   SAP Web AS is a reliable, scalable component platform that assumes a central role in the SAP systems environment, and that supports all major standards for enterprise applications either directly or through connectors.

No matter which path you choose, however, it is clear that the conventional client/server concept will have to give way to a services-oriented architecture. Communication in the client-server concepts is controlled either by the application or through transaction processing. In a service-oriented system, a powerful application server is responsible for controlling communication between the client and back end.

9.7   Composite Application Framework

The *Composite Application Framework* (CAF) is surely one of the most interesting components within SAP NetWeaver. It makes it possible to build entirely new applications from existing applications such as SAP R/3 or Web services. This component is described in detail below.

9.7.1   Market and Solution Requirements of the Composite Application Framework

Evolution   As Chapter 8 explained, the transition from a client/server architecture to ESA (enterprise services architecture) will require several changes to the IT landscape. This transition is not comparable to the switch from mainframe to client/server architecture, however, which represented a revolution in enterprise IT that required the wholesale replacement of system landscapes. Instead, it involves the further development of existing systems, based on three steps:

▶ Identifying the most important application services

▶ Creating the necessary enterprise services based on the identified application services

▶ Closing the functional gap between the enterprise services through the use of composite applications (CA)

Toolkit for SOAs   It is readily apparent that every software vendor that plans to offer an SOA (service-oriented architecture) will have to provide a tool—or an entire set of tools—to meet these requirements.

Such toolkits make it possible to build new, process-oriented user interfaces and systems. These new systems will give users optimum support for process execution and monitoring.

9.7.2 The SAP Solution in Detail

The Composite Application Framework (CAF) is SAP's platform for developing and operating enterprise services. As we mentioned above, nearly every enterprise is faced with the challenge of building enterprise services based on the application services, as well as implementing any necessary functional enhancements. This is done in the CAF.

But how are applications like this set up, and how do interaction and integration take place between the involved systems? Figure 9.18 emphasizes the dependencies between the applications.

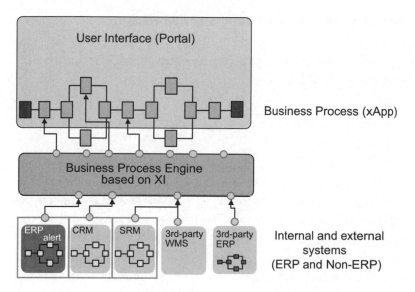

Figure 9.18 xApps in the Context of the Overall Solution Landscape

Several facts are apparent in the diagram. First, there are no longer any direct user interfaces for the ERP and non-ERP systems. All information flows through the *portal* user interface (also see Section 9.3.2). In addition, the XI component described in Section 9.5 increases in importance, because it represents the connection between the systems and the user interface (SAP Enterprise Portal in this case). The business process then runs visually in this user interface (all user interaction that is necessary for the entire process is done via a single user interface (the portal). The necessary business process logic is concealed in systems like SAP XI (specifically Business Process Management) and the involved applications.

User Interface Portal

The model in Figure 9.18 clearly indicates that systems have to be interconnected in a large number of places. Previously, users had to "commu-

"Human Integrators"

nicate" directly with each individual system. They entered data, analyzed situations, and made decisions based on their process knowledge. We speak of "human integrators" in this context. Today, most enterprises have yet to integrate the requirements of the individual "human integrators" in a business process. The Composite Application Framework is perfect for this task.

xApps   Applications that are created using the CAF are called *xApps*. This is a proprietary SAP term that describes an application created using enterprise services. xApps are developed in SAP NetWeaver Developer Studio.

Delimitation of Individual Services and xApps

To classify the xApps and the other terms mentioned above, a summary of the different services appears below (see Section 8.4.2 for a more exact delineation and description).

▶ **Service**
A service is a function within a program.

▶ **Web service**
A Web service is a service that is available through use of Internet technology and that can be addressed externally. It communicates using open standards and has its own logic for addressing the underlying application. In most cases, it also has its own data retention.

▶ **Application service**
An application service is a Web service that is offered by an ERP application. The term "application service" is used primarily in the context of SAP ERP and non-ERP systems (such as CRM).

▶ **Enterprise service**
An enterprise service groups a number of application services together to create a logical unit, such as the "business partner" object. An enterprise service contains only the logic, but does not have its own data retention, which remains in the individual subsystems.

▶ **Cross-applications—xApps**
Cross-applications, or *xApps* in the SAP context, are applications that are more than mere enterprise services. While they use the same logic, they have a more powerful scope, and differ from applications that are wholly implemented in a single system. An xApp is a composite application that SAP has filled with content.

xApps in Practice

To examine xApps in practice, we need to define an additional term: *packaged CA* or *packaged xApps*. Both describe an xApp supplied by SAP.

Packaged xApps

These packaged xApps are the first applications that were developed completely based on SAP NetWeaver. This new type of application is not shipped with the existing SAP solutions (mySAP ERP or the mySAP Business Suite), but instead is sold separately. These applications use the data layer of the existing systems (i.e., SAP and non-SAP systems) and are used to realize a new process (or processes) that uses different source systems and crosses the boundaries of those systems.

Several xApps that SAP is already shipping are listed below. They illustrate the potential of xApps in general:

Available xApps

▶ **SAP xApp Product Definition**
This application supports the first phase of the product development process, which is product definition. It establishes a connection to the ERP system, CRM system, and office applications, letting you execute the definition process much faster and more transparently.

▶ **SAP xApp Employee Process Management**
This xApp represents an extended interface to the existing Manager Self-Services (MSS) and Employee Self-Services (ESS), by including the work center-relevant areas that come before the actual HR activities.

▶ **SAP xApp Resource and Portfolio Management**
These applications let yon control employees, projects, and other resources in a targeted manner, resulting in improved, more efficient project execution.

In addition, a wide range of SAP partners have also begun developing and selling xApps for specific industries.

xApps make it possible to link the systems that are already deployed at an enterprise, to model new processes that have not been implemented yet in this form. An xApp always consists of the following components:

Components of xApps

▶ Data access
▶ Business process management, based on XI
▶ User interface

These components are implemented with the NetWeaver landscape.

Data access is implemented via XI or its various adapters. Business process management lets you create processes and integrate them in the systems graphically. You can also use the Business Process Repository to implement any missing functions. The user interface for all xApps is the same: a portal is always involved—SAP Enterprise Portal in this case. This portal integration lets xApps capture entirely new groups of users, who can now manipulate content in the system without having power-user skills. xApps make new applications easier to use and represent the processes more clearly. xApps help you create "people-centric" applications—applications that are highly tailored to users' needs, and provide ideal support for day-to-day work without system gaps (switching between different user interfaces and application logic).

Outlook for xApps

The possibilities that xApps offer can help an IT department solve inter-system integration issues within a process in a more targeted, cost-effective manner.

Focus: Business Process xApps unify both technical access to the system and the business processes in a unique way, although the primary focus of an xApp is always a business process. Enterprises can now start using xApps to implement new processes based on their internal ERP/SAP systems to replace the "human integrators" with a software solution that models a process completely and holistically.

Thanks to XI, this procedure does not end at company boundaries—it also reaches the last system in the supply chain. As a result, each enterprise and its users can control, measure, and optimize the processes they are responsible for.

Requirements More time will surely pass before these systems come into practical use, however, as many customers still use ERP software that provides only a few Web services, or none at all. But Web services are a prerequisite for building xApps and addressing the data in the individual systems.

Software vendors, particularly SAP, are responding to these developments and equipping their applications with Web services—such as in *mySAP ERP*. This development will intensify in the coming years as more and more software is converted to Web services.

Accordingly, the early adopters of this new platform will benefit most from this development, as they will be able to model new, improved processes with xApps. They will have a head start on their competition and will benefit from all the advantages described in Chapter 3.

9.8   SAP Solution Manager

SAP Solution Manager plays a special role within SAP NetWeaver, as it is not used to implement (cross-enterprise) business processes, but instead focuses on managing the software. SAP Solution Manager is a component of SAP NetWeaver, but is a tool that's mainly used for operating SAP installations—especially SAP software, and of course all NetWeaver components.

Like *SAP NetWeaver Developer Studio*, SAP Solution Manager is a tool that supports the use of IT systems. SAP positions Solution Manager as a supplement, not a competitor, to other vendors' solutions in this area. SAP Solution Manager is included in the maintenance fees for an SAP installation.

People frequently misunderstand the objectives of SAP Solution Manager: Because one of its functions lets you centrally manage the SAP Service Marketplace messages your company submits to SAP, this is often mistaken as its main task. In fact, however, SAP Solution Manager has much more comprehensive functions that go beyond the conventional definition of software logistics. It offers tool-based support for the entire life cycle of a business process—that is, it supports the management and optimization of the processes in all five of the phases described below, which are illustrated in Figure 9.19:

Support for the Complete Product Life Cycle

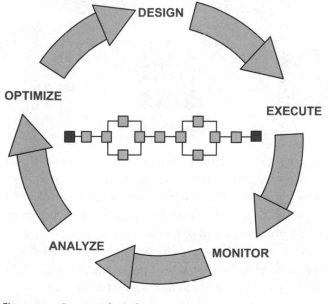

Figure 9.19 Process Life Cycle

- Design
- Operation
- Monitoring
- Analysis
- Optimization

While its positioning results in a focus on the implementation and operation of SAP software, the integration of other systems is explicitly supported. As Figure 9.20 shows, it does not matter whether the software in question stems from a third-party vendor or is a proprietary development. SAP Solution Manager provides support for all life cycle phases of a process (and the systems required for a process step), from design to optimization.

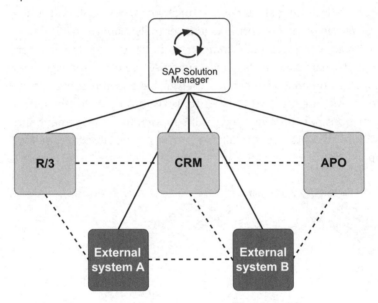

Figure 9.20 System Landscape Integration in SAP Solution Manager

Predefined Business Content Most of the IT tools you get are "empty"—you need to add specific data (i.e., regarding processes, etc.) first before you can use them. SAP Solution Manager is different. It is shipped with a wide range of predefined Business Content, such as process descriptions, links to customizing entries, and prototype documentation of the business processes in nearly all SAP solutions. Best-practice processes and workflows are predefined, and just have to be adapted to individual requirements (if necessary). At the same time, SAP Solution Manager can be considered the successor to ASAP, SAP's implementation methodology. It contains all the content required for methodical support (such as templates for project plans or checklists).

It is important to understand that SAP Solution Manager is focused on two main elements: *processes* and their *life cycle*. In actuality, this means all documentation and implementations of SAP Notes are based on processes. All information is arranged and saved within a three-level hierarchy (scenario, process, and process step). Different functions are available for the individual elements of this hierarchy, depending on the project phase. Whereas the blueprint phase concentrates more on the documentation and creation of concepts, the emphasis later is on distributing the Customizing settings, for example.

Every enterprise that uses SAP Solution Manager can freely select the project phases and scope for using the tool. Some customers use only SAP Solution Manager to document business processes, while others use nearly all its options. The major benefit of comprehensive Solution Manager use is that all information is available for the respective business process. Because the documentation, SAP Notes, Customizing settings, and test information are available at the process step level in this case, this collected knowledge base is also available in the downstream maintenance and upkeep phase.

Scope of Use

9.8.1 Support in the Process Life Cycle

In line with the different requirements in the different phases of the life cycle, SAP Solution Manager offers support in several different forms, which are described below:

Phases of the Process Life Cycle

1. **Design**
   During the design phase, support is provided as documentation at the business process level and through the graphical display of processes as swim lanes that enables the assignment of process steps and systems (for Business Blueprint, Customizing, and so on). During this phase, Solution Manager supports you through its documentation capabilities and via the graphical display of processes, which occurs in the format of "swim lanes" that enables the assignment of process steps and used systems (Blueprint, Customizing etc.) Predefined content from SAP can be used. SAP Solution Manager also offers testing support for the Going Live phase.

2. **Operations**

SAP Solution Manager supports the rollout of software implementations for additional countries through the distribution of Customizing settings and transports (referred to as *software logistics*). An interface to the *SAP Tutor* e-learning product lets you save e-learning content at the business process level.

3. **Monitoring**

SAP systems can be monitored by function modules (Remote Function Calls, RFCs) or *agents*. Non-SAP software can also be monitored by agents, which collect information at the operating system level and display it centrally in SAP Solution Manager.

4. **Analysis**

Integration of a support desk lets you process and categorize all reports with problems entered by end users centrally. Assignment to certain processes, or even process steps, simplifies analysis. In addition, SAP offers services to help customers analyze their systems.

5. **Optimization**

During system operation, improvements can be implemented in the form of *SAP Notes*, which are documented and saved in SAP Solution Manager. During updates and upgrades, Solution Manager compares the existing system landscape with the planned installation and indicates any components that are missing or have an outdated version number.

In addition, support is also provided during the setup phase—for example, SAP Solution Manager can exchange information regarding the system landscape with SAP XI, saving you from having to maintain this data redundantly.

9.8.2   Process Modeling and Management

As a result of the all-encompassing approach that SAP has selected, issues involving the life-cycle management of business processes overlap questions from other areas in some cases. Process modeling is a particular focus.

Avoiding
Integration Gaps

In the past, the modeling of business processes made a fairly clear distinction between design and implementation. The concepts were first "written down" and worked out on a purely theoretical basis. As soon as this phase was complete, the concepts were implemented in the system—but there was no link between the paper-based concept and the process implementation. This represents an actual integration gap, and the associated inefficiencies harbor great potential for implementation.

Graphical tools such as Microsoft *Visio* were often used to model the processes. Another such widespread tool is *ARIS* from *IDS Scheer*, which has its roots in the academic work of Professor Scheer[6] and offers comprehensive support for the *design*, *analysis*, and *optimization* phases. ARIS features a powerful range of functions and has a correspondingly steep learning curve. But even ARIS is an isolated tool to date. It's not integrated in the overall design process. The information created with ARIS has no direct connection (no interface) to what happens in the (SAP) systems. Therefore, there is still a divide between the theoretical design work and the subsequent development.

SAP Solution Manager features an interface to ARIS that lets you compare the modeled business processes with the (predefined) content. This comparison is possible in both directions, which means you are assured an up-to-date, uniform data pool. (Both systems are using the same data without one of them getting outdated—even after changes.) SAP cooperates with IDS Scheer in this area to avoid functional overlaps between the two tools. Their announcement to pursue joint developments in this area and promote "ARIS for NetWeaver" opens up interesting possibilities for the future—particularly in the context of the transformation of IT architectures to ESA.

9.8.3 Outlook

Tighter integration of Solution Manager and ARIS is planned for the future. The interface between these two tools will become less visible and more seamless to users. Far more important than these "conventional" integration efforts, however, are changes in the implementation methods: Close integration between ARIS and SAP Solution Manager could facilitate a change in the design paradigm for business processes itself. If modeling is performed in ARIS and the processes can be developed further in SAP Solution Manager—without integration gaps!—you would have a true visual approach to business process programming. The foundation for this fundamental change lies in a direct link between the graphical display of a process step and the corresponding enterprise service. Figure 9.21 illustrates this connection.

---

6 IDS Scheer, Annual Report 2003. Page 11 (available online at *www.ids-scheer.com*).

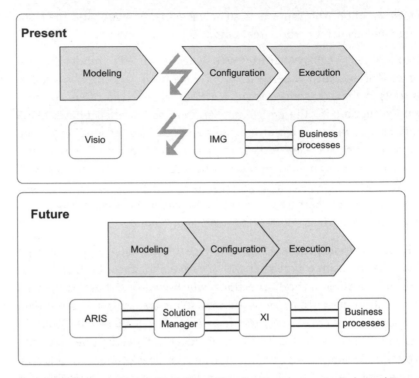

Figure 9.21 Business Process Modeling and Further Development—Today and Tomorrow

Prerequisite: Enterprise Services Architecture To enable this transformation in managing business processes and enable graphics-based programming, however, an ESA is required to support the extensive use of enterprise services. These enterprise services are used on three layers, whose context is illustrated in Figure 9.22:

1. **Process architecture**
   When designing a business process, ARIS offers the existing enterprise services as modules that can be used for modeling.

2. **Process configuration**
   In SAP Solution Manager, the process and its process steps are configured, and this configuration is distributed throughout the system landscape.

3. **Process execution**
   The Composite Application Framework and SAP XI execute the process by utilizing the individual enterprise services.

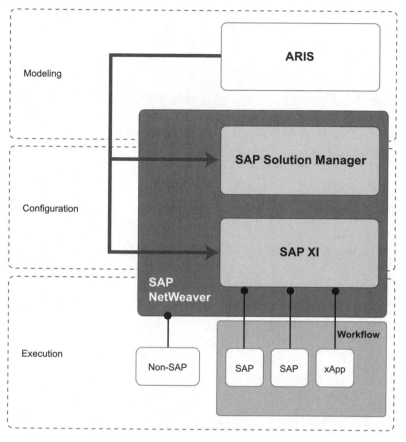

Figure 9.22 Process Architecture, Configuration, and Execution

Accordingly, issues involving the life cycle of a business process and its modeling become very important as a result of the transition to a service-based architecture. By establishing a direct link between process step and enterprise service, the graphical modeling of a process can fundamentally change how processes are defined and modified; at the same time, this process paves the way for the spread of cross-applications.

10 Final Considerations

Cutting costs, increasing flexibility, and reducing time to market for new products by 50%—these are the expectations linked to the introduction of SAP NetWeaver.

What does an IT world with SAP NetWeaver look like? Will all challenges be mastered, or will there be a significant improvement in some areas only? When will the first companies have completed the redesign of their client/server landscape into an SAP NetWeaver landscape? These are the questions we have to answer and evaluate to obtain a holistic picture of the ESA strategy and SAP NetWeaver. When approaching a new concept, it is always helpful to think of it in terms of what is "really new" about it and what is "familiar." This is what we will do in the following two sections.

10.1 Familiar Applications As a Basis

Among the things we are already familiar with are all those applications within SAP NetWeaver that have been used by customers for several years. These applications used to be standalone ones, that is, they had been installed as individual applications and were mainly used by individual departments or business areas. Within the respective departments or areas they were of great use, but unfortunately their full potential has never been completely exploited. The following SAP NetWeaver applications have been in use for quite some time now:

▶ *SAP Business Information Warehouse* (BW)

▶ *SAP Enterprise Portal* (EP), *including Knowledge Management* (KM)

▶ *SAP Solution Manager*

▶ Various predecessors of XI in the form of pure EDI solutions such as *SAP Business Connector*

▶ *SAP Web Application Server* (Web AS)

Hence these applications form the basis for a company to consider an SAP NetWeaver solution. In this context, it makes a lot of sense to opt for a step-by-step approach in which the IT landscape is redesigned in individual subprojects. The scenarios in Chapters 4 through 7 illustrated the way in which such a project approach can be handled.

Starting Point for Using SAP NetWeaver

10.1.1 SAP Business Information Warehouse

BW as the Basis
for an Enterprise
Data Warehouse

In order to have a decent and functioning reporting system, every company needs a data warehouse. As a matter of fact, most companies already use one, even if it is simply in the form of a collection of Microsoft Excel documents distributed throughout the company. However, as time progresses, there is a growing need to develop a solid basis of data, and only a data warehouse can offer such a basis. In its current release, SAP NetWeaver provides a platform that helps you map almost all reporting activities. And due to the enhancement of SAP BW with the planning functionality from SEM, the planning aspect has now also been addressed.

10.1.2 SAP Enterprise Portal

Today, most companies use an intranet solution. In many of them, the intranet serves as a place where employees can get information about the cafeteria menu or receive the latest news from the board of directors. The actual business processes take place in the email system and in the individual applications, which, in many cases, pertain to how individual processes work. Yet even in this area we see the first signs of change, as there is a growing number of companies that have implemented portal solutions for their staff.

These solutions are primarily applications for leave, travel expenses, and messages to the HR department in the context of Employee Self-Service (ESS).

The next step to take in these companies is to make new services available to management too, which can be done by introducing Manager Self-Service (MSS).

10.1.3 Predecessors to XI in the Form of Pure EDI Solutions

Even before the hype that was triggered by Enterprise Application Integration (EAI), companies used to exchange data electronically. This was frequently done using third-party software and with the objective of accelerating parts of processes (for example, delivery requests triggered by manufacturers for their suppliers to ensure just-in-time delivery). However, what all these solutions had in common was the fact that they established only a point-to-point connection between the participating systems. Although the implementation of these connections could take place quickly and cost-effectively, maintaining them generated high costs.

10.1.4 SAP Web Application Server

Until now, in many companies, SAP's basis system—SAP Web Application Server (Web AS)—and its predecessor (R/3 Basis) have been used to operate only SAP applications. When it came to new developments that went beyond the scope of a pure SAP application, a different server platform was chosen.

Web AS now provides a comprehensive development environment for application development and implementation. It contains everything you need to develop a modern application, and with its two engines (ABAP and J2EE), it enables you to develop your applications in both the "old" SAP world and the Java world.

Web AS was created based on the old R/3 base functionality; it contains all the basic R/3 functions that you're familiar with, and furthermore, all the features you need to operate a Web server. Web AS serves as a platform on which you can operate all the various SAP components as well as develop your own solutions.

10.2 New Components in SAP NetWeaver

But what is really new in the SAP NetWeaver landscape? The answer is clear: the strict orientation toward a service-oriented architecture— Enterprise Services Architecture (ESA). All SAP NetWeaver components have been designed based on this architecture. The primary advantage of ESA is that you can reuse objects and processes, which, in turn, are no longer tied to individual applications.

ESA is what is really new in SAP NetWeaver, and in the context of xApps, it serves as a basis for all future applications that are developed in SAP NetWeaver. The entirely new components in SAP NetWeaver are:

ESA As a Direction

▶ *SAP Exchange Infrastructure* (XI) with *Business Process Management* (BPM)

▶ *SAP Master Data Management* (MDM)

▶ *SAP Composite Application Framework* (CAF) as a basis for *xApps*

No IT department in the world will restructure its system landscape toward services and thus toward xApps in the twinkling of an eye. Nor will existing interfaces be migrated to XI in one go. But in future projects and decision-making processes, every IT department should ask itself if there is the potential to use SAP NetWeaver. The first applications that include components such as XI, MDM, or xApps will certainly be pilot applications, but in three to four years' time, some processes will definitely be based entirely on this technology.

10.2.1 SAP Exchange Infrastructure

Centralized Business Objects

SAP XI provides a comprehensive range of functionalities that enable companies to map their centralized business objects and establish a data exchange between the individual sub-systems. The logic of business objects enables the harmonization of a company's master data and the data of customers and suppliers, without having to redesign all applications involved. If in addition to this you use Business Process Management (BPM), you will have a solution that enables you to model, monitor, and accelerate (in "real time") the entire business process.

10.2.2 SAP Master Data Management

Homogeneous Master Data on the Basis of Business Content

As an application within the XI landscape, SAP MDM enables the harmonization of a company's master data as well as all data from systems that have been linked via XI. In doing this, SAP MDM ensures the distribution of new master data to all systems involved, as well as the synchronous implementation of changes in all these systems. Included in the MDM release is the "Business Content," that is, certain rules according to which you have to harmonize your business objects.

10.2.3 SAP Composite Application Framework (CAF)

Services Melt into xApps

CAF is the development platform for new applications that are tailored precisely to the business process. Such applications are used for connecting existing applications with each other so that, as a result, new applications are created that support the processes in a more extensive and integrated way. SAP already delivers some of these applications called xApps. xApps utilize the services available from other applications and link them with each other to create new processes. Therefore, they are a main component of ESA.

Hence, CAF is a development platform that utilizes the full functionality of SAP NetWeaver. However, it will still take several years until customers use it on a broader basis. As already explained in Section 9.7, the reason for this is not CAF itself, but rather the many changes that are necessary on the customer side to move from a client/server architecture to ESA. CAF uses Web Services. If you change your architecture so that it can be used with Web Services, you'll automatically get an ESA. Therefore, using CAF automatically means changing to an ESA implementation.

10.3 Advantages for "Early Birds"

As we already described in the project scenarios in Chapters 4 through 7, the change in direction for the IT landscape is from a client/server architecture to an Enterprise Services Architecture. This means that every CIO needs to plan how he or she wants to move in this direction. In this book we described several different strategies, which were evaluated with regard to added value and TCO. It is now up to the responsible IT managers to decide which way they want to go.

It is certainly useful to become familiar with new technologies in the context of pilot projects. Such an approach helps the IT department learn how new scenarios are to be handled on the project management side, and also where the benefits for the company are. It then quickly becomes very clear that IT will be able to add value to the various departments if it uses the ESA strategy instead of an architecture that is completely based on a client/server technology. Therefore, the IT department will move away from the "reactive" role it often assumes and move toward an "active" role, enabling it to again promote IT innovation within the company.

Pilot Projects Guarantee a First Success

The first steps toward ESA could consist of pilot projects that are used for specific services or mapping interfaces internally or externally with an XI solution. But there's also no reason why a company-wide implementation of SAP Enterprise Portal or BW shouldn't take place, provided the restructuring doesn't end here. If you don't want to lose ground, you have to continue on.

SAP NetWeaver provides a great opportunity to restructure the IT landscape in order to enable companies to implement their strategies even faster and more cost-effectively than ever before, and thus guarantee a lasting success. Of course, you'll find alternative solutions for each subcomponent of SAP NetWeaver on the market; however, none of these solutions provides this wide range of functionalities and the profound integration of individual solutions that are possible with SAP NetWeaver.

Don't Miss the Train to the Future

The change toward the new IT architecture will take time, and those who start early will finish early, which might become the deciding factor for companies when it comes to gaining a competitive advantage.

Changes Take Time

Of course, those who switch to SAP NetWeaver now will be among the first ones to try out new functionalities. In the beginning stages, this will lead to increased costs that wouldn't have occurred otherwise. However, you will benefit in the long run from starting early and thus making an earlier transition from the client/server architecture, and the cost savings realized in the future will far exceed what you spend to get started. The benefits found in a continuous decrease of TCO are important, but become less significant as soon as the company's profits return to normal. Then, the benefits in terms of flexibility and the time it takes processes to run will come to the forefront. Whenever you gain time—whether in selling products or in the development process—it can be converted into a competitive advantage, which will add to a continuously growing company value.

Thus the question is not whether SAP NetWeaver should be implemented, but rather when and how to begin its implementation.

A Sources and Further Reading

English Texts

▶ Austvold, Eric; Shepherd, Jim: *SAP NetWeaver 2004*. AMR Research Report.

▶ Banking Technology Magazine: *In Profile*. March 2004. *www.bankingtech.com*.

▶ Berger, Roland: *Nine Mega-Trends Re-shape the Automotive Supplier Industry—A trend study to 2010*. Roland Berger & Partner GmbH, Munich 2000.

▶ Bloomberg, J.: *Principles of SOA*. In: *Application Development Trends*, No. 3, Vol. 10., pp. 22.

▶ Bussler, Christoph: *B2B Integration – Concepts and Architecture*. Berlin/Heidelberg 2003.

▶ Chakravorti, Bhaskar: *The New Rules for Bringing Innovations to Market*. Harvard Business Review, March 2004, pp. 60.

▶ Collins, Heidi: *Corporate Portals – Revolutionizing Information Access to increase productivity and drive the bottom line*. AMACON – American Management Association, New York 2001.

▶ European Central Bank: *Structural Analysis of the EU Banking Sector*. 2002.

▶ Färber, Günther; Kirchner, Julia: *mySAP Technology Roadmap*. Bonn 2003.

▶ Leymann, Frank, et al.: *Web Services Platform Architecture: SOAP, WSDL, WS-Policy, WS-Addressing, WS-BPEL, WS-Reliable Messaging and More*. Prentice Hall 2005.

▶ Porter, M.; Millar, V.: *How information gives you competitive advantage*. In: Harvard Business Review (HBR), 7/8 1985.

▶ SAP AG: *mySAP Mobile Business – Statement of Direction*. Whitepaper, Walldorf 2003.

▶ SAP AG: *SAP NetWeaver – Statement of Direction 2004*. Whitepaper, Walldorf 2004.

▶ Woods, Dan: *Enterprise Services Architecture*. Sebastopol 2003.

▶ Woods, Dan: *Realtime: A Tribute to Hasso Plattner*. John Wiley & Sons Australia, 2004.

Sources only available in German

▶ Bestmann, Uwe (Hrsg.): *Kompendium der Betriebswirtschaftslehre*. München, Wien 2001.

▶ Bieber, Gerald: *Mobile Computer*. Frauenhofer IGD Rostock, INI-GraphicsNet, Darmstadt 2003.

▶ Burkhardt, Bärbel; Laures, Guido: *SOA – Wertstiftendes Architektur-Paradigma*. *http://www.sigs-datacom.de*, 21.7.2004.

▶ Cherdorn, Malte; Stahl, Konrad: *Fusion in der Automobil-Zulieferindustrie: Fallstudie und Theorie*. 2003.

▶ Dudenhöffer: *Automobil-Zulieferer im Wachstumsstress*. GAK 1/2002.

▶ FAZ: *Flottengeschäft sorgt für Plus im Neuwagenmarkt*. 22.05.2004.

▶ FAZ: *Handbremswende bei der Elektronik*. 22.05.2004.

▶ Fröschle, Hans-Peter (Hrsg.): *Web-Services*. *HMD Praxis der Wirtschaftsinformatik*. Heidelberg 2003.

▶ Junior Beratung Bayreuth e.V (JBB): *Studie über die Automobilzulieferindustrie in Oberfranken*. Bayreuth 2004.

▶ Fröhlich, Mike: *Evaluierung und prototypischer Einsatz eines XML-basierten EAI-Gateways im validierungspflichtigen Umfeld*. Konstanz 2003.

▶ Kearney, A.T.: *Management Consultants*. München 2001.

▶ Keller, Wolfgang: *Enterprise Application Integration – Erfahrungen aus der Praxis*. Heidelberg 2002.

▶ Kinkel, Steffen; Lay, Gunter: *Automobilzulieferer in der Klemme*. Fraunhofer Institut Systemtechnik und Innovationsforschung (ISI), PI-Mitteilung Nr. 32, 2004.

▶ Koch, Andreas: *Allgemeine Einführung in adaptive Computersysteme*. Abteilung Entwurf integrierter Schaltungen EIS, Technische Universität Braunschweig 2004.

▶ META Group Deutschland GmbH: *Market Research 2003 – IT-Trends in Branchen*. 2003.

▶ Perez, Mario; Karch, Steffen: *WebBusiness mit SAP*. Bonn 2002.

▶ Puschmann, Thomas: *Collaboration Portale*. Bamberg 2003.

▶ RölfsPartner Management Consultants und Center Automotive Research FH Gelsenkirchen: *Befragung von 82 Zulieferunternehmen*. In: Dudenhöffer: *Automobil-Zulieferer im Wachstumsstress* GAK 1/2002.

▶ SAP AG: *Exchange Infrastructure: Prozessorientierte Integration und Zusammenarbeit*. Whitepaper, Walldorf 2003.

▶ SAP AG: *Portalinfrastruktur: Benutzerorientierte Integration und Zusammenarbeit.* Whitepaper, Walldorf 2002.

▶ SAP AG: *SAP Business Connector. Lösungen im Überblick*, Walldorf 2003.

▶ SAP AG: *Web Application Server: Technologie und Web Dynpro Version 1.1.* Whitepaper, Walldorf 2003.

▶ Schmitz, Andreas: *Festgeknüpft und doch flexibel.* In: *http://www.cio.de*, 21.7.2004.

▶ Schwab, Frank: *IT-Strategie.* In: *www.4managers.de*. ILTIS GmbH, Rottenburg 2004.

▶ Volkrath, Rudolf; Vettinger, Thomas: *Economic Value Added (EVA)*. Universität Zürich 2000.

B About the Authors

Figure B.1 The writing team (left to right): Andreas Hardt, Christian Bernhardt, Andreas Mayer, Loren Heilig, Frank Heidfeld, Roland Pfennig, Steffen Karch

Steffen Karch is a senior business consultant for SAP Business Consulting at SAP Deutschland AG & Co. KG. Previously, he was IT Project Manager at Pixelpark AG in Munich.

His project work concentrates on strategic IT consulting with special emphasis on matters of integration. One focus is the prioritization of projects using operational value analyses.

Steffen Karch has nine years' experience with SAP and has worked as a consultant for the last four years. His book *Web Business with SAP* came out in 2002 (also from SAP PRESS, co-written with Mario Perez). His contributions to the present book include the *Introduction*, the chapters *SAP NetWeaver in 20 Minutes* and *Roadmap to SAP NetWeaver at ABC Bank*, and the Solution Manager portion of Chapter 9, in addition to coordinating the entire project.

Loren Heilig is founder of IBSolution GmbH and has been its managing director since 2003. IBSolution GmbH is an innovative SAP NetWeaver service provider, and has made a name for itself on the SAP consultancy market, due in large part to its title, *SAP BI Special Expertise Partner*.

Before founding IBSolution GmbH, Loren was a project leader at SAP Systems Integration AG and SAP AG. There he was responsible for setting up an SAP BW consultancy team focusing on human resources, and he coordinated the BW/HR projects at Saudi Aramco (Saudi Arabia). He received a degree in industrial engineering from Karlsruhe University of Applied Sciences.

Loren gained wide-ranging experience with enterprise data warehouses through his work on many Business Intelligence projects, which primarily focused on SAP HR. Since in most cases these projects demanded more than just a BI solution, comprehensive restructuring of the business process was often required, along with constant attention to the exchange of information between non-SAP systems.

Loren also works as an instructor at SAP AG, where he trains BI consultants.

Loren contributed the chapter *Roadmap to SAP NetWeaver at Automotive Inc.*, the sections on Process Integration and Composite Application Framework in Chapter 9, and the conclusion. He also initiated the writing of this book along with Steffen Karch.

Christian Bernhardt is an industrial engineer. In his role as a senior business consultant at SAP Deutschland AG & Co. KG, he has become an expert in SAP NetWeaver. His consultancy work focuses on the area of company portals, from determining the benefits of a portal installation to implementation and rollout.

As a project manager, Christian oversaw international CRM development projects that focused on the development and implementation of e-commerce shopping solutions using SAP software. His work has been published by SAP PRESS once before, as he contributed to the book *Internet Selling*.

Before joining SAP, Christian worked at Plaut Management Consulting AG in Munich as an SAP consultant for sales and financial controlling. The area he focused on there within the context of R/3 implementations was the mapping of modern cost accounting systems, such as the marginal costing of Plaut and Kilger. He has broad experience in the mechanical engineering, automotive, and financial services industries.

In this book, Christian's knowledge was applied to the sections on people integration and value analysis.

Economist **Andreas Hardt** is a senior consultant at IBSolution GmbH. He specializes in the design, planning, implementation, and management of Business Intelligence projects. One of his customers recently went live with the ramp-up of SAP BW 3.5. He is also an instructor at SAP in Walldorf and delivers various in-house training courses.

Before working at IBSolution GmbH, Andreas spent 18 months as a senior consultant at SAP Systems Integration AG. In that role, he oversaw Business Intelligence projects in the retail, healthcare, and insurance sectors.

After his studies, Andreas began his career with Germany-headquartered Burda Group, where he spent three years in application development and then went on to spend another six years in enterprise financial controlling in the MIS department. There he was responsible for the introduction (in 1999) of a controlling information system based on SAP BW.

Due to the knowledge he gained from his major field of university study, "Management Information Systems," he has been able to bring a great deal of expertise to his projects, as reflected in the chapter *Roadmap to SAP NetWeaver in an Automotive Supplier Company* and the sections on information and application integration (in Chapter 9).

Business information technologist **Frank Heidfeld** is a senior consultant at Capgemini Deutschland GmbH. Previously, he worked as an SAP consultant at Bertelsmann.

His project work entails the implementation of business processes with SAP R/3 across the entire supply chain. In particular, he focuses on procurement, including e-procurement. His work in this area covers process design, change management, and system integration.

Frank has more than eight years of SAP experience and has worked as a consultant for six years. He co-authored the book *Web Business with SAP* (also from SAP PRESS). He contributed the chapter *Roadmap to SAP NetWeaver for United Gas* to this book.

Dr. Roland Pfennig is Professor of Business Informatics at Ravensburg-Weingarten University of Applied Sciences. His teaching specialties are Business Intelligence, standard software for business, and business processes. His research interests include the complex set of topics surrounding the sustainability of an information society.

In his doctorate studies, as part of the research project "Eco Rapid" for the German Federal Foundation for the Environment, he developed an information model for sustainable management of economic activity, the "Material Information Factory."

Before this, he spent 14 years as a consultant, mainly focusing on Business Intelligence (SAP BW), Human Resource Management (SAP Personnel Management, Payroll Management, and Time Management), material flow optimization, company modeling (ARIS), and workflow-based system operation. Finally, he assumed the role of team coordinator for Business Intelligence in the Human Resources department at SAP Systems Integration AG.

Dr. Pfennig contributed the chapter ESA—Enterprise Services Architecture to this book.

Andreas Mayer has more than ten years' experience in IT architectures, honed at well-known companies of differing sizes and in various industries.

Andreas co-founded IBSolution GmbH at the start of 2003 together with Loren Heilig and Oliver Donner. He's responsible for business development for the SAP NetWeaver areas of information integration and process integration.

Drawing on his broad practical experience, Andreas provided important insights and suggestions during the writing of this book, which were used in the structuring of the book, the scenario descriptions, and also in achieving an overall view of the entire architectural process—from initial implementation to a complete SAP service-oriented architecture.

Index

Gain in-depth knowledge on SAP's new UI technology

356 pp., 2005, US$ 59.95
ISBN 1-59229-038-8

Inside Web Dynpro for Java

www.sap-press.com

Chris Whealy

Inside Web Dynpro for Java

A guide to the principles of programming in SAP's Web Dynpro

This unique book on SAP's new Java-based user interface (UI) technology teaches readers how to leverage the full power of Web Dynpro. You'll start with a detailed introduction to the Web Dynpro basics. Then, benefit from expert guidance on how to create your own Web Dynpro applications, with volumes of practical insights on the do's and don'ts. The authors provide you with detailed sections on the use of the Adaptive RFC layer, as well as Dynamic Programming techniques. This exceptional book is complemented by an in-depth class and interface reference, which further assists readers in their efforts to modify existing objects, design custom controllers, and much more.

Interested in reading more?

Please visit our Web site for all
new book releases from SAP PRESS.

www.sap-press.com